Flight Lessons 5: People

*How Eddie Learned
Crew Reource Managemnt*

James Albright

Copyright © 2020 James Albright

All rights reserved.

ISBN: 978-0-9862630-9-5

Acknowledgments

Thanks to Chris Manno for over thirty years of trading aviation stories, writing techniques, and for permitting my blatant grand larceny of his artwork without complaint. Thanks also to Chris Parker for all the fact checking, sense of grammar, and style pointers. If he's told me once, he's told me a thousand times to avoid hyperbole. (This book makes a thousand and four.)

Thank you especially to Grace (*The Lovely Mrs. Haskel*) for proofreading this more than a times and living through it the first time.

James' Lawyer Advises:

Always remember that James, when you get right down to it, is just a pilot. He tries to give you the facts from the source materials but maybe he got it wrong, maybe he is out of date. Sure, he warns you when he is giving you his personal techniques, but you should always follow your primary guidance (aircraft manuals, government regulations, etc.) before listening to James.

Contents

Prelude: A New Life	7
Part One: Masters of Ocean Flying Boats	17
1: The Ground Up	19
2: No Soup for You!	31
3: The Check Ride	41
4: The Missed Approach	51
5: Deposed	63
6: The Chain of Command	75
Flight Lesson: The Days Before CRM	87
Part Two: The Captain	93
7: The Regal Captain Returns to Earth	95
8: Everybody is a Captain, Nobody is Crew	109
9: The Oblivious Captain	125
10: The Captain Has Gone Too Far	139
11: The Captain is Dead, Long Live the Captain	151
Flight Lesson: First Generation CRM	167
Part Three: The Crew	169
12: First Officer	171
13: Captain	185
14: Instructor	191
15: Manager	199
16: "He Who Be In Charge"	209
Flight Lesson: Second Generation CRM	225
Part Four: Management	231
17: Top Draft Pick	233
18: Coaching	253

19: Rebuilding Seasons	265
20: The Team	287
21: Free Agent (At Last)	297
Flight Lesson: CRM Beyond the Textbooks	313
Postscript	317
CRM Case Studies	319
References	321

Prelude: A New Life

The Summer of 2000

Santorini Sunset (Eddie's Photo)

When I'm on the road, I normally switch from tourist mode to pilot mode the moment I get the next flight plan in my hands. The photography, gastronomy, and mixology objectives effortlessly transform to weather, fuel, aircraft, and air traffic control. But the switch requires the flight plan and I didn't have it yet. Gary took the faxed copy from the hotel clerk and immediately stashed it in his brown leather brief case. It was like a military top secret.

"Where is he?" I asked.

I was standing on the tarmac, having just completed the external preflight. Helen Fuhrman looked down the airstairs from her perch in the galley to me, and then she shifted her gaze to above my head. "See those shipping containers along the fence?" I spotted the containers. "There is some smoke coming from behind the last one."

I looked at the container and then my watch. I would have no choice but to confront him. Lieutenant Colonel Gary Storm, United States Army (Retired) took over the flight department just before I arrived. I left my United States Air Force lieutenant colonel rank behind after 20 years in uniform. When I got hired by Q-Tron Computers out of Hanscom Field, Bedford, Massachusetts, I thought I had won the lottery. Q-Tron was a big name in personal computing and the industry became what it is because Q-Tron was able to break the monopoly of the "big box" makers. Q-Tron used three state-of-the-art Canadair Challenger 604 business jets to visit plants and customers throughout the world. My starting pay was about what an Air Force Four-Star general made. When I interviewed, the chief pilot had all the markings of the best boss I would ever work for. But in the two months from when I signed the contract to when I finished aircraft initial training, the old boss retired, and I found myself working for Gary Storm. After my first two trips with Q-Tron, I was recommended for immediate upgrade to an international captain. Gary said he would be the judge of my fate and that's how we ended up flying to Santorini, a beautiful Greek Island in the Aegean Sea just 118 nautical miles southwest of Athens. In the week since we left Boston, I had come to know Gary all too well.

I made my way to the shipping container, trying to be as conspicuous as possible. I adjusted my ground track to allow Gary to catch a glimpse of me as soon as possible, and I was careful to make it appear I wasn't looking directly at him. That would give him the chance to snuff out the cigarette so he could maintain the illusion that he wasn't a smoker, something Q-Tron would frown upon. The fact he wreaked of tar and nicotine didn't seem to faze his self-delusion.

"What the hell do you want?" he asked when I came within a few paces. "I already told you we don't start the APU until fifteen minutes prior."

Gary was in his late fifties, had the weather-beaten face of a life-long smoker, and stood just over five-foot-six. I was forty-three, six-foot-even, and more of a youngster when compared to my boss. He went absolutely ballistic the first time I fired up the APU on time, even when we were caught behind the power curve when our passengers showed up early. I had resigned myself to the routine. "I was hoping to see the flight plan so I could pull the charts."

He reached into his brief case and pulled the envelope that must have been delivered to him by the hotel, hours earlier. "Here," he said.

I reversed course back to the airplane and started to read. Our flight plan from Santorini Airport (LGSR) to Athens, Greece (LGAV) required a turn west on a Standard Instrument Departure (SID) to join the arrival flow using a Standard Terminal Arrival Route (STAR). The routing added 15 minutes to our flight time but was the most expeditious way to travel a short distance into a very busy international airport. You have to get in line. I pulled out the low altitude en route charts, the SID, and the six possible STARs into Athens. I filed everything away in the right seat of the cockpit, knowing things would go more smoothly if Gary flew while I negotiated with the Greek air traffic controllers. I positioned the checklist on top of the throttles, wanting to get everything ready for when Gary finally gave me permission to start the APU. Our company rulebook said we had to be ready for the passengers 30 minutes before the scheduled departure time, but Gary said that would waste jet fuel. The fact our passengers routinely showed up 15 minutes early didn't deter him at all. I studied the STAR again, trying to memorize the names so I could more easily understand the controllers.

"Put those away," I heard from behind me. Gary lowered himself into his seat. "We are going direct, no need to waste any time on such a short distance."

"There is no way Athens is going to allow that," I said. Gary started to speak but Helen interrupted.

"They're here," she said. I looked up to see the black limousine approach. I opened the checklist but heard the APU starting. Gary's hands were ablaze with motion and I struggled to keep up. I heard the limo's door open downstairs and the sounds of Mr. Samuel Therianos, his wife, and their bodyguard greeting Helen. Except for the last-minute rush, it was all very normal in the life of a business jet crew. Subtracting from what little normal we had that morning, Mr. Therianos, the Q-Tron Chief Executive Officer, stopped at the cockpit.

"Lydia would like to sit in the jump seat for takeoff," he said. "Would that be okay?"

"Of course, Mr. Therianos," Gary said. "Eddie, set up the jump seat and a headset for Mrs. Therianos."

I got out of my seat, greeted Mrs. Therianos, and pulled the jump seat into position. I gave her a quick lesson on how to get out of the jump seat in an emergency and how to use the jump seat interphone panel. As I returned to my seat, I heard the right engine spool up.

"I'll close the door," Helen said.

I looked down to the blank FMS, the Flight Management System, and was grateful to see the Inertial Navigation System had just a minute to go before completing its alignment, but less happy to realize not a single line of the flight plan had been entered. I considered my typing chores but opted to catch up on the engine start checklist first.

"Get me my taxi clearance," Gary said. "Let's go."

"I'm not ready," I said. "I need a few minutes."

"Santorini ground," Gary said while keying the radio, "Bravo Zulu 604 ready for taxi."

In a sign that Murphy must have been Greek, ground control cleared us to taxi and Gary released the brakes and we started to move at Gary speed. There is an old Air Force saying that you should never taxi faster than the wing commander could walk. Gary wasn't an Air Force pilot. I got the critical items on the taxi checklist and returned to the waiting FMS. The Challenger 604 can fly without it, but navigation becomes a problem.

"Call tower," Gary said. "Get me my takeoff clearance."

I looked to my left and saw that he was serious. We were moving at about 30 knots and would be at the end of the runway in seconds. I knew that Gary's first reaction to not getting his way was a string of "F-bombs." I wasn't a stranger to the F-word, but had never heard it called the "F-bomb" before showing up at Q-Tron. In the week since I started flying with Gary, I became acquainted with the F-word in all its derivations. Gary would use the word as a noun, verb, adverb, and adjective; sometimes all in one sentence. Mrs. Therianos crossed her legs, getting my attention and giving me an idea.

I extended my legs and applied the wheel brakes. I brought the airplane to a stop and locked my knees, placing my hands above them to emphasize the point. "Gary," I said over the interphone in my calmest voice. "I am not ready. I will not be ready for another five minutes. I need five minutes."

Gary looked at me, mouth open. I could see the F-parade was queuing up but also that he had given Mrs. Therianos a sideways glance. "Okay, Eddie," he said. "You take all the time you need."

Flight Lessons 5: People

I pulled out the flight plan and started to type. While I typed, tower offered our air traffic control clearance, which I accepted. Mercifully, it matched what our dispatchers had filed and included the STAR I had clipped to my yoke. I added the STAR to the FMS, looked up to our navigation displays and saw that life was sane again. I relaxed my legs. "Your airplane, Gary." I then let tower know we were ready for takeoff and in less than two minutes we were airborne.

Mrs. Therianos thanked us for the jump seat and retreated to the cabin. I was bracing myself for Gary's wrath, but he just gave me a sneer and said, "get me direct the airport."

"Gary, that's not going to happen," I said.

Gary keyed his microphone and made the request himself. The air traffic controllers said something that could have been the Greek version of the F-bomb and ended with "maintain assigned course."

Gary released a tirade of the American version of the F-bomb, but without keying his microphone. I acknowledged the instruction and busied myself with the checklist. While it would be true to say Gary's behavior was a surprise, it would be stretching things to say I was unfamiliar with this kind of conduct. During my twenty years as an Air Force pilot, I had flown with more than a few general officers with similar dispositions. I knew the best course of action was to keep one step ahead of the child in the left seat and prompt them to make the right decisions at the right times.

I programmed the FMS for the instrument approach and got the navigation radios set up. As long as the course needle was centered or Gary's flight director was aligned for the task at hand, he kept quiet and flew the airplane. Once we were on the ground, he directed his ire towards whomever he decided was in the way. Athens isn't a particularly dangerous city, but it always pays to be polite when a visitor. Once secured in his hotel room, Gary normally kept to himself. That meant Helen and I became a crew of two.

"How do the other pilots manage?" I asked that night at dinner. "I don't think I can put up with this much longer."

"You aren't alone," she said. "Gary has gotten worse since he took over. The other pilots just put up with it in front of him and grumble about it behind his back. I've never seen any of them confront him like you did today."

Helen was part of the original cadre at Q-Tron, having stood the flight department up with its first airplane and first three pilots. She was the least talkative of our three flight attendants and that counted as a plus. I let the conversation drop until she saw fit to restart it.

"There is a definite seniority system in this flight department, just like an airline," she said. "Length of service means everything. Nobody ever questioned the old boss. Now that he's retired, nobody ever questioned Gary. Until now."

The Q-Tron flight department had a good reputation and when I interviewed, everyone seemed to be on the same team. The old chief pilot was an Air Force veteran and the atmosphere appeared to be, in a word, collegial. I had only met four of the nine pilots, but they talked about great trips, well-maintained airplanes, and a no-nonsense leader. But all that was before Gary's reign as the chief pilot.

The rest of the week included overnights in Munich and London. We delayed our APU start each morning, but the passengers obliged us by being late each time. A week before, I was in the left seat when we crossed the Atlantic going east and kept my mouth shut as Gary ignored all our rules about oceanic plotting procedures. But going west I was in the right seat and resolved to do everything by the book.

The book, for the Q-Tron flight department, was written by Bravo Zulu Aviation, a management company based in White Plains, New York. BZA had more than 200 clients, including Q-Tron. They wrote our Flight Operations Manual, supervised all our training, handled our licensing, provided our dispatchers, and did everything an airline would do when managing a fleet of aircraft. BZA rules were our rules. More importantly, BZA rules made sense.

"Put that away," Gary said as I started to plot our oceanic route. "Can't you see the FMS does that automatically?"

"Plotting is a check of the FMS," I said. "Flying domestically, you have radar controllers doing the check. Oceanic it is up to us."

Flight Lessons 5: People

"Suit yourself," he said. "I thought you Air Force pilots had more sense than that. But don't you think for a moment we are paying for that chart."

The atmosphere in the cockpit had turned icy ever since our Santorini debacle. While crossing the pond going east Gary relaxed noticeably after our first leg from Bedford, Massachusetts to Shannon, Ireland. He talked about how we military pilots were a cut above our civilian counterparts and that since we were both lieutenant colonels – he used that in the present tense – we had something in common. But every little thing became a confrontation after Santorini.

"I don't know why you insist on wasting the company's money," he said as I turned the radar to its standby position. I looked around the cockpit for clues but came up empty.

"You are going to have to help me out here, Gary," I said. "How am I wasting money?"

"The damned radar!" he said. "You know the weather is good so you should leave it off!"

"The manual says we should never fly with the radar in the off position to protect the radar plate from turbulence when it isn't powered," I said.

More F-bombs flew but Gary eventually satisfied himself by reaching cross cockpit to switch the radar off. I left the radar alone. Gary kept quiet as I busied myself with my right seat chores until I switched the radios from Shanwick to Gander Radio. The name "Shanwick" is a kludging together of Shannon, Ireland and Prestwick, Scotland. Gander is based in Newfoundland. The switch from one oceanic control area to the other is a ritual made at 30 degrees west longitude; it had been that way for many years before my first North Atlantic crossing in 1980. The High Frequency radios are noisy and a nuisance to monitor. Our radios included a Selective Calling (SELCAL) feature which listened to the static for us and allowed the controller to call us specifically using one of 10,920 combinations of four tones made to sound like two. Our radios listened for the tones and alerted us when being called. The system usually worked but had to be tested.

"Request SELCAL check," I said to Gander Radio. In less than 30 seconds the tones came up, the crew alerting system reported "SELCAL," and our cockpit chimed. "SELCAL received," I said.

"You already did that," Gary said.

"That was with Shanwick," I said.

"Doesn't matter," he said. "You already proved it works."

"I proved the radio works," I said. "But I also have to prove the connectivity between transmitters. It says so in the regulation. Besides, it's in the BZA manual."

More F-bombs. "You got an answer for everything," he said. "To think, you were an Air Force colonel!"

Gary kept to himself until after we landed and shut down in front of our hangar at Bedford. Helen opened the door and our passengers said goodbye as they left. Gary collected his gear and got out of the seat, but not before leaving me with one more thing to consider. "I don't think you have what it takes to fly for Q-Tron," he said. "I'm going to call BZA to see if they can find you someplace else that can deal with a crybaby like you. You better get your resume updated but don't use me for a reference. Anybody calls me about you and they are going to get an earful."

After I finished with the cockpit, I got up to see Helen stacking the last dish into a plastic bin. "Need help?" I asked.

"Take this, please," she said. I carried the bin and followed her to the hangar kitchen. Another flight attendant greeted her with the news we had missed while we were gone.

"Three pilots just quit," she said. "They gave a month's notice."

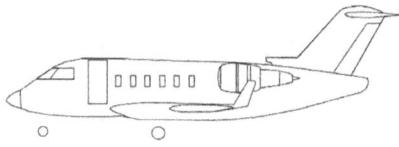

Flight Lessons 5: People

After twenty years as an Air Force pilot I was hired to fly a Canadair Challenger 604 for a major computer company. It was my first job as a civilian pilot but not my first flying what many call VVIPs, Very Very Important Persons. Through it all, I learned how to fly airplanes, how to instruct, and how to lead men and women in large and small flight departments. I also thought I knew the art of what has become known as Crew Resource Management, or CRM. But I was wrong.

CRM in a military environment is different. If the commander of the operation buys into CRM, everybody buys into it or is shown the door. I suppose the same would be true with a very large airline. But when dealing with a smaller, civilian flight department, things get complicated. You want to get along and the feelings of the person in charge are not enforced by a rigid command structure. You end up with pilots that can ignore rules they don't agree with or do things situationally. You fly so as to get along with whomever is in the other pilot's seat.

Even pilots who think they have fully embraced CRM may be deluding themselves to thinking their particular version of CRM is good enough, or better than what the next pilot believes. But there is a secret to better CRM. My only regret is it took me another twenty years to discover that secret.

The story is presented in four parts, each with a flight lesson that follows.

The flight from Santorini really happened as I've related, as did all of the flying events that follow. I've changed some of the locations, reordered and changed some of the events, and combined many of the characters. You cannot assume any of the characters in the story that follows are faithful representations of actual people. All this is an effort to focus on Crew Resource Management and to protect the identities of some very fine men and women.

Oh yes. All of the names have been changed, even my own.

Part One

Masters of Ocean Flying Boats

1: The Ground Up

April, 2000

A Boeing 314 "Clipper" NC18607 circa 1941 (US Library of Congress)

We sat at the kitchen table, rereading my resume designed to hide the fact that I held my most recent job for only a few months. We had two kids in school and *The Lovely Mrs. Haskel* was halfway through nursing school. Our mortgage was brand new. Our savings were old, but paltry.

"It's not too late to go to the airlines," *The Lovely Mrs. Haskel* said. "In fact, you have a couple of open invitations, don't you?"

"Not interested," I said.

She bit her tongue, starting to voice her thoughts but realizing they would not be helpful. We went through the discussion twice before, in the weeks after I put in my request to separate from the Air Force and the day I had officially retired. We had both agreed the airlines would have bored me, having to commute from wherever we decided to put down the new homestead would be brutal, and having to spend a few years waiting for the pay to catch up would have been a financial burden. Starting pay at Q-Tron dwarfed any other offers I had, but now that was coming to an end.

Being asked to leave an assignment was nothing new for me. I had several Air Force commanders over the years tell me that I should find another job.

But in each of those instances, a higher-level commander overruled them, and I ended up in a better situation than before. But getting on the wrong side of one's boss is never a good thing. I left the cockpit three times in the Air Force, each time thinking there was more to an Air Force career than flying airplanes. But just as Michael Corleone could never leave "The Family," just when I thought I was out, they pulled me back in.

"We should do a postmortem," she said.

"I'm not dead," I said.

"When you were in the Air Force you always finished every assignment with a notepad of lessons learned and reasons things turned out the way they did," she said. "In medical jargon, that is a postmortem."

"Ah, so," I said. "Let me think about it." In many of our previous lessons learned sessions I had to admit that perhaps, just maybe, I could have been less confrontational to my superiors. Yes, I did tend to find fault in those giving me orders, but there were faults to be found. I suppose the sheer number of confrontations would argue that the problem wasn't necessarily one-sided, but the fact I kept rising from the ashes had to argue otherwise. I thought about my "*Friend* versus *Foe*" ritual about these things, one of my few secrets that The Lovely Mrs. Haskel knew nothing about, would disapprove of, and therefore would never know.

"No," I finally said. "Gary's actions left me with no recourse. I would make the same decisions all over if presented with the same situation. That's a key pillar of Crew Resource Management. You have to stop the captain before he does something that can endanger you, your passengers, or the airplane."

The next three days were spent on the phone and the Internet. The Boston public school system said I was qualified to be a high school science teacher and they had immediate openings. So we wouldn't go hungry; but we wouldn't get rich either. The following day the U.S. Treasury department asked for a copy of my resume and the day after that invited me for an interview. It would have meant a small pay raise but not enough to justify the move to Washington, D.C. Through it all, the thought of leaving aviation was enticing, but the thought of moving was not. In twenty years, the Air Force had moved us thirteen times. But now both kids were getting to the age where uprooting from school would be traumatic.

Flight Lessons 5: People

On Friday morning I decided to fly down to D.C. for the interview, but my decision was OBE, overcome by events. The BZA dispatcher called to ask my seating preferences for an airline flight to White Plains, New York. I was scheduled for a week of indoctrination training at company headquarters. It seemed Q-Tron couldn't live without me after all.

The short flight from Boston to White Plains was aboard a Canadair Regional Jet, the same basic tube as our Challenger 604s with the same engines, but less sound insulation. I stole a quick look into the cockpit and realized that my life as a corporate pilot wasn't so bad after all. They had the most basic avionics I had seen in a decade. As the stuffed airplane made its way to the runway I listened carefully to the creaks and moans, wondering about the metal fatigue of the undercarriage and the human fatigue of the two occupants in the two front seats. I closed my eyes and thoughts of a story I had read years ago returned to reteach me the lesson I needed at that precise moment.

It was a cold winter's morning in a lonely, fog-shrouded West Virginia cemetery. A black lacquer casket was lowered into the ground as men and women dressed in black looked on. After the last bit of earth was returned to the hole the family walked away, silently. "At least dad died doing what he loved doing," the oldest son said.

"What are you talking about?" the widow said, looking at her son. "What did he love doing?"

"You know," the son said. "He was a coal miner all of his life and it was only fitting that the last day of his life was in the mines, where he wanted to be."

"That's ridiculous," the mother said. "He hated everything about mining. He started in the mines when he was fifteen and he died when he was only fifty. He knew the mines were going to kill him, and by God they did."

The son stopped, incredulous. "I never heard him say he hated his job. If he hated it so much, why did he spend his whole life doing it?"

"Because that's what men do," she said. "They don't complain, they realize they have an obligation to their family and they do what they have to do to put food on the table. He never finished high school and this job was the best he could do. Yes, he never complained. But that doesn't mean he was happy being a coal miner. He was putting food on the table. That's what men do."

The next morning, I was in a classroom at the BZA-USA headquarters, housed on the third floor of a large office building in an industrial park, about a ten-minute drive from the White Plains Airport. I got to the classroom about 30 minutes early, seeing five rows of tables with a stack of books and a name tag at each seat. Everyone had an indoctrination book and the flight operations manual. About half of us also had an international operations manual. I had the room to myself and started to read. The indoc book and FOM were very good, neatly printed, and full of excellent content. The IOM was laughable: out of date, poorly printed, and filled with errors.

"You must be Eddie," I heard as she entered the room. "I am Debbie Lynn, your instructor for the day. It is always good to have an Air Force pilot in class. You guys keep me on my toes."

She sat on the table opposite mine and read the notes I had scribbled on the pages of the IOM. "Are you going to be a troublemaker, colonel?"

"Not at all," I said. "I go by Eddie, by the way, and I am here to learn."

She was extraordinarily short for a pilot, someone you would joke about having to sit on phone books to see over the glare shield. She had the face of a much older woman, but judging by her voice and language, she was probably about my age. I guessed her normal disposition was to scowl, but as each new pilot walked in her warm smile reminded me never to judge a book by its smirk.

As the classroom filled, it became obvious I was flying a middle tier airplane in a top tier mission. Q-Tron flew all over the world; many of my peers were domestic only operators. The Challenger 604 is either at the high end of the mid-range aircraft grouping, or the bottom end of the long-range birds. Most of the class were flying Learjets and Citations, the short-range-aircraft. The second largest grouping was the Gulfstream crowd, the long and ultra-long-range set. About a half of the class was younger than me.

"Welcome to Bertrand Zacherie Aviation, USA," Debbie started. Her voice carried well and she wielded a PowerPoint slide clicker with the authority of a veteran speaker. "Monsieur Bertrand Zacherie founded Bravo Zulu Aviation thirty years ago in Paris. He changed the name of the company to Bravo Zulu after he acquired several U.S. corporate aviation management and charter aviation companies in 1985. We are now the largest corporate aviation management company in the United States. You will not find another aviation company in the world that takes safety more seriously."

We spent the morning going over the standard operating procedures in the FOM, spending most of our time covering duty limits. BZA rules were well written and quite conservative. But I realized that many of my flights in the past month violated the maximum permitted duty period for a basic crew (14 hours in a day), the maximum flight hours for two pilots (10 hours in a duty period), and the minimum rest requirements between duty periods (10 hours). But the real news was the fact no flights as a BZA crewmember were permitted until indoctrination was completed. I was rapidly filling a page of my own non-compliance to SOPs in my first month as a civilian pilot.

Though we were all new hires, it seemed many in the class knew each other. With each new topic some of my classmates would grumble about the tight controls BZA was placing on their new lives. It all seemed rather relaxed compared to my Air Force upbringing. But the BZA waiver process appeared to be flawed. I held my fire until the lunch break and negotiated my way through the company cafeteria to have a seat next to our instructor.

"You have been taking a lot of notes," she said as I sat opposite her. "I am either captivating you with my speaking style or you are getting ready for the mother of all critiques."

"Could be both," I said. "Or maybe I am wondering if Q-Tron really is a part of BZA."

I explained how I had already been flying the line for a month, despite having never been to indoctrination training. "But what I am really interested in is why our chief pilot has the waiver authority to extend our duty day indefinitely and is able to disregard other manual requirements without the check of any higher level of management."

"That's a problem unique to Q-Tron," she said. "And maybe three or four other bases. BZA acquired Q-Tron and a few other flight departments from another management company that called each base's manager a chief pilot. BZA has Part 91 and Part 135 operators. A 'chief pilot' has a specific meaning in the 135 world. So, we call the person in charge of a flight department the base manager. The waiver authority in the manual belongs to the BZA chief pilot, not to individual base managers." A Part 135 flight department operated under Part 135 of the federal aviation regulations commercially, for compensation or hire. Q-Tron operated under the less restrictive rules of Part 91, for general aviation.

"But the guy in charge of our outfit calls himself a chief pilot," I said. "And he waives things all the time."

"We know that's a problem," she said. "But I didn't know anyone was taking advantage of the loophole like this."

The afternoon included three hours of first aid training and an hour about scheduling. After the very long day Debbie reminded the class that we were to meet the next day at 0900, sharp. As I gathered my things and got up, Debbie approached. "Kari Owens would like to meet you tomorrow morning for breakfast, in the cafeteria at seven. Can you do that?"

"Sure," I said. "Who is Kari Owens?"

"He's the BZA director of operations," she said. "I told him about your waiver questions. He pulled up your resume and said he wanted to meet with time to talk."

I spent the night reading the Flight Operations Manual more closely and remained impressed. I cracked open the International Operations Manual and wondered what ten-year-old they had contracted the work to. I started to write on the manual itself with a red pen, correcting spelling errors, grammatical mistakes, and inconsistencies. By the time I was done it was 2 a.m., leaving me just a few hours before my working breakfast.

With 200 aircraft and ten times as many people, Bravo Zulu Aviation was about the size of an Air Force fighter wing. So, meeting the director of operations was like meeting a wing commander or maybe the vice commander. And I was just a line pilot, so let's say I was the equivalent of a lieutenant or captain. I wasn't sure what to expect, but I certainly didn't expect Mr. Kari Owens to be standing outside the cafeteria, waiting for me.

"Colonel Haskel!" he said, extending a hand. "I've been looking forward to meeting you. Let's get some eggs and coffee."

I followed Kari to the cafeteria and chose the hot foods line where an omelet cook stood ready behind an array of meats, cheeses, and vegetables. Kari went to the fruit and yogurt bar and quickly ended up at a table overlooking the BZA parking lot. He was slender, about five-foot-eight, fully gray, with

Flight Lessons 5: People

bifocals that suggested he was in his mid to late fifties. As I approached the table his smile reignited.

"Debbie tells me you have met all our expectations and more," he began. "I only wish we could take advantage of you beyond just one flight department."

"I am surprised to hear you had any expectations at all," I said. "I'm just a line pilot."

"You are more than that," he said. "All pilot hires go through us here and we read every resume. You have quite a background and we think you are going to be good for Q-Tron."

"I don't think Gary Storm agrees with you," I said. "I think he wanted to fire me before the last three guys quit."

"I heard," he said. "Gary and I are college classmates, we talk a fair bit."

My internal warning triggers elevated to full alert. Was I talking with a Gary Storm confidant? Would Kari be a *Friend* or yet another *Foe*? The two appeared to be the same age, with Kari being the healthier looking and friendlier acting version of Gary.

"VMI," he said. "The Virginia Military Institute. I went to the Navy to fly fighters and Gary went to the Army to fly helicopters. The Navy taught me how dangerous things can be if you don't do them right, the Army taught Gary how to be dangerous because that's what they do for a living."

Alarm bells cancelled. Kari spoke freely about his passion for standard operating procedures and the BZA standardization program. "We have about twenty pilots who are check airmen for the commercial side and standards pilots for everyone else. They are a good bunch of gals and guys but few of them have your background in standards. You should think about joining the group."

"I'll give it some thought," I said. "But I'm brand new here. I'm just trying to survive Q-Tron at the moment. That flight department is a bit of a shock after the Air Force. I only found out yesterday what a chief pilot is and that our chief pilot isn't really a chief pilot. But he has the waiver authority of one."

"We are about to unveil a fix to that," Kari said. "But until yesterday I didn't know just how far off the reservation Gary had gone. We pulled the last three months of flight logs at Q-Tron. I'm going to have a long talk with Gary this afternoon."

"I guess I'll be looking for a new job after all," I said.

"No, you won't," Kari said. "Gary and I go way back; I'll talk some sense into him. We are both sons of Pan American World Airways pilots, guys who made the transition from the first airliner seaplanes. Do you know what they called them?"

"No," I said.

"They were 'Masters of Ocean Flying Boats' in the words of Juan Trippe," he said. "Trippe was the founder and CEO of Pan Am and, in his view, the aircraft captain was like an ocean liner captain. Nobody dared question the man in charge. Believe it or not, the U.S. Navy doesn't believe that. But there are pilots out there that do."

"Like Gary," I said.

"Like Gary," he agreed. "But you are going to fix that."

Flying for Pan American World Airways had been a boyhood dream of mine. Growing up in Hawaii I remember seeing the blue globe on the tail of Pan Am Boeing 707s as they graced our island skies. I knew also that Pan Am barely escaped shutdown because they were crashing those Boeing 707s all over the world. The blame was usually placed squarely on captains who didn't listen to their crews or crews that didn't confront their captains.

The year I started flying, 1979, was also the year the National Aeronautics and Space Administration issued a study on why airline cockpit crews were often dysfunctional, leading to avoidable crashes. Their study became the first generation of what was known as "Cockpit Resource Management," or CRM. The resources were people and captains needed to learn how to better utilize those resources.

"I don't want to steal Debbie's thunder," Kari continued, "but starting next month all our base managers will be called client aviation managers, or CAMs. It doesn't exactly roll off the tongue, but it will straighten out the waiver authority mess."

Flight Lessons 5: People

The morning was taken by the BZA version of Crew Resource Management. (The industry agreed the "cockpit" should be "crew" to emphasize the role of non-captains in the CRM equation.) We were combined with a class of flight attendants and mechanics and after a few hours of class were broken into groups for some role playing in specific situations. It was much like CRM training in the Air Force. It was good, but it was preaching to the choir. Those of us who got it, got it. I think those who didn't get it were just playing along because they knew it was a box on their indoc forms that had to be checked.

The afternoon was spent at a nearby pool, commandeered for water survival training. After Debbie dismissed us for the day, I retreated to my hotel room with a new red pen and finished my assault on the IOM. The next day was all about international operations.

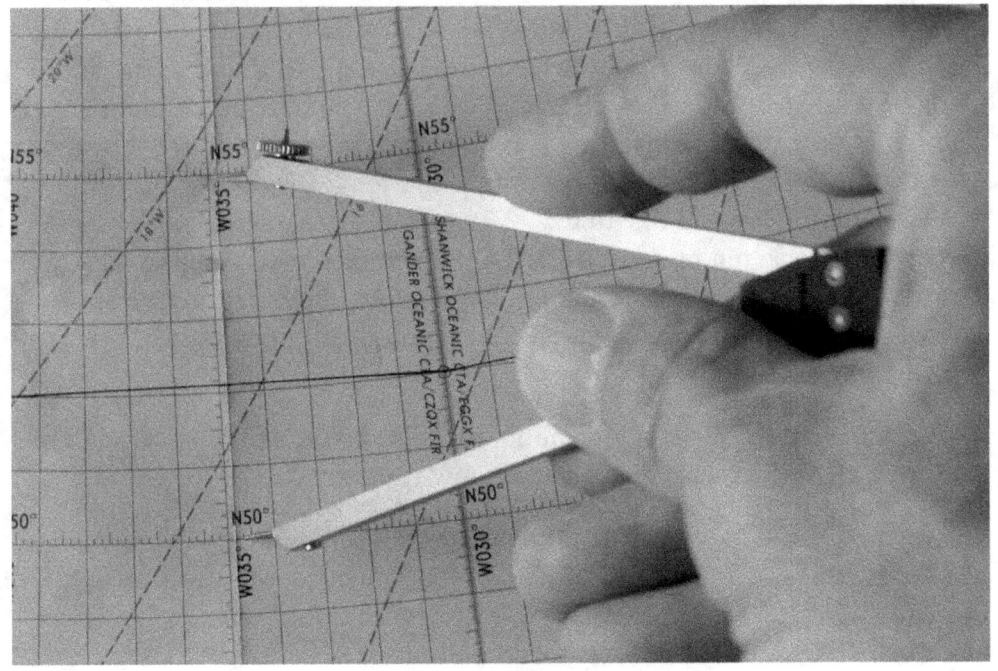

Navigation dividers

I entered the classroom as the instructor wrote on the whiteboard on the front wall. He pretended I wasn't there and continued to write. According to the white board, his name was Captain Chip Dawson, based in Bedford, Massachusetts, and he was an international captain flying a Gulfstream GIV.

He listed the topics for the day, including one full hour devoted to introductions. An hour? I immediately started to hate Chip Dawson before he uttered a single syllable.

Once he was done writing he sat down, facing the classroom, but remained silent. He appeared to be staring just above my head but didn't appear to recognize that I was there or any of the other students filing in. He was dressed in a faded polo shirt that had the letters "GVL" stitched over one breast. But the most striking thing about Captain Dawson was that his face was divided by a diagonal line right through his nose, left upper left side covered by a red birthmark and the lower right by his pasty white skin. I willed myself to avoid staring at the red signpost that appeared to scream, "look at this!"

Once the second hand on the clock indicated it was 0900:00, Chip began talking. He gave us his life's story that included his attendance at the Vermont Technical College, his first job flying a DC-6 in Malaysia, a Part 91 job flying a Dassault Falcon 20, and his current gig as an international captain flying the Gulfstream GIV. When faced with such an introduction, my first reaction is to record the start time. As the introduction continued, he said, "We fly over 700 hours a year, most of that charter. Why do I put up with that schedule? Because I like to fly." Parts of the class laughed politely. I rechecked the clock: ten minutes so far. A few minutes later – at last, I thought – he started talking about international operations and his vast experience. "Why do I teach this class?" he asked. "Because BZA pays me and I like to eat." A little less laughter this time.

At 0922:20 he said, "Well enough about me." He pointed to the person in the front row, rightmost seat. "Let's get to know you."

The intros continued. I had a technique for these situations but that only worked if I was the first person called. My introduction was the same even if I wasn't the leadoff audience member, but the technique really depended on being called first. At 0935:17 my turn finally came. "I'm Eddie Haskel. I was an Air Force pilot for twenty years. Now I'm flying Challengers for Q-Tron computers." I looked to my left, making way for the next introduction.

I was pleasantly surprised to see the remainder of the class adopted my technique and we were done with introductions well ahead of Captain Dawson's schedule on the board. "Well, let's take an early break and be back here by 10:15." Dawson wasn't going to be taken off his schedule.

Flight Lessons 5: People

The rest of the day was consumed with Chip Dawson speaking, us listening. My notebook filled with his techniques and to many of those I added question marks. Chip said, "you must plot whenever you do not have a VOR or NDB needle in range." I knew that was wrong, but I wasn't positive. I reminded myself that the best way to learn in a new environment was to listen, refrain from arguing, and wait. Judging by the examples he cited, Chip certainly had more experience than I. Once he dismissed us for the day I approached, careful to look into both eyes, not just the one outlined in red.

"Who wrote this manual?" I asked.

"That would be one Rebecca L. Cherbourg," he said. "A neat lady who has been running her own international procedures program since Moby Dick was a minnow."

"Where do I send corrections?" I asked.

"Beats the heck out of me," he said. The next day I asked Debbie Lynn the same question.

"Just put it on Kari's desk," she said.

I found Kari's office where he was on the phone. He gestured me in and to a seat opposite his desk. "As a matter of fact," he said to the phone, "he just walked in. Gary, this is going to work out great. And I'll get you more pilots. Don't worry about it." He cradled the phone.

"Eddie, good to see you," he said. "I hope you packed enough underwear for another week. We are sending you to Dallas next week for check airman's school. The class is three days and it just so happens we are having a standards group meeting in Dallas next Thursday and Friday. It's just like it was meant to be."

The check airman course was my third time learning to be a standards pilot and was easily better than any Air Force class on the topic. The standards group meeting was even better. I learned that BZA took standard operating procedures very seriously and backed that belief up with a cadre of highly professional pilots charged with enforcing those SOPs. They had willingly given up several high-profile clients who refused to fly by BZA standard operating procedures. I returned to Bedford with a renewed hope for my new life at Q-Tron Computers.

2: No Soup for You!

May 2001

Two Challenger 604s (Eddie Photo)

Gary seemed to settle on a sort of detente with me whereby we never flew together and while at the hanger he stayed in his office and I stayed out. The pilot situation helped with our separation. In the next year we lost two more pilots, so I went from the newest to number three in seniority virtually overnight. Of nine pilots, we were down to only five captains, so most captains only flew with first officers. The three of us who were qualified as international captains were on the road almost continuously, my only breaks coming when assigned to fly a check ride for BZA. I was also tasked with training and checking each new pilot who showed up to match our continuing turnover.

"This is Linda, your dispatcher," she said over the phone from White Plains. Every conversation with her began the same way.

"This is Eddie, your pilot," I answered.

"I see you signed Sidney Justice off as a first officer," she said. "We have you and he scheduled for Paris Le Bourget next week. He's finished all of his international procedures training and all his documentation is in order. Besides, he was an international captain at his last job."

"Okay," I said, ignoring the sales pitch. She always thought of everything and it really didn't make sense to play twenty questions with her. The Bedford to Le Bourget run was an easy one with a tailwind for the Challenger 604. Coming back could be a problem; going east was easy.

Training a first officer for his or her first oceanic crossing isn't that tough either, you just have to do everything expected of both pilots while offloading the first officer tasks at a rate commensurate with that pilot's ability to learn. The fact we were cycling through pilots so quickly complicated matters, in that we wanted them to grow up very quickly. Based on his performance during our first training flight, I knew Sid would be a quick study. He seemed to have the right attitude, but the Challenger 604 was his first airplane with a glass cockpit. Most of his jet time was in the earlier 601, an airplane with what we had come to call "steam gauges."

I put Sid in the left seat so all he had to do was fly the airplane, something he did very well. From the right seat I talked through each step of the process of doing an oceanic crossing in a two-pilot flight deck. He listened intently as I covered the mechanics of ensuring the FMS was indeed navigating in accordance with our cleared route. I carefully plotted our route along a large North Atlantic chart, along with the routing of the competing lanes of the North Atlantic Track System, called the NATS. Though I had the correct format of the High Frequency radio calls memorized, I went through the details a minute before the actual call. Ten minutes after each waypoint, I plotted our position on the chart to verify we were headed correctly to the next waypoint. Sid took copious notes at each new nugget of information. In years of doing this kind of instructing, I never had a more attentive student.

The approach into Paris was routine for France. It took several tries to interpret the English part of the Automated Terminal Information System and many of the radio calls to Paris Control and Approach Control had to be followed by, "Say again, slowly." But once we were on the ground life became sane again and Sid turned out to be an excellent bar companion.

A born and raised New Englander, Sid spoke without any kind of Boston or New York accent. At six-foot-four, he towered over me in stature. Five years my junior with an easy smile, he attracted the attention of many of our

Flight Lessons 5: People

waitresses. It was especially fun witnessing his easy banter with any bartender. Sitting at the bar, for the first time, became entertaining. I decided that I liked Sid. *Friend.*

I put Sid in the right seat for the flight home and continued the instruction while flying the airplane. Sid was unable to properly build the plotting chart, plot our positions, or make basic position reports. I wrote out a basic position report with blanks for where the applicable information had to be, but even his last position report of the day was poor. I decided I no longer liked Sid. *Foe?* Too soon to tell. Once we returned to radar-controlled airspace, however, Sid was back in his element.

"Hey great flight, Eddie," he said as I sat at the flight department's flight planning table with a stack of paperwork to complete. "See you next time."

"Not so fast," I said. "We need to work on a few things." Sidney looked like I had shot his dog. He put his briefcase down and pulled up a chair. We spent the next hour going over oceanic crossing procedures and compiling a list of study materials. When I finally finished and "dismissed" my young charge, he repacked his briefcase and got up to leave. He hesitated and looked at me.

"Eddie," he said, "thanks for taking the time. I need to step up my game."

I decided I liked Sid again. *Friend.* "We all start out the same way," I said. "But even old guys like me need to keep learning."

When I came home that night *The Lovely Mrs. Haskel* asked how the trip went. "Nothing new," I said. "No wait. Something new did happen. The other pilot thanked me for being a jerk."

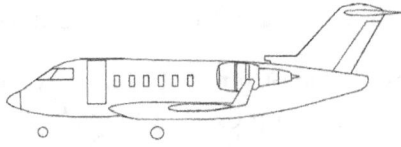

Flying all over the world, fifty hours a month, and throwing in a check ride or two was becoming routine. Routine as in safe, not routine as in boring. Q-Tron had offices in Australia, China, Japan, Brazil, England, France, Germany, and Italy. The Challenger 604 was poorly suited for such long distances and we had to airline crews to intermediate stops days ahead of crew swaps, so that the passenger made it from Boston to their destinations in minimum time. I was racking up an impressive number of airline miles and hotel bonus nights. BZA tried to weave in check rides for days when I was airlining home. All told, I was averaging twenty days a month on the road.

Our three youngest pilots were not progressing as quickly as we would have liked, not upgrading to domestic captains as quickly as predicted. Q-Tron had paid for my move to the Boston area, but the company's bottom line had gotten worse over the two years since. We were now only hiring local talent and, paradoxically, that meant a greater diversity of talent.

"Aileron into the wind?" Jeff Lombard asked.

"Yes," I said. "And then rudder to align the aircraft."

It was an absurd conversation; crosswind landing procedure is normally reserved for a student pilot's first few flights in a single-engine prop. But Jeff was a good pilot with an Air Force pedigree.

"This airplane lands just like a T-37," I said.

"That was ten years ago for me," he said. "I haven't touched the rudder in all these years, except maybe in a dogfight."

Of course, it all made sense now. After the T-37 Jeff would have flown the T-38, like me. But from there he went to the F-16 fighter. The T-38 and F-16 both land in a crab, with the nose pointed into the wind. These aircraft didn't really align themselves to the runway until the nose gear was down. But their main gear were relatively sturdy, beefy affairs that could take the punishing sideloads. Jeff tried to do that in our Challenger and I took the airplane from him before the wheels touched. The main landing gear on the Challenger could have collapsed if subjected to a sideways landing.

After a few phone calls with the other captains it became apparent that they too had noticed his sloppy technique, or perhaps better said, his lack of technique when it came to crosswind landings. I dug up my notebooks from many years ago and reviewed the basics. The next Monday I sat down with Jeff and spoke from those notes and coached him through the ancient art of chair flying, going through the motions on the ground in a hope to instill some muscle memory.

After three practice landings Jeff seemed to have learned what he needed to do, and I signed him off. "Say that's a pretty handy notebook you got there,"

Flight Lessons 5: People

he said. "Mind if I borrow it for a while to study?"

"Not at all," I said. "But I want it back." A month later we were scheduled to fly from Anchorage to Tokyo to Shanghai and back to Anchorage, as part of a trip from Massachusetts to Japan and China. We would airline to Anchorage with Diane Malcomb, our flight attendant.

I didn't pay enough attention to the airline arrangements and didn't realize we were seated together going west. I ended up in the middle seat somewhere near the front of our Boeing 757. Jeff was seated to my left and Diane to my right. I'm not sure how that happened, the travel department knew we would be sealed up in the same aluminum tube as a flight crew and wanted nothing to do with each other while deadheading. I wanted to trade, but Jeff was too big for the center seat and Diane insisted on the aisle. Oh well.

The good folks at Continental Airlines presented us with a mystery meat with mystery potatoes and mystery soup for lunch. Jeff finished the meat and potatoes off in no time flat, while I poked at the meat wondering what it was. "You want this?" I asked. He reached over and took the tan brown concoction; too dark for chicken too light for cow. I polished off the potato and left the murky bowl of broth unmolested. "You want my soup?"

Jeff declined. "Nah." He looked over and saw untouched bowls on all three of our trays. "No soup for you!" he proclaimed.

Diane laughed, "no soup for you!"

"What's so funny?" I asked. They both looked at me like I was asking about the orbit of the earth around the sun.

"Seinfeld," they said together.

It would seem I was the only person in the northern hemisphere who had never watched an episode of Seinfeld. Diane and Jeff traded lines from their favorite episodes as I tried, in vain, to nap.

Twelve hours later I was asleep in my hotel room when the phone on the night stand came to life. "No soup for you!" It was Jeff.

"I'm sleeping."

"No you're not," he said, "you're talking to me. Besides, Seinfeld is on in two minutes. Turn on channel seven."

I said that I would, knowing I would not. But, lying in bed, wide awake now, I knew I had to. It was the Soup Nazi episode. Kismet? Maybe. Serendipity? To be sure.

Our Challenger arrived at Anchorage on time and we flew on to Tokyo. Over the next five days Jeff learned the finer points of Japanese and Chinese air traffic control while I got reacquainted with the foods of my youth. All things considered, it was shaping up to be a good trip. We almost always ventured outside the hotel for dinner but I usually made an exception for the night before a long flight. From Shanghai to Anchorage with a fuel stop at Sendai, Japan it would be a full day so no sense wasting time in a cab. I wanted dinner, a few drinks, and bed.

I exited the hotel elevator on the lobby level moments before another elevator deposited Jeff and Diane. "To the bar!" they said together, as if rehearsed.

We walked through a double set of glass doors into a darkly lit barroom dominated by a long, mahogany bar behind which stood a mirror-lined wall of Scotch Whiskey. "You got any Scotch?" Jeff asked with a grin. The bartender flipped three menus deftly in front of us, each landing on the table unfolded to the precise page. "Two hundred, seventeen, all in stock, you name your desire."

I won a bottle of Scotch in pilot training, shared half of it with my classmates and drank the other half in about a month. I've never been able to touch the stuff ever since. Jeff and Diane, it would seem, were both Scotch Whiskey Connoisseurs and set up themselves the task of trying all two hundred and seventeen. We ended up eating dinner at those very bar stools.

I do enjoy a beer or three, and sometimes I'll follow that with a glass of red wine. The scotch afficianodos stayed true to their chosen drinks and I resisted the urge to count drinks. Bravo Zulu Aviation rules said all drinks stop twelve hours prior to takeoff, the so-called "bottle to throttle" rule. Our takeoff was scheduled for 0900. As the clock neared 2100 I made a grand show of checking my watch, asking for the check, and paying off our tab.

"Twelve hours prior to takeoff," I announced, "and just about bedtime for me." Jeff and Diane made no gestures towards following my lead. "I shall see you both tomorrow at oh seven hundred, bags in hand."

Flight Lessons 5: People

The next morning, we three assembled and were whisked away to our waiting aircraft. Jeff and Diane seemed perfectly rested and the flights to Sendai and Anchorage were routine. The relief crew was ready for us and we waited until the aircraft taxied from sight. "Back to the Captain Cook Hotel," I ordered the driver. I looked to the back seat of the van, Diane's eyes were closed, and Jeff looked like a zombie. "You guys up for Simon and Seafort's?"

"Okay." It was hardly the enthusiastic response I was hoping for. The best crab legs in Alaska deserved better. Within an hour we had checked in, changed clothes, and walked down the few blocks to the eatery. The maître de gave us a table with a view of the Cook Inlet, the only ugly view of water in the state. No matter, it was a good table for a good meal to serve as the capstone for a good trip. Jeff and Diane still seemed readier for bed than dinner. They opened their menus, and each lit up, "Scotch!"

Simon and Seafort's did not have hundreds of varieties of Scotch, but the seven on the menu all met with the approval of the critics at our table. I joined in the revelry with yet another glass of Shiraz. We weren't flying the next day, after all. Well, we were flying, but we would be flying as passengers to Seattle and back home to Boston. We had to get up early again, but there weren't any company or FAA rules on how late the bar light could stay on. And it stayed on a very long time.

The next morning everybody was in place at the appointed time, but that was about all that could be said in our favor. My throat felt like I had swallowed some 80-grit sandpaper. Diane was dressed in jeans, highly unusual for her on an airline day. Jeff's eyes were puffy slits and it looked like he forgot to shave. No matter, we were members of the traveling public. I was happy to see our seats were spread far apart, Jeff in seat 12A, me on the opposite side at 14F, and Diane in back. My only worry now was that Jeff's snoring two rows ahead would keep me from finding the magical R.E.M. sleep I so desperately needed.

R.E.M. was exactly where I was at when I felt the tap on my shoulder. "Captain Haskel," I heard, "you are Captain Haskel aren't you?"

It was an Alaskan Airlines flight attendant. How did she know who I was? I wasn't in uniform and the "captain" title is not something branded on my forehead. "Yes?"

"Your flight attendant just passed out in the galley."

I rushed back and there was Diane, sitting on the floor with an Alaska Airlines flight attendant steadying her against a galley cart. She smiled weakly, started to speak but stopped.

"What should we do, captain?"

It was a ridiculous question. I wasn't the captain, I was passenger 14F. "Well," I said, "I would call forward to Seattle and have medical help waiting for us. I would keep her comfortable here until then."

After landing, while we taxied in, the public address system came to life. "Ladies and gentlemen, we have an injured passenger in the aft galley of the aircraft. EMTs will be meeting the aircraft so we ask you to please remain seated until we let you know the EMTs have reached the back. Thank you for your cooperation."

That ain't gonna happen, I thought. But it did. Everyone remained seated until the EMTs made it to the back. I waited until the last passenger made it past my row and made my way back. There I found Diane where I last saw her, but this time with a smile. "I'm okay," she said.

"She's severely dehydrated," one of the EMT's said to me, "you need to pump her with liquids before your next flight."

"We have three hours," I said, "will she be okay to go on to Boston after that?"

"Sure," the EMT answered, "just get those liquids into her. The best thing for her would be a nice warm bowl of soup."

I spun on my heels and knelt down to Diane's face, "no soup for you!"

Diane smiled but the look from the Alaska Airlines flight attendants hit me cold. To this day I am sure they still tell the story about how harsh corporate captains are. By the time we left Seattle for Boston, Diane was looking much better. We talked the airline into seating us in the same row so we could keep an eye on her. She asked for the window seat so she could doze. I read for a while, at least until I got to the last page. I looked at my watch and estimated another two hours with nothing left to read.

"Now what are you going to do?" Jeff said, with a laugh.

Flight Lessons 5: People

"Go crazy," I said. "Do you have my notebook?"

"Sorry," he said. "I left it at home. You don't spend a lot of time at idle, don't . . ."

"I don't."

"Can I ask you a question?"

"You just did," I said.

"Ah humor," he said. "Me and the other pilots were wondering . . ."

"What other pilots?" I asked.

"Well, all of us, actually," he said. "All of us meaning all of us who aren't you or Gary."

"Ah . . ."

"Were wondering," he continued. "If you are planning on killing the king, we want to know how we can help."

"Kill the king?" I asked. "What are you . . ."

"You know," he said. "Everyone knows you two don't get along. The flight attendants say you don't put up with any of his bullshit. We thought that since you are a check airman, and since you have connections at BZA . . ."

"Gary works at the pleasure of Q-Tron," I said. "BZA would have a hard time getting rid of him, even if they wanted to."

"Dammit," he said with another laugh. "Oh well, it was worth a try."

"Why would you think I would condone a mutiny?" I asked.

"You know . . ." he said.

"I don't."

"You are the giant killer," he said. "My Air Force buds tell me you did this all the time."

"Mutiny?" I asked.

"No, not mutiny," he said. "You know what I mean."

I knew exactly what he meant, but I never talked about it to anyone. As an Air Force squadron commander, I had the misfortune of working for a psychopath general officer. He wasn't the first or the last *Foe* in my Air Force career, but he was the worst of them. My prime motivation became to protect the squadron from him. In a classic "keep your enemies closer" move, he reassigned me as his personal assistant. A few days after my change of command the squadron crashed an airplane with the loss of all 35 on board. The ensuing investigation resulted in the general's firing and what amounted to a pat on the back for me for my resistance efforts. If my peers thought of me as a giant killer, they were misinformed. That was five years ago but the scar tissues remain.

I pulled the airline magazine from the seat pocket; Jeff took the hint. By the time we landed in Boston, Diane seemed to be back to 100 percent. We shared a limo from Logan International back to our hangar at Bedford and she immediately dialed up our dispatcher. "Not so hot," she offered after the dispatcher's first question. "I think I'm going to need a week off before I can think about getting on another airplane. Sure, he's right here." She handed me the phone.

3: The Check Ride
June 2002

Taking notes from the jump seat (Photo: Mark Eisner)

"This is Eddie," I said, "your pilot."

"This is Linda, your dispatcher," she said. "Bravo Zulu wants you to fly a check ride from Nantucket to Vancouver tomorrow morning. But they promise you all of next week off."

"Okay," I said. "Who is it?"

"It's not good," she said. "It's a Falcon 900 crew from Wayland Hospital Group. Kari said you should call him as soon as possible."

I promised Linda I would do all that and handed the phone back to Diane. I pulled out my own phone and selected Kari Owen's name from the directory.

"You ever hear about Stefano Wayland, Eddie?"

"Rich guy," I said. "He owns a bunch of hospitals."

"Yeah, that's him," Kari said. "We manage his flight department of five Falcons. His pilots are forever getting into trouble for one thing or another.

In the last five years Bravo Zulu has only had two pilots violated, both were from Wayland. Hank had a visit with Mr. Wayland last week and said we need to give each of their pilots a look before we can renew our contract." (Hank Callaghan was the president of Bravo Zulu – USA. He made a point of being on a first name basis with everyone in the company.)

"Hank's willing to give up such a big contract?" I asked.

"It's going to cost us if we do," Kari said. "But we can't have pilots that don't fly by our rules. They set you up with their top pilots tomorrow, Eddie. Be fair but be thorough. Give me a call from Vancouver."

The next morning, I met the crew at their hotel in Nantucket. Both pilots were about my age or younger, the flight attendant was definitely younger. The captain briefed me that the weather was okay from departure through destination, no worries. We chatted over breakfast and the ride to the airport. Both pilots were from the airlines and seemed to have the kind of experience that usually means comfort with standard operating procedures. I started to relax. Just as we pulled into the airport parking lot the captain's phone rang. "We'll be ready, sir," he said. He looked at the rest of us, "They are early. They'll be here in thirty minutes."

"Forget I'm here," I said. "Just do what you need to do and we can brief everything once we are en route."

I tried my best to blend into the background as the crew got their airplane ready. The passengers showed up early, as promised, and we were airborne without any drama. I recognized Mr. Wayland from the many news photos over the years. He was controversial, to say the least. He was a medical doctor who put together a group of physicians to take over a hospital in Chicago. They cut the staff mercilessly, came up with innovative ways to reduce patient-doctor contact, and turned the hospital profitable. In ten years he had repeated the prescription all over the United States and Canada and became a multi-billionaire.

I made myself comfortable in the jump seat for the six-hour journey west, from Nantucket to Vancouver. The jump seat in the Falcon 900 isn't the best, but it isn't the worst either. I checked their paperwork and spotted the arrival forecast immediately as something less than okay: CYVR 191738Z 05004KT 1/2SM OVC002 FM190200 07002KT 1/4SM OVC 001. The

Flight Lessons 5: People

destination airport was at minimums (one-half statute mile visibility with an overcast ceiling of 200 feet) when we took off and would go below minimums before we got there. The alternate, Abbotsford, was just thrity miles to the east but was practically clear. They had violated our company rules by taking off, but we would be okay at the alternate. Technically speaking, I should not have allowed them to takeoff, but I had assumed the captain's "weather's okay" statement was true. The fact I also made a mistake could not be ignored. But as long as the rest of the ride went okay, I would make this a critique item but not a "bustable" offense.

Passing 10,000 feet both pilots removed their headsets and turned the cockpit speakers on. I knew some companies allowed this, but Bravo Zulu required the use of headsets except when oceanic. I kept my headset on. The cockpit was noisy enough that the speakers were difficult to understand from the jump seat.

"Bravo Zulu nine oh one," I heard from the headset, "climb to and maintain flight level three six zero." The two pilots continued their discussion about the pros and cons of direct drive motorcycles.

"That was for us," I said.

"Huh," they said together.

"Climb to and maintain three six zero," I said.

The first officer answered the call and the two reset their autopilot to make the climb. "These speakers aren't the best," the captain said.

"Then why don't you use the headsets?" I asked.

"They are too uncomfortable," the captain said. "Besides, it isn't a problem above 10,000 feet."

"Didn't one of your guys get an altitude bust last year for this very problem?" I asked.

"Well that's Joe," the captain said. "That poor guy is snake bit."

I decided to drop that matter for now. I had saved them from some embarrassment but maybe they would have caught the controller's second or third attempts. Hour after hour, the two pilots chatted happily, oblivious to the weather in Vancouver. Center called up and finally asked, "Vancouver airport is closed, say intentions?"

The two scrambled, papers flew, the weather was requested via data link, and the approach plate was examined. Finally, center called in with more help, "Bravo Zulu nine oh one, hold at point WHATS, left turns, ten-mile legs."

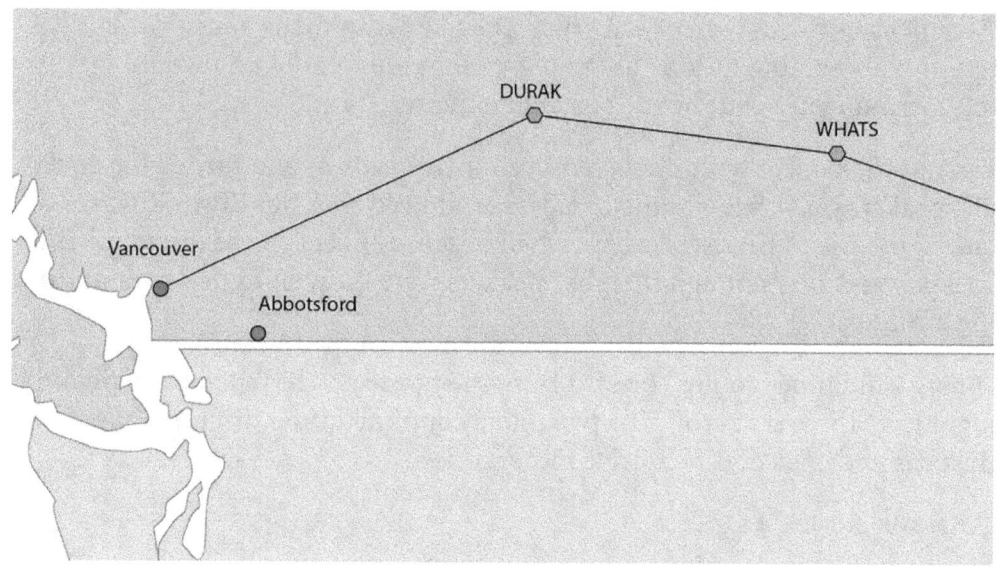

Route to Vancouver with WHATS intersection

I looked up to the FMS and watched the point pass behind us. The first officer swore an oath at the box and told the captain he would have to manually enter the point. I restrained myself from giving him a two-keystroke answer to all his problems and watched him build the holding pattern from scratch. The captain, very smartly, commanded a manual left turn on the autopilot and hit the timer on his clock. Well done, I thought. Finally, the first officer got the holding pattern done and was ready to tell the FMS to override the previous instruction. Just then the captain turned back to the point and saw WHATS in the box and commanded his FMS to proceed direct. The captain hit the final key on his FMS a split second before the first officer okayed the holding pattern, erasing the holding pattern from the FMS.

There was more swearing from the right seat and another manual turn from the left. Bravo Zulu discouraged flying with both FMS in "sync mode," but allowed the practice. Synchronized or not, we required coordination between pilots whenever navigation changes are made. This would be another strong critique item. I was getting ready to intervene when center cancelled the holding pattern and said they could try the approach if they wished.

Of course, they wished, again violating a company rule forbidding these "look see" approaches. The critique items were stacking up.

Just as forecast, Vancouver was below minimums, nevertheless, the crew shot the approach, saw nothing, and went missed approach. Twice. Finally, they asked for vectors to the alternate. Climbing through two thousand feet we were again in sunlight, and just ten miles to the east we saw the ground.

The first officer asked the captain to monitor the radios as he set up the avionics for the approach into Abbotsford. The first officer spoke as he covered each item: the inbound course, the decision altitude, and so forth. Center directed a descent to 2,000 feet, the captain acknowledged and set the altitude alert system to 2,000 feet, but as his hand was moving from the altitude knob to the autopilot's vertical command knob the first officer briefed the ILS frequency. The captain immediately set that in his radio and forgot to command the descent.

I counted silently to myself. At sixty seconds I would say something. The two pilots finished the approach briefing as I finished my count. "Captain," I said, "you need a vertical mode you were cleared to a new altitude."

Just then center asked, "Bravo Zulu nine oh one, say altitude?" The first officer looked up at the altimeter just as the captain spotted the runway to our left. With his left hand the captain disengaged the autopilot, banked sharply to the left, pushed the nose over hard, and keyed the mike, "Airport in sight, going to tower." With his right hand he reached over and extended the landing gear, the flaps, and zeroed the autopilot altitude. The first officer looked up from his approach plate and said simply, "What?"

"Call tower," the captain said.

Dutifully, the first officer called and tower cleared us to land. I bit my tongue and tried to see if either pilot would give even a second thought to what they had just done. It seemed all very normal to them, which made their crimes that much worse. "How'd we do?" the captain asked as we got into the limo for the hotel.

"I think I can sign you off for single pilot operations in the Falcon 900," I said. "But only if you promise to do that for another company."

He laughed. After we got to the hotel, I excused myself, saying I had some phone calls to make. The first was to Kari.

"Unbelievable," he said after I gave him the full accounting. "No, it is believable. It confirms everything we've been hearing anecdotally. I need to have a long talk with Hank. Keep your phone nearby."

I spent most of the night on the phone with the rest of the standards group who collectively agreed the two pilots I had flown with should be fired and the rest of the Wayland pilots all needed check rides. The only decision left was what to do with the ongoing trip. Mr. Wayland would be stranded in Vancouver without any qualified pilots to fly him home.

"It was a Hank Callaghan to Stefano Wayland decision," Kari said during the last phone call of the night. "We let his crew fly him home tomorrow and then we terminate our contract with Wayland Hospital Group."

"Does this happen often?" I asked.

"Maybe once every two years," Kari said. "Bravo Zulu is in the business of moving people safely. We can't have rogue operations in the system like this. The only thing unusual about this is Mr. Wayland's reaction. He isn't used to having someone push back at him. He said he's going to get even with Bravo Zulu." I let his words sink in. "Don't worry about it Eddie," he said finally. "You made Bravo Zulu a better company today."

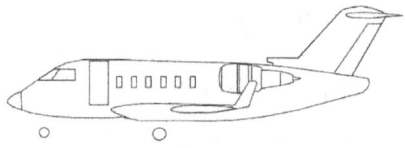

"I'm sorry, Eddie," Jeff said. "I can't find it anywhere. Are you sure I didn't already return it?"

"I guess you must have," I said. "Maybe I lost it." Of course, that wasn't true. The notebook had taken me twenty years to compile and I had lent it out many times. It was only a matter of time for it to grow legs and walk off. It was a seven-ring binder of half sheet pages, 5.5 x 8.5 inches. On each were

Flight Lessons 5: People

handwritten notes about everything I had learned over years about how to fly airplanes. I had about ten other notebooks which were the primary sources – the notebooks I brought back from various schools and flights – but the notebook had it all. I set out to recreate it.

Other than my missing notes, life at Q-Tron was becoming fun and I thought for the first time since leaving the Air Force that civilian life was going to work out. We got several of our first officers upgraded to domestic captains while Gary mysteriously lost his taste for international travel. That meant that we three remaining international captains spent most of our time overseas and avoided flying with Gary. It was a détente I could live with.

Of course, I knew the reason for Gary's sudden desire to remain U.S. bound but was sworn to secrecy. During his most recent return from Europe, he became impatient with an unforecast increase in headwinds and sped up, in violation of what is known as the Mach Number Technique. Despite the word "technique," it is a mandatory procedure. The North Atlantic can become so tightly packed with airplanes that each is required to adhere strictly to an assigned crossing speed measured as a ratio of the speed of sound, known as Mach number. If the winds change, the timing changes; but the timing changes for everyone so spacing is maintained. When Gary sped up without authorization, the separation from the airplane ahead became compromised. The international regulatory agency investigation placed the entire fault on Gary's aircraft, the U.S. Federal Aviation Association tasked Bravo Zulu to explain, and that task fell to me. A quick look at their paperwork and an interview with Gary and his copilot answered any questions I had. I was hoping the FAA would pull Gary's license, but they agreed to let him continue to fly so long as Bravo Zulu restricted him to flying in the Continental United States. In the months that passed, my life had become suddenly serene.

But not everything was tranquil. Every three months the Q-Tron shareholders were treated to a predictable news cycle that began with disappointing earnings performance and ended with Mr. Therianos announcing a new strategy to turn things around. His latest belt tightening plan included sale of one of our three airplanes with two pilots, without a reduction in the flying schedule. I came back from one trip from South America with a day off before a weeklong trip to Paris and London.

The flight to France was uneventful but wasn't really complete until the aircraft interior was cleaned and made ready for the next flight. Most of our passengers were very neat and respectful of the aircraft's cleanliness. The biggest exception was Mr. Therianos, who tended to leave wads of tissues, trails of crumbs, and wine stains wherever he went. "How do you get red wine off white ultraseude?" I asked.

"You don't," Diane said while bundling the last bit of trash. "We'll have to leave that for the mechanics. I think they have some kind of machine for it. We have a bigger problem. Mr. Therianos wants Beluga caviar for lunch on the London flight. Have you ever heard of it?"

"Sure," I said. "I've never seen it, though."

We found it the next day, acting on a hint from the hotel concierge. It was just over $400. "That can't be right," I said, "let's keep looking." But it was the best price we could find anywhere in the city.

"I can't afford that," Diane said.

"You can expense it," I said.

"But it will put my card over the limit," she said.

"I'll pay for it then," I said. That chore completed, we returned to our normal Paris tourism routines. We walked from meal to meal and took up the time in between visiting bars.

"This is the best part of flying for Q-Tron," Sid Justice said between sips of his Kronenbourg 1664 beer. "If I could just avoid the domestic trips with Gary, I would be a happy camper."

"You just need to upgrade to international captain," I said. "With our turnover you will be one of our senior pilots soon."

"That's going to take too long," he said. "I might have to jump ship before that."

It was becoming a pattern. We hired inexperienced pilots, got them qualified in our high-tech cockpit and flying internationally, and then they left. I couldn't blame them. Having to fly with Gary almost chased me out too.

Flight Lessons 5: People

The flight from Paris to London is usually a busy one for pilots; it only takes an hour and you move from the climb to cruise to descent phases almost seamlessly. There was no time to eat but since the galley is just aft of the cockpit, you heard the meal preparation noises and smells. And sometimes, you got a look. "What do you think?" Diane said, showing us a tray with a tin of Beluga caviar positioned on a paper doily on one of our smallest china plates.

"I wouldn't mind some of the leftovers," I said.

"You will eat his scraps?" she asked.

"I've never had four-hundred-dollar caviar," I said.

Just as we started our descent, Diane tapped me on the shoulder. "Sorry," she said, holding the empty tin that must have been licked clean. "He wants five more tins."

As easy as finding Beluga caviar was in Paris, it was a challenge in London. After a few hours search, we found a shop with three tins at $500 each. We struck out for the rest of the day. On day two we found another shop with two tins at $550 apiece. "More credit card points," I said to Diane as I handed my Visa card to the salesclerk.

The flight back to Bedford was easy, given that we were an hour closer when leaving from London and the winds were light. Sid had mastered the art of making HF position reports and plotting, and eagerly asked for the duty both east and westbound. I had very little to do but watch and enjoy the smells coming from the galley.

"Here you go," Diane said. "I saved you just a little before I served it. He's got another four tins after all." It was a small ramekin with a dollop of glossy sturgeon eggs sitting on no more than half of a silver teaspoon. I took the ramekin and gestured to Sid.

"No thanks," he said. "I know how much you are looking forward to this."

I placed the spoon into my mouth and let the eggs linger. "Good," I said. "Five hundred dollars good. Maybe he'll leave more scraps on the next four tins."

But it wasn't to be. I asked just prior to starting our descent back into Bedford. "No more caviar for you!" Diane said in her best Soup Nazi voice. "He wants them packed up so he can take them home."

"Oh well," I said.

Our ritual after a return from overseas started once the last passenger was gone. The PIC started the mountain of paperwork while the other pilot raced to get the airplane cleaned and all the dirty dishes into the hangar dishwasher. The last step of the process for everyone is to get their expense reports finished and on Gary's desk so they could get his signature on the way to the Bravo Zulu accounting department. Placing everything into his inbox was the only time I spent in his office, unless things had gone horribly wrong.

"Haskel!" I heard as I entered the office the next day. "Get in here!"

"You called?" I asked, peering into Gary's office.

"Did you spend three thousand dollars on caviar?" he asked.

"Yes," I said. "Mr. Therianos asked for it."

"That doesn't mean you have to do it," he said.

"Yes, it does," I said.

"We'll see about that," he said. He yelled to the outer office to his secretary, "Get me Therianos on the phone, right away!" He scowled at the expense report in his hand and then at me. "Get the hell out of here."

4: The Missed Approach
February 2003

On approach to Eagle Airport (KEGE), Colorado (Eddie photo)

"Have you flown into Eagle before?" I asked, looking up from the flight plan and our crew trip sheet.

"Many times," K-Square said. Kevin Knox was our newest pilot but had quickly built a good reputation.

"Okay, then," I said. "Why don't you fly us there and I'll fly us back."

"Deal," he said.

It wasn't a frequent destination for Q-Tron but we knew all about it; getting in could be a challenge even with good weather. Getting out was next to impossible with a low ceiling. Our Challengers didn't have the best avionics for getting in and couldn't outperform the mountains getting out. I had probably tried to get in about ten times and had to divert to another airport three or four times. I had spent many hours on the ground waiting for the ceiling to lift, but these were expected complications for this airport.

K-Square flew precisely and according to our Standard Operating Procedures and I was able to relax a bit for the several hours before the descent into the Colorado mountains. I got the weather and started to type a text message to our dispatcher. The available letters, numbers, and symbols on our FMS keyboard made for terse communications, but it was easier than picking up the phone.

WX KEGE MARGINAL, PREP KRIL GND TRNS FOR POSSIBLE DIVERT.

K-Square looked cross-cockpit and smiled. "What?" I said.

"I heard from the others that you divert to Rifle while the others prefer Centennial," he said. "It's funny how in a flight department where so much is standardized, the captains still have personal preferences for these things."

"Rifle is closer to the passenger's home," I said. "The traffic is easier than from the Denver area, and they won't have to cross those mountain passes where the roads are closed now and then because of snow."

"No, I get that," K-Square said. "I diverted to Centennial with Gary once and told him the way it was snowing the passengers would have a rough time getting to Vail. He didn't care."

"That's surprising," I said. Gary was my most current *Foe* but he was the boss and it wouldn't do to badmouth the boss in front of the troops. "I suppose he has his reasons," I said.

The published weather minimums for our approach into Eagle was a ceiling of 2,400 feet and a visibility of 1-1/4 miles. Because of the mountainous terrain, the approach was considered a circling maneuver. Most pilots considered the approach far too steep to fly directly to the runway and instead maneuvered down a valley north of the approach course. In order to do that, I wanted to see the runway no later than the waypoint POWRS, which we would cross at 12,000 feet. That meant any ceiling lower than 12,000' minus the field elevation of 6535', which equals 5,465', could be a problem. The automated weather system had it right at 5,000 feet.

"If we don't see the airport at POWRS, let's not mess around, we'll head for Rifle," I said.

"Sure," K-Square said. "Gary takes it to AWACC, but I like your plan better."

Flight Lessons 5: People

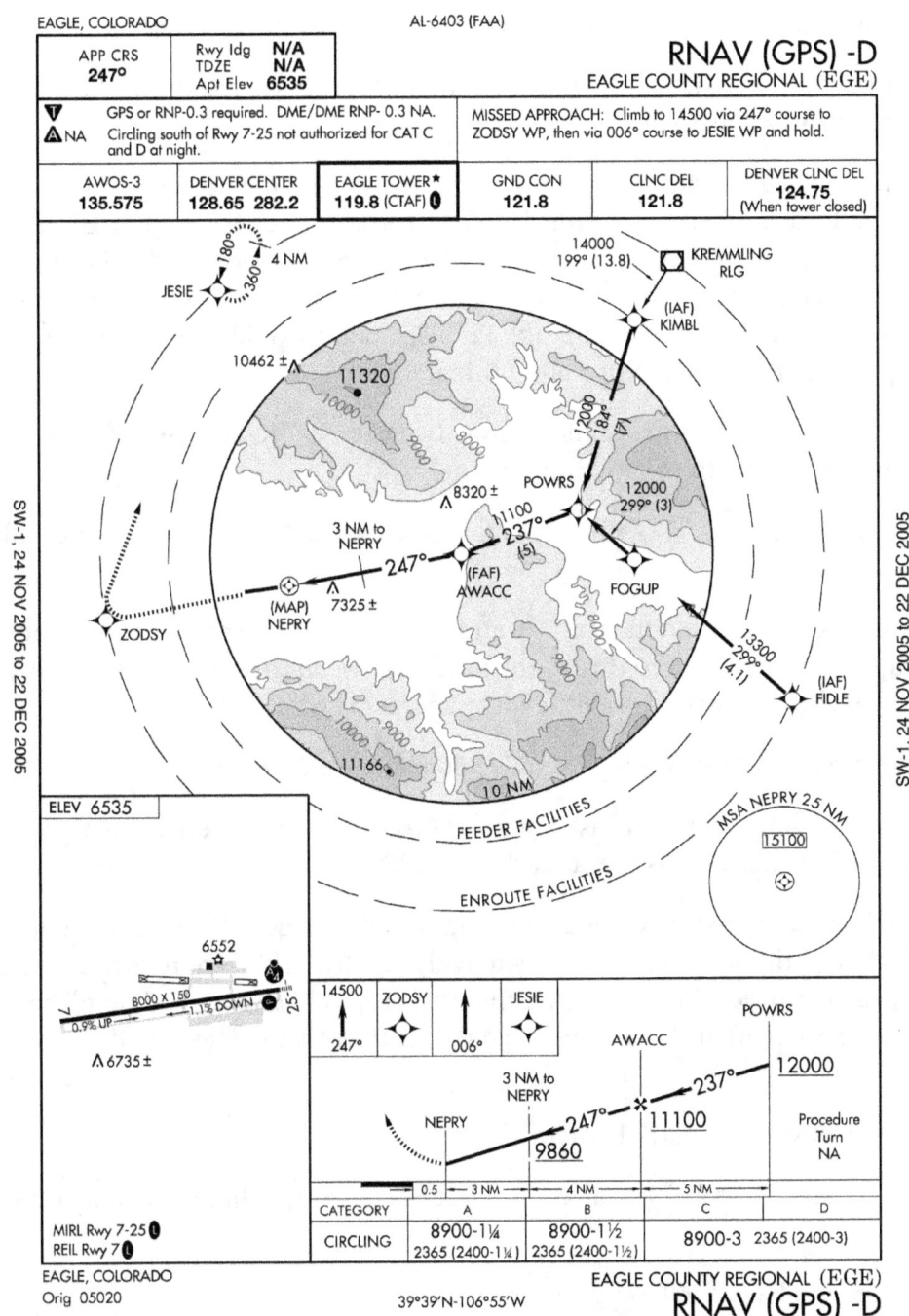

The approach into Eagle, (FAA instrument approach plate)

"Doesn't the ground prox go crazy over the mountains?" I asked.

"It sure does," he said, "but what'cha gonna do, ground prox does what ground prox wants to do."

"So fly somewhere the ground prox is happy," I said. I let him consider that while he studied his approach chart. The airplane's Ground Proximity Warning System, GPWS or "Gyp Whiz" in our pilot jargon, had a database of terrain around the world. If the airplane got too close, it had varying levels of audible warnings. The "Pull up! Pull Up!" alert would be loud enough for the passengers to hear. Not a good thing.

"That's why you want to see the runway by POWRS," K-Square said. "So you can maneuver north of those mountains."

"Very good," I said. "No sense getting anyone upset by the GPWS, especially me."

At POWRS we spotted the runway and were cleared for the visual approach. K-Square turned right to thread the needle between the two mountain ridges. "Let's head downstairs a little more aggressively," I said.

"The min altitude at AWACC is only 900 feet lower," he said.

"We are no longer on that instrument approach," I said. "Let's make this visual as normal as possible, as early as possible."

"Cool!" he said, instantly understanding the advantages. We were on a normal glide path for the runway very quickly and the GPWS remained thankfully unemployed. "That was the smoothest arrival I've ever had here," he said after we landed. "I just wish I could get the other captains to do it this way."

"Why can't you do that?" I asked.

"I fly the way I'm told," he said. "You last longer in any flight department that way."

"We need to have a talk over a beer," I said.

As we drove to our hotel it dawned on K-Square that we weren't headed to Vail. He read his trip sheet with renewed interest. "Glenwood Springs? Why Glenwood Springs?"

Flight Lessons 5: People

"It's a nice little town with lots of history," I said. "It is halfway between Rifle and Eagle, so even if we couldn't make it in to Eagle our hotel reservations stay the same. Besides, we are staying at the hotel where Doc Holliday died."

"The Hotel Glenwood burned to the ground forty years ago," K-Square said. "Lots of places claim to be that hotel, but there's some kind of mountaineering shop there now. I can show it to you if you like."

"Really!" I said. "That would be great. I've been to Glenwood Springs three or four times; I never knew that. Are you a history buff?"

"Yeah," he said. "I especially like the Old West."

We spent the next two days going to historical spots and a few of the local places calling themselves museums. I saved our CRM talk for the night before our flight home. We were at the Hotel Denver restaurant, the place I thought was Doc Holliday's hotel of choice, overlooking the Colorado River. "Tell me about how you got to flying Challengers for Q-Tron," I said.

K-Square revealed that he was Kevin Knox for most of his flying career, which began as a flight instructor in his hometown of Fitchburg, Massachusetts. He gave flight lessons for the owner of a local business who ended up buying a King Air turboprop and wanted a pilot to fly and manage it. That job blossomed into a fleet of King Airs until the owner decided he would be better off contracting flight services with a fractional ownership company. But, in gratitude, he agreed to buy Kevin a training slot for a corporate jet. Kevin chose the Learjet 35 and was almost immediately hired by another company at the same airport. His new flight department was run by several ex-fighter pilots who insisted everyone needed a call sign, so Kevin became K-Square.

"Don't get me wrong, Eddie," he said. "They were a great bunch of guys and I learned a lot. But it seems to me being a first officer for ten years is a bit much. It was time to move on."

"How was the CRM in a flight department of fighter jocks flying Lears?" I asked.

"Not too bad, I guess," he said. "We all got along, and the old guys would listen to us younger pilots. But once they made a decision there was no going back. They fired one or two who started arguing in the cockpit."

"Arguing about what?" I asked.

"Oh, I don't know," he said. "Just stuff. Things like how much fuel to put on the jet, how much rest we needed between flights. Standard stuff."

"How are we at Q-Tron?" I asked.

"About the same," he said. "Maybe a little better. We have six young guys and the three of you who have a lot more experience. So it's only natural that the three of you know what you are doing and the rest of us are absorbing all that."

"But us old guys make mistakes," I said. "What do you do when you see us miss something or make a bad decision?"

"I've never seen anything like that," he said. "Believe me, if I saw something unsafe I would say something."

"Isn't flying low enough over a mountain to set off the GPWS unsafe?" I asked.

"Yeah," he said. "I guess I never thought of that."

"That's part of our job in a two-pilot airplane," I said. "It is up to us to monitor the other pilot and to speak up if things aren't as they should be. Don't be afraid to speak up."

"Okay," he said. "I get it."

I wasn't sure that he got it at all. K-Square was the sharpest of our new hires and if he didn't get it, we had a problem.

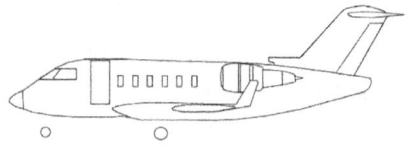

The next day the ceiling was low enough where our aircraft would have problems outclimbing the mountains if we lost an engine. I called our passenger and recommended a two-hour delay; he agreed to another two hours of sleep. After stowing our bags on the airplane I prepped the cockpit while K-Square completed the external preflight. I came down the stairs to find him staring at the low cloud cover.

Flight Lessons 5: People

"Why do we have to assume we are losing an engine?" K-Square asked. "I know everyone says that, but how often do we lose engines on takeoff?"

"Well commercial rules require it," I said. "Bravo Zulu applies those rules to even non-commerical operations as a 'best practice.' Let me get my notes." I pulled my latest edition of notes, no longer in a weather-beaten leather seven-ring binder but in a shiny, brand-new leather seven-ring binder. I managed to recreate the lost original, but I could not be sure I got everything.

"Do you mind if I read your notebook while we wait?" he asked. "I might as well make use of the time."

"No problem," I said. "I'm going back to the FBO and find a cup of coffee." I returned to the Vail Valley Jet Center and found a pot of coffee that smelled like it had been made the day prior and decided on a comfortable seat with a view of the flight line.

"Eddie!" I heard from the doorway across the room. I looked up to see Hank Callaghan, dressed in jeans, cowboy boots, and holding his cowboy hat in his hands. I got up, shook his hand, and gave him my best "what are you doing here?" look without actually saying that.

"I was enjoying a few days in Vail with the family," he explained. "I was doing some business with the office and your name came up. I asked them where in the world you were today and, lo and behold, they said you are right next door. "Sit down, sit down," he said. "Let's talk a bit. It sure is good to see you. We hear nothing but good about you at Q-Tron and the standards group always sing your praises."

"Good to hear," I said. "But I gather something more important is up."

"Yes, of course," he said. "There is a congressional aviation oversight committee asking questions about BZA. They have deposed various people in accounts, manuals, and standards. We are not sure what they are looking for. Have you ever had to testify in court, Eddie?"

"Yes," I said. "We had a crash in one of my squadrons and families of the deceased took our vendors to court."

"How did that go?" he asked.

"Okay," I said. "The thing I learned is that most of these lawyers have only a superficial understanding of aviation. I just did my best to be honest. In the end the case was dismissed."

"That's good," he said. "Your name is on the list of possible witnesses. I don't know who the target of all this is, but I just want everyone they depose to know we at BZA have always placed safety as our top priority. We just want everyone to be as honest as possible, speak their minds, and let the chips fall where they may."

"I can do that, Hank," I said.

He asked about *The Lovely Mrs. Haskel* and the kids. I didn't know anything about his family so I could only counter with, "So how are things with you?" It was a weak rejoinder, but he responded cordially.

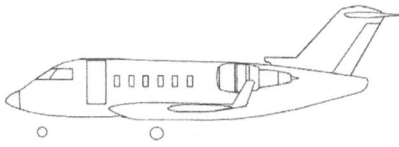

The ceiling finally lifted and we flew back to Bedford, Massachusetts, albeit three hours late. The weather was going to be a problem.

"Winds are calm," I said after listening to the automated weather report. "They are using the ILS 11, and we have the required weather, but just barely. Set me up for that, please," I said.

"Sounds like a plan," K-Square said. I studied the approach again, just to keep it fresh in my mind. The Instrument Landing System broadcasts two signals left and right of centerline. Our aircraft radios would turn the strength of those two signals into a lateral display allowing me to keep the aircraft on course. The ILS shot two more signals above and below an ideal three-degree glide path, allowing me to fly a precise descent. At 383 feet above sea level, or 250 feet above the runway, I would have to spot the approach lights ahead of the runway to continue. At 100 feet above the runway, I had to see the runway. Failing either test, we would execute a missed approach.

The Challenger 604 makes short work of most instrument approaches. You just need to get it established early, get it configured early, and be gentle with power changes on the way down. If you could get the needles centered early,

Flight Lessons 5: People

you had a good chance of being precisely on runway centerline and on the correct glide slope at minimums. Being too abrupt or late with power or flaps or gear would make the "on course, on glide slope" objective more difficult. But we did everything right.

"One hundred to go," K-Square said as the altimeter descended below 490 feet. With one hundred feet to go, we had about ten seconds to spot the runway lights and the runway. Each needle was exactly where it needed to be.

"Decision altitude, nothing," K-Square said.

"Going around," I said. I pushed both throttles forward, pulled back on the yoke and watched the altimeter reverse its descent. I looked up briefly to look out of the window to see nothing, of course, and back down to the instruments. "Climbing to 2,000 feet, set me up on the missed approach."

K-Square did as requested while reporting our missed approach to Boston Approach Control. "Tower says they can turn the airport around if you want to try Runway 29," they said.

"Sure," I said.

"Requesting that," K-Square said over the radio and then got busy programming our navigation system to do just that. Turning around the airport at Bedford required the tower controller to flip a few switches to deactivate the ILS on Runway 11 and activate the same for Runway 29. The weather minimums were lower so our odds were improved.

I reengaged the autopilot and pressed the radio button for Bedford Tower. "Anybody make it in recently?" I asked.

"We haven't had any arrivals since the ceiling fell," the tower controller said. "The transmissometer says you got a mile, so it ought to work."

Looking at the approach plates I had to agree. We had just shot the ILS to Runway 11 where you needed a mile of visibility to spot the runway. Now on Runway 29, we needed less visibility. It should work. But it didn't.

"Minimums, nothing, go around," K-Square said.

"Going around," I said. "Let's go to Logan."

"You got it," he said

Fifteen minutes later we were on the ground at Boston Logan International Airport. I escorted our passengers to the Fixed Base Operator, or FBO, and helped arrange limousines and taxis for each passenger. With that completed, I arranged two hotel rooms for us pilots. K-Square put the airplane to bed and came in with both our bags. "Dinner at any bar works for me," he said.

That night, at the airport hotel bar, we dined on steaks, bypassing the lobster special. "We did a good job tonight on all three instrument approaches," I said. "You did especially well on the missed approaches and getting us set up for next second approach at Bedford and the divert here. You seem very comfortable and competent in the jet."

"Thanks, Eddie," he said. "That means a lot."

"Is there anything we could have done better?" I asked.

"Nah," he said, "it was textbook."

"Strange how we never spotted the runway the second time around on a runway with lower minimums," I said. "One of these days I'll understand weather better than I do."

"That's kind of the way it is at Bedford on days like these," he said.

"What do you mean?" I asked. He looked at me and started to talk but stopped. I could see he was trying to measure his words.

"I'm no weather guru either," he said. "But I've noticed over the years at Bedford that when the winds are calm, the reported visibility isn't as good as they say it is, especially on Runway 29."

"Why is that?" I asked.

"I think it has something to do with the Shawsheen River," he said. "It sits right off the approach end of Runway 29. I've noticed that when you have fog on a calm wind day with the temperature well above freezing, if Runway 11 doesn't work Runway 29 won't work either."

"So we should never have made the second approach," I said.

Flight Lessons 5: People

"I wouldn't say that," he said.

"If you were the pilot in command, what would your decision have been?" I asked.

"I wasn't the PIC," he said. "You were. And all your decisions were good."

"But for the sake of scientific exploration, let's say it was your decision," I said.

"Eddie, I don't want to second guess you," he said.

"K-Square, we have a fundamental misunderstanding here," I said. "I have more experience than you in many ways, no doubt about it. But you have more relevant experience at Bedford. You need to speak up."

"But everything was fine," he said. "If you aren't unsafe my job is to back you up, no questions asked. Shooting an extra approach isn't unsafe."

"That may be so," I said. "But every approach to minimums includes some risk. If I knew what you knew, my decision would have been different."

K-Square sat silently, rearranging the uneaten peas on his plate. He appeared injured by my rebuke. "Eddie it's easy for you to say all that. You have all that Air Force history and Bravo Zulu puts you on a pedestal. Only you can talk to Gary with any kind of attitude and get away with it. It isn't so easy for the rest of us. This is a pretty good job and the pay is decent. We have to think about these things, even if you don't."

Now it was my turn to do urban planning on my plate. K-Square, of all pilots. But more than just him. None of our first officers were old enough to have ever been exposed to the grizzled old captains of the flying boat days. The tenets of Crew Resource Management had been around for as long as any of them had been flying. Each passed a test on the subject and were examined for it every six months in the simulator. But, worst of all, I had been blind to it all.

James Albright

5: Deposed

June 2003

A courtroom (Photo: Michael D. Beckwith)

The summer of 2003 marked my third appearance at the Bravo Zulu standards group meeting which had grown from 20 to 30 pilots, keeping pace with the rapid growth of the company itself. We normally picked a central location and rented a hotel conference center with 20 or so rooms, simplifying logistics on multiple levels. Our increased size meant multiple Dallas area hotels and a conference room in what looked to be a city hall for rent. It took three orbits in the parking lot to figure out I had the correct location and those orbits cost me an on-time arrival.

I peered into the appointed room through a glass window and spotted Kari addressing the group. There was a massive table surrounded on all sides by identical chairs. I recognized half the faces and realized I had no choice but to embarrass myself. I opened the door which was mercifully quiet, but Kari stopped midsentence and looked right at me. "And here he is!" he said. "Eddie, your reputation precedes you."

"That can never be good," I said, to just a few polite laughs. I found the only empty seat next to a pilot whose name I had forgotten but whose face I would never forget.

"Chip Dawson," he said, offering a hand.

"We've already done our intros, Eddie," Kari said, turning in my direction. "We just graduated ten new standards pilots from the simulator and we are hoping you can give them the final standards group blessing."

"I can do that," I said.

Kari continued with the topic of the moment, which appeared to be the need to reduce the excessive number of call outs in our manuals. A "call out" is something one or both pilots had to verbalize at various times in a flight. They were a great help to standard operating procedures unless there were too many. It was a subject I was very interested in.

"Look at this," Chip said in a whisper. I looked down to see a crude drawing of what looked like a microwave oven with squiggly lines around a spindle and connected to a meter. I ignored him and returned my gaze to Kari.

"It's an ammeter connected to the microwave's turntable," Chip whispered. "I can measure the current draw from the motor."

"Why?" I asked.

"So I can figure out when my coffee is warm," he said.

"My microwave has a temperature probe," I said.

"I don't want to contaminate my coffee," he said. I ignored him for the rest of the session. After we broke for lunch, Chip followed me to the cafeteria and followed me to my seat. It was a table of six, I knew four of the other pilots pretty well. "So what do you think," Chip said, placing the drawing in front of me."

"The current draw isn't linear," I said. "The amperage will vary with the temperature of the motor, the friction of the turntable bearings, even the weight of the coffee cup. There are too many variables."

"We knew you two would get along," one of the other pilots said. "You engineers are all alike." Chip smiled broadly.

The rest of the standards group meeting was more of the same. It seemed Chip was my new best friend and whatever meeting, meal, or informal get-together that included me, included Chip. Kari thought highly of Chip, saying he logged more charter hours than any other pilot at Bravo Zulu and

Flight Lessons 5: People

that was only going to continue as his company transitioned from the Gulfstream GIV to the longer range GV. When addressing the group, Chip tended to have meaningful things to say and was at his best when talking about international operations. But one-on-one it was difficult to tell if he was joking or really being a jerk.

"What's your opinion about the latest news in string theory?" he asked.

"I don't know anything about it," I said. Chip looked at me with a raised, red, eyebrow.

"Haven't you read Stephen Hawking's latest book?" he asked.

"I managed to finish the first chapter in the bookstore," I said. "Then I decided it was hogwash."

Chip's insults for others were usually at a less scholarly level. We were at a dinner with several pilots, including Kari. Kari was proudly talking about a house he was building, providing great details about his decisions for a 10-foot ceiling throughout the house and lower, split level living room.

"When you said you are building a house, do you mean you are physically doing the building or are you paying someone to do the actual construction?" Chip asked.

"Well of course I am not hammering and framing the house on my own," Kari said as the rest of us politely laughed.

"I built my own house," Chip said while polishing his nails against his shirt. "You can't really say you are building your own house."

"That's great," Kari said. "Tell us about it."

Chip began to bore us with chapter and verse of his house building experience while the rest of us made mental notes to avoid having dinner with Chip in the future.

That night, after I provided the play-by-play, *The Lovely Mrs. Haskel* couldn't stop laughing. "And he kept going?" she asked.

"I think that he thinks we were all impressed that he dug his own septic tank," I said.

"It is pretty impressive," she said. "But not after telling someone they really didn't build their house."

The next day I taught a class to the "newbs," including Chip, about how to give a Bravo Zulu check ride from the jump seat of an aircraft they were not qualified to fly. The idea was to ensure our crews were following company standard operating procedures, provide useful instruction, and give the standards group feedback. In very rare cases, we reported problem crews for further evaluation. "But you must always be courteous and tactful," I said, emphasizing the last word for Chip Dawson.

As I concluded the last item on my lesson plan there was a knock at the classroom door. I looked up to see Kari.

"When you get done, Eddie, I need to see you," he said.

"I think we are done now," I said. "May I present to you a new cadre of standards pilots."

There were smiles all around and each new standards pilot filed out, shaking my hand and then Kari's. As the last of them left, Kari closed the door and sat down. "The Q-Tron CEO called Hank directly and said he wants us to replace Gary. It had something to do with caviar, if you can believe that."

"I can believe just about anything when it comes to Gary," I said.

"Well try this one on for size," Kari said. "We want to nominate you to take his place."

"I don't want the job," I said.

"Now I'm the one who is surprised," Kari said.

"Most of the flight department has been beaten so hard for so long that I doubt they will ever function as a team again," I said.

"I think you are just the guy to put all the pieces together," Kari said. "It will be about a thirty-percent increase in pay. You can make a difference, Eddie."

"No thanks," I said. "Q-Tron is a sinking ship and it is only a matter of time before we will all be looking for jobs."

Kari drove his eyes down to his desk. "That puts us in a bind, Eddie." In a few seconds his smile returned. "I understand, you have to do what is right for you."

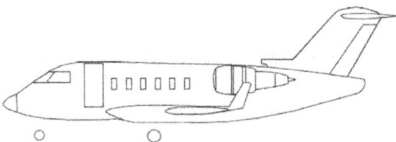

I wasn't surprised when the registered letter showed up in the mail, just perturbed that it meant a trip to the post office to sign for it. I knew I was to be deposed in the case against Bravo Zulu Aviation, thanks to Hank's heads up. But I still didn't have a clue as to what it was all about.

I showed up to the deposition on time, after having squandered any pad I had trying to find a taxi from Reagan National to the offices in Crystal City, just south of the Pentagon. The cabbie dropped me off at the correct location, but it may have been the back of the building. It was a warm Washington, D.C. day and I wanted to get there early to acclimatize in the air conditioning. "Don't let them see you sweat," seemed like a good plan. No matter, I rushed through the building and presented myself to the receptionist on time, perhaps perspiring a little. She ushered me into a conference room where four officious looking men and one equally officious woman arrayed themselves behind a table with a lone chair opposite, obviously meant for me.

It was a large room, but the table was arranged so that the five lawyers were on one side with their backs to the window that ran the width of the room. A court reporter sat at the end of the table. The morning sun beamed into the room and the seat opposite was hit by the light, as if this was to be an interrogation. They wanted me in the "hot seat" and the intent was all too obvious. I wiped the sweat off my brow and laughed, causing each of the five to stare in disbelief. They introduced themselves, made me swear or affirm my fealty to the truth, and asked me to sit. There were two men flanking each side of the woman in the middle. Each had in front of them a notepad and a pen. The woman also had a stack of other papers.

The center lawyer, the lady, pushed a photocopy of a flight log with my name listed as "EP" just below two other names listed as "CA" and "FO" and a column for a number of passengers, of which there were seven. Below that were four more flight logs. "Let the record show we are entering as evidence five aircraft flight logs of dates spanning the years 2001 through 2003 with the name of Edward Q. Haskel listed as evaluator pilot. Captain Haskel are you familiar with these flight logs."

I looked at each log, cross checking my name, the names of the crews, and the city pairs. "I am," I said.

"What was your capacity aboard these flights?"

"I was assigned by BZA to administer a line observation to these pilots," I said.

"For the record this is for Bravo Zulu Aviation, USA," she said.

"It is," I said.

"Let the record also show we are entering into evidence five check ride reports submitted by you to Bravo Zulu, USA, one for each of the flights," she said. She thumbed through the pages and pointed to the signatures on the last page of each report. "Are these your signatures."

I took the papers, thumbed through the pages, and returned the bundle. "I think so," I said.

"You aren't sure?" she asked.

"I am not," I said. "I have a copy of each with me, if you allow me to compare your copies with mine and I can tell you with greater certainty."

"As you wish," she said, returning the report.

I pulled out my laptop and placed it to the right of the stack of papers. I had to fish through a number of check rides, but they were organized by date and finding each report wasn't a problem. It took the computer several seconds to open each file. The lawyers shifted in their seats and the lady opposite me sighed audibly. "These look like my reports and my signatures," I said.

The lawyer seated to her right took the stack of reports. "We will accept your reports as your true observations on each flight," he said. "We have asked you to appear today to give us a sense of why you were sent to do these, what did you call them?"

"Line observations," I said.

"Yes," he said. "Do you know why we singled out these five line observations out of the over one hundred on file that you administered?"

"No," I said.

"These were typed," he said. "The others were handwritten. Why is that?"

"Most line observations are fairly routine," I said. "If I can complete the paperwork on the spot, I try to do so. It puts the pilots being observed at ease and it gets it done. If a line observation requires further research or includes a recommendation that needs the company's attention, I'll complete those later."

"Why would you need further research," another lawyer asked. "You don't know all the facts once you finished these observations?"

"I do not," I said.

"Isn't it your job to be the expert?" he asked. "You are after all being placed in a position to pass judgment on these crews."

"I am not sure I would call myself an expert," I said. "but I certainly don't have everything I need to know memorized."

"That seems a bit irresponsible," he said.

"Just the opposite," I said. "I can't know everything." All but the lawyer on the far-left started writing. That lawyer shook his head in disbelief.

"That sounds, if you don't mind me saying, irresponsible," he repeated.

"I don't mind you saying it," I said. "You don't appear to know what you are talking about."

"Let's move on," the lawyer on far left said. It was his first utterance. He nodded to the center lawyer.

"Let's look at the observation dated October 3rd, 2003," she said. "Are you aware of what happened to the pilot as a result?"

"As a result of what?" I asked.

"As a result of your written report," she said.

"I don't see the cause and effect," I said.

"You wrote that she did not have the judgment necessary to hold her position as a pilot in command of a company airplane," she said, raising her voice. "She was fired as a result!"

"She was fired as a result of her performance," I said.

"Let's move on," the mystery lawyer said again. The center lawyer pulled the next report in the stack.

"Here is another case where Bravo Zulu Aviation not only fired the pilots, but terminated the contract with the client," she said, pushing my report. "What were your specific instructions prior to the conduct of this line observation?"

"I don't remember," I said.

"How can you not remember?" she asked.

"I've given over a hundred of these," I said. "This was four years ago. I don't remember."

"Can you speculate?" he asked.

"No," I said.

"Let me try it this way," the lawyer to her left said. "Did management at Bravo Zulu Aviation give you any reasons for this line observation that may have been out of the ordinary?"

"Yes," I said.

"I don't understand," the center lawyer said. "A second ago you said you don't remember and now you do?"

"You first asked me what my specific instructions were," I said. "I don't remember. Then you asked if I was given any reason for the line observation that may have been out of the ordinary. Those are two different questions."

"Fine!" she said, raising her voice, and then blushing.

The lawyer to her right stared daggers at me, his face flushed. Control your breathing, I said to myself. Keep your volume under control, I thought. Make sure your facial muscles are relaxed, but don't feign a smile. That will

Flight Lessons 5: People

drive them crazy.

"Fine," she repeated in a more even tone. "What were the reasons for this line observation that may have been out of the ordinary?"

"This was four years ago but I believe I stated those reasons in the report," I said, pulling the report and scanning the first page. "First page, second paragraph. This flight department had two FAA violations in a three-year period, had no line observations in the two years prior, and were recently the subject of an FAA altitude deviation investigation which had the potential of becoming the third certificate action against this flight department. The FAA asked the company to investigate. The company directed our standards group to look at the flight department."

"Three of the eight pilots of this particular flight department are, as of this date, unemployed," she said. "The other five found other positions at greatly reduced salaries. Did you know that?"

"No," I said.

It took the rest of the morning to cover the three remaining line observations. Only the first two resulted in the dismissal of pilots. The third resulted in a reprimand of two pilots, the fourth in one pilot losing his status as a captain, and the fifth with no action taken by BZA.

"This last case is interesting," the center lawyer said. "Were you disappointed there was no action taken?"

"No," I said.

"How can that be?" she said. "Isn't it a personal rebuke to you?"

I pulled the report, a one-page, single-spaced, typed onto a standard form. "I didn't ask for any action."

"Why not?" she asked.

"Sometimes having the problem pointed out is corrective action enough," I said.

"You castigated these pilots for twice improperly planning their descents into busy airports," she said. "In one case it required a 360-degree turn to lose altitude and in the second it left the airplane at a lower than necessary altitude.

You said this exposed them to crowded airspace unnecessarily and wasted fuel. That sounds like serious stuff."

"They were new to that airplane," I said. "They didn't understand that a simple mistake in a FMS entry would cause an erroneous top of descent cue. In other words, they were relying on the computers to determine when to start their descents."

"Garbage-in, garbage-out?" she asked.

"Basically, but more complicated than that," I said. "There is a lot going on and a lot of data so it is easy to miss. I gave them a simple technique that allowed them to prevent this. They didn't know the technique before, now they do. No further action needed."

"Then why did you go through the trouble of typing this report out?" she asked.

"I wanted to give them chapter references to their manual," I said. "I had to look those up."

It was noon, the sun was no longer in my face, but I was getting hungry. They gave everyone a bathroom break halfway through, but I was ready for another. "Let's take two hours for lunch," the mystery lawyer on the far left said, reading my mind. "We will reconvene at 2 p.m."

The lawyers all rose but didn't move from their places. I got up and left through the door I had entered. There was a sandwich shop on the first floor and I ate alone, watching a sea of lawyers enter and leave the building. Each male lawyer was dressed in the same dark blue suit with a red, gold, or black tie. The women tended to favor knee-length skirts, a suit jacket, and heels that made it obvious they were heels, but not conspicuous. They were not in uniform, but they might as well have been. A two-hour lunch left me with far too much time to eat and lawyer-watch. My laptop battery had died and I had nothing else to read.

I timed my return to the 30th floor office room precisely but it seemed the gang of five had never left. They reseated me, reaffirmed me, and restarted from where we left off.

"We only have one question left, Captain Haskel," the center lawyer said. "Did any company officer prepare you for your deposition?"

Flight Lessons 5: People

"Yes," I said. All five lawyers looked up at once.

"Who?" she said.

"Hank Callaghan," I said.

"How did he prepare you?" she said.

"He told me to be as honest as possible, speak my mind, and let the chips fall where they may," I said. "And I have done that."

"He didn't say anything else?" she asked. "He didn't give you any ideas about what we have discussed today?"

"No," I said.

"Can you excuse us for a few minutes, captain?" the mystery lawyer on the far left said. "Just wait in the receptionist's room for a bit."

I got up and did as instructed. After about ten minutes the lady lawyer appeared. "We have what we need from you today, Captain Haskel. Thank you for appearing today. Please remain in the local area and call in tomorrow at nine. We'll let you know if we need any further testimony. Goodbye."

I resisted the urge to call Hank until I made it back to the hotel. He picked up on the first ring. "So tell me everything," he said. I did so. "That gives us a few places to look," he said. "Perhaps this is coming from one of those five companies. Thanks, Eddie."

6: The Chain of Command
November 2003

Arnold Palmer at Hilton Head Airport putting green (Photo courtesty hhigolfvacations.com)

Just as I turned down the promotion to Gary's job, so too did every other pilot. Q-Tron summoned Gary to company headquarters for some counseling and decided a second chance was in order. Since every one of his pilots was offered his job, he had to have known his near firing was public knowledge. We all were left to guess how Gary would handle the humiliation. I drew the first trip after his brush with career death.

After three years at Q-Tron I realized I had never flown with Gary Storm since our trip to Santorini. I heard my fill of Gary stories from the other pilots and flight attendants, but I was somehow spared the experiences. I had also never flown any trips to Hilton Head, a regular trip for our golfing CEO. The airport's 4,300-foot runway required a BZA waiver which depended on day-only operations with a highly experienced captain at the controls. Gary liked Hilton Head and took all the trips there. I had been lucky, but my luck had run out.

The first leg of the trip was to Houston where Gary retreated to his hotel room, leaving the flight attendant and I to find a restaurant for dinner. The next day I sat quietly in the right seat as Gary flew us east. The weather was great, and we could see all of South Carolina from a great distance out. Savannah Approach cleared us direct to the airport with about a hundred miles to go. Gary entered a waypoint 2 miles north of Runway 21, setting us up for a right base to that runway. Gary was a frequent visitor to Hilton Head and I had never been. But a right base would be unusual for an airport without a control tower.

I called ahead to the airport's Common Traffic Advisory Frequency and heard there were three airplanes in the pattern, all flying left traffic, meaning each turn was made to the left and the pattern was counter-clockwise. After Savannah approach released us and wished us a good day, Gary directed me to dial 1,500 feet in our altitude select window. His plan was now unmistakable. "It's left traffic at Hilton Head," I said. "You should turn right a few degrees to overfly the airport for the left downwind entry."

"We don't do that in jets," he said. "We're gonna make a right base."

"You can't do that," I said. "There are three airplanes in the pattern, all making left traffic."

"What kind of stupid are you?" he asked. "We are in a damned jet."

"Gary, non-towered airport rules apply to us too," I said. "The rules were changed two years ago and if you don't want to overfly the airport, you can fly an instrument approach straight-in. But you are going to have to turn left to the final approach fix."

Gary let loose with a tirade of F-bombs loud enough for the passengers in back to hear. He realized this and "shut the F up" as I programmed the FMS to turn the airplane left for the localizer approach. I made the appropriate CTAF calls and the other airplanes acknowledged. Without a control tower it was up to us airplanes to make sure the sequence was okay. At twice their speed, the light aircraft would have to watch out for us. But being predictable on the instrument approach made everything easier. And safer.

As we passed the airport on our way to the instrument approach fix to the north, Gary couldn't take it any longer. "To hell with this!" he said while smashing the autopilot disconnect button. "I'm turning base."

I looked up to see a Cessna 172 opposite us on the left base turn. "Bravo Zulu 604 is entering a right base, sorry about this but we are opposite you, Cessna."

"I see you, Bravo Zulu," the Cessna said. "I'll just do a 360. Thanks for the warning."

I noted the sarcasm, but my attention shifted to the steep approach Gary had in store for us. He planted the airplane and brought us to an unceremonious stop. The F-bombs reignited, and I was to blame for the approach and landing. Unlike our first trip together, the threat was no longer about my employment but about Gary's vow to never again fly with me. *Foe.*

Mr. and Mrs. Therianos left the airplane without looking into the cockpit. The bodyguard looked directly at me and shook his head in what had to be a mixture of pity and disapproval. "I was seated all the way aft," Helen Fuhrman said that night at dinner. "I could hear him, so you know the passengers heard him. It was awful."

Helen was our best flight attendant and had something in common with the other two; they also hated flying with Gary. "Don't feel bad, Eddie," she said. "He yells at the other pilots too."

We flew back to Bedford in silence. I witnessed a few cockpit shouting matches in the Air Force over the years, usually one-sided affairs led by general officers. But this was a first for me as a civilian. Gary simmered in the right seat. I bit my tongue a few times as he tried and failed to push our way around air traffic control. After we landed and after the last passenger departed I pulled out the paperwork while remaining seated. Gary started to get up but stopped. "The thing you don't understand, colonel, is the chain of command," he said. "But it's even worse than that. Your paycheck isn't signed by Uncle Sam it's signed by me. Don't expect any pay raises or bonuses because your boss doesn't believe you deserve any." I nodded, silently. "If you want to survive around here you need to get one thing straight," he continued. "I am in charge. Me. Never forget that. Just because I don't like flying with you doesn't mean I don't have my eye on you."

We lived just north of the Massachusetts – New Hampshire border and the drive usually took an hour, which gave me just enough time to replay the arrival into Hilton Head in my mind. Gary and I had both failed our responsibilities to manage our crew resources. I had seen CRM failures before, but never this bad.

"At least you won't have to put up with him again," *The Lovely Mrs. Haskel* said that night. "In a way it works out in your favor."

"Yeah, I suppose." I said. "But the other pilots are going through this too. It can't make the passengers feel safe. I should have been able to deal with this before the shouting. Besides, flying opposite air traffic is a recipe for disaster. If he's unsafe, don't I have a duty to speak up?"

"You do," she said. "This sounds just like some of your experiences in the Air Force with those general officer jerks. Gary sounds just like Skeletor."

"Indeed," I said. "I guess we didn't have a monopoly on jerks."

Friend or *Foe*. I knew many general officers in the *Friend* category but just three who were *Foes*. General Skelton, Skeletor in my personal slang, was in neither category. He was a jerk, a lousy pilot, and one of the worst Chiefs of Staff in Air Force history. But he never treated me badly out of a personal vindictiveness, he was a jerk to everyone. Even when I worked for him at the Pentagon, there was little I could do to impact Skeletor. There is no point having a *Foe* you can't influence. With Gary, I had some influence.

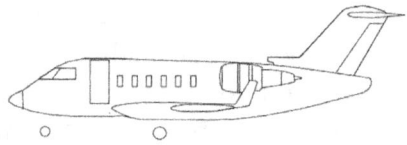

Q-Tron closed out its fiscal year on the last day of September and we braced ourselves for Mr. Therianos' next idea to turn the company around. Ten years after the rest of the industry decided making computer components in the U.S. was a losing game, Mr. Therianos decided Q-Tron would outsource the complete computer to a plant in Taiwan. "Shipped as a complete unit from our plant directly to your door," the advertisement read. "We save, so you save." Our competitors were buying silicon chips and small components from Taiwan, we were buying the whole thing. I wondered about how quickly Q-Tron could react to the rapidly changing computer world while depending on a single supplier on the other side of the globe. I didn't normally devote a lot of thought to Q-Tron parts suppliers, but I was spending half my time in Taiwan, so these kinds of thoughts became the norm.

We usually staged people in Anchorage, Alaska for the crew swap and rotated staging and staged crews to even out the time away from home, airline miles, and international experience. But we were spending so much time in Taiwan and had lost so many internationally qualified crews that it became

Flight Lessons 5: People

more cost effective to leave me in Anchorage after returning from Taiwan, ready for the next go around. In just a few months it became my new normal and I had forgotten most of the flight department was busy flying other trips.

"This is Linda, your dispatcher," she said.

"This is Eddie, your pilot," I said.

"I imagine you are pretty tired of Taiwan by now," she said. "How about a week off in Hawaii?"

"Sign me up," I said.

"It is going to be you, Sid, and Helen staging to Long Beach next Wednesday," she said. "Another crew brings the airplane to you Thursday at midnight, and then you fly it to Maui. The following Tuesday you turn around without the crew swap and come home."

"Who is the captain from Bedford to Long Beach?" I asked.

"It's Gary," she said. "Is that a problem?"

"Not at all," I said. "Sid is right here, I'll brief him. Thanks."

The following Thursday night, about midnight, Sid and I were sitting in a Long Beach FBO's lounge, waiting for our inbound aircraft. "They've landed but we have to park them on another ramp," the FBO representative said. "We'll give you a ride out there." Sid pulled out his crew swap checklist and reviewed our roles and responsibilities. As the PIC of the second leg, my role was to review the mission and any airplane problems with the arriving PIC and then get the FMS set up for the next leg. Sid would ensure the fuel truck had the correct quantity in mind and would help Helen prepare the galley.

They drove us out to the airplane, parked in the darkest part of the airport. We got there just as the airplane's main cabin door was opening. Two passengers assisted Diane as she carefully negotiated the stairs. I hadn't seen her that unsteady since her Soup Nazi incident. Helen rushed forward to help. The fuel truck showed up and Sid went off to supervise the refueling. I boarded the airplane and tapped Gary on the shoulder.

"What happened to Diane?" I asked.

"Diane?" Gary said. "Diane is fine. She's just a drama queen."

"Any problems coming in?" I asked.

"None at all," he said.

"Any problems with the airplane?" I asked.

"Nope," he said. "I predict smooth sailing from here to Hawaii."

Something implied but not explicitly stated in our crew swap checklist was the need for speed. Everyone had to do everything as efficiently as possible to minimize the passengers' delay. Any experienced pilot looking at the flight log would see the airplane had spent nearly 45 minutes on the ground. That was a poor crew swap time for many airplanes but not the Challenger, which has a reputation for slow fueling. Once we were headed west at 36,000 feet, Helen came forward with a cup of coffee.

"What happened to Diane?" I asked.

"I don't know," she said. "I asked, and she was babbling something about falling. The passengers said it was pretty bumpy. I'll see if I can get any of them to talk."

We landed in Maui before sunrise and parked under a sea of lights near the FBO. The marshaller crossed his arms as we inched to our parking spot and then pointed to our aircraft's nose. "What's that all about?" Sid asked.

"I don't know," I said. But I soon found out. As soon as our passengers were gone, I went outside to the front of the airplane. Q-Tron's aircraft were all painted dark blue, but the nose of our aircraft was mostly blue with hundreds of pock marks of silver dents. Tracing the damage aft, the dents stopped but the missing paint continued along the fuselage and to the wings, where the dents continued.

"Hail damage," Sidney said.

"Yeah," I said.

"Helen found out what happened to Diane," he said. "The passengers said it was the roughest air they had ever seen. They said Diane got thrown around the cabin like a ping pong ball. All the passengers were belted in, thankfully."

Flight Lessons 5: People

It was already business hours in White Plains, so I called Bravo Zulu Aviation immediately. They dispatched a "go team" of Canadair specialists to fix the airplane. I then called Gary to ask again about the weather and all I got was, "it was a little bumpy."

"I noticed the radar was in the off position," I said. "By the book it should have been in standby. Did you have it on at all during the flight?"

"I don't like your tone," he said. The line went dead.

I documented the damage in the aircraft forms, grounding it. The next day, Helen, Sid, and I flew home as passengers aboard a United Airlines Boeing. I got back to our hangar to confront Gary again but found myself in an empty office. Everything was gone.

"Fired," his secretary said. "He didn't waste any time hanging around."

Sid and I took the remaining airplane and returned to Maui to pick up our passengers. Before we left, Kari called to offer me the Base Manager position again. "We need you to step up to the plate."

"I'll think about it," I said. During the trip back from Hawaii I gave Sid the rundown of Gary's fate and Kari's offer.

"You going to take the position?" Sid asked.

"No," I said. "It would be like being the captain on a sinking ship."

"Well as long as we are talking about sinking ships, Eddie, I have a confession."

"That can't be good," I said.

"You guys have done a lot for me and I've learned a lot," Sid said. "But I've accepted a position with another company at Bedford. I'll be flying a GIV."

"That's great!" I said. "You are going to like flying Gulfstreams. Having excess thrust is good. Having an airplane with redundancy is really good. When do you start?"

"Soon," he said. "They wanted me to start right away. I told them I wouldn't feel right with less than a month's notice."

"That's good," I said. "We are going to miss you."

81

When we got back to Bedford, Mr. Therianos followed his usual "good bye" with "it was nice to have known you."

"What was that all about?" Sid asked.

"I don't know," I said. "But it continues." I pointed to the hangar where a Q-Tron lawyer I recognized from previous trips was standing. He was carrying a briefcase and the look of bad news.

"Who died?" I asked as he approached. He stopped, mouth agape, but then recovered.

"I guess we all did," he said. "Q-Tron declared bankruptcy this morning and I've been ordered to impound the airplane and everything associated with it. You and your crew are to surrender your aircraft keys and any supplies that belong to Q-Tron."

Driving home from the airport it was hard not to have those "what am I going to do now?" thoughts. After three years with Q-Tron we hardly made a dent in the principal on our mortgage. We had a son about to start high school and a daughter just three years behind. Savings? Not enough. On the plus side, *The Lovely Mrs. Haskel* was working full time as a Registered Nurse, so we wouldn't be penniless. I planned on spending the day on the phone, secluded in my home office. I grabbed a second cup of coffee and joined *The Lovely Mrs. Haskel* at the kitchen table.

"Postmortem?" she asked.

"Well it was in the cards," I said. "The computer industry has been changing and the pace of change has been accelerating. They just couldn't keep up."

"I meant a postmortem on the flight department," she said.

"Oh," I said. "I guess that would be helpful." I thought for a few minutes. She was good about keeping silent and staring into space at these times. "Remember Pan Am?" I asked.

"Just from our high school days," she said. "We would sit on your father's deck and watch the airplanes takeoff and land at the airport. Whenever it was a Pan Am airplane, you got a little more excited."

"I used to think they were a great airline," I said. "They practically invented the international airline business. But when they moved up to jets, they crashed more of them than practically anyone else. Turns out their pilots had this ocean liner captain mentality. They didn't tolerate dissent and anyone who dared was immediately fired."

"Those days are long gone," she said. "Aren't they?"

"For most airlines they are," I said. "The Feds threatened to shut Pan Am down and that finally got the message across. Pan Am fired all those old captains and their safety record after that point was quite good. But in the end, they couldn't survive the crash at Tenerife or the Lockerbie bombing. A few years after Pan Am folded, the airlines in the U.S. and most of the world adopted Crew Resource Management. That fixed a lot of problems."

"So what about corporate aviation?" she asked.

"Most of us get it too," I said. "But we still have a few that never got the word, a few that pretend to agree with CRM but are just play acting, and those that are cut from the old captain mold. I think that was Gary."

"So how do you fix that?" she asked.

"From what I saw in the Air Force and now in my only civilian experience is that it has to come from the bottom," I said. "The younger generation that gets it has to force the older pilots to either get it or retire. In a cockpit, the crew has to assert itself. The captain either listens or is shown the door."

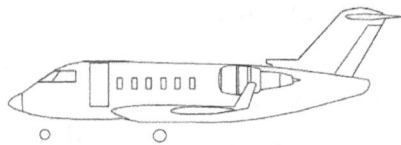

I overslept the next morning and was jolted awake by the phone; it was Kari. "I got two things to talk about," he said. "I heard about Q-Tron and want you to know we are going to find you another job, don't worry about it. But before we get to that, hold on to your hat. Gary is interviewing for the chief pilot position at a competitor and was hoping someone at BZA would write him a letter of recommendation."

"Which competitor?" I asked.

"IFE," he said.

"They deserve each other," I said. Kari's laughter was explosive. International Flight Enterprises had more airplanes than BZA, but they were mostly small, domestic aircraft. Our annual revenues dwarfed theirs.

"I can't think of anything positive to say about the man," I said.

"Yeah," he said. "I'm getting that from everyone who knows him. So that will be a 'no' from Mister Haskel then." Another *Foe* vanquished, I thought.

"Okay, that's taken care of," Kari said. "I have no doubt there are a ton of flight departments who would love to have you on their payroll. What is your preference?"

"Back to Gulfstreams," I said. "I don't want to move the family, but I might consider commuting."

"I am happy to hear that," Kari said. "Let me work on it."

"It's me," I heard after picking up the phone on the first ring.

"You'll have to do better than that," I replied to the unknown voice.

"Bravo Zulu standards group," he said. "I'm the guy who keeps coming up with good ideas for you to shoot down."

"Chip?" I asked.

"So you admit they were good ideas then," he said.

"If you ever come up with one, I'll let you know," I said.

"Well try this one out for size," he said. "We just had a pilot quit and I heard from Kari Owens you are looking for a new job. Mr. Viceroy has time to meet you tomorrow."

"That would be great," I said. Chip gave me Mr. Viceroy's office address, told me to wear a coat and tie, bring a resume, and remember, don't be afraid of lions.

Flight Lessons 5: People

"What lions?" I asked.

"You'll see," he said.

It was a typical Chip Dawson phone call. He never gave direct answers and always tried to leave something unsaid. In the years I had come to know him, I knew the job would have a long list of pros and cons.

"Okay, let's hear them," *The Lovely Mrs Haskel* said. "Pros first."

"It's a Gulfstream," I began. "Not only that, the best Gulfstream out there today. The pay is higher. We don't have to move." I thought for a bit. "That's about it."

"Cons, then," she said.

"The flight department tends to run through pilots," I said. "I think they last no more than a year each."

"Why is that?" *The Lovely Mrs. Haskel* asked.

"According to Chip, it's the owner," I said. "They do a lot of charter, 700 hours a year. That isn't as bad as it sounds, since the airplane does a lot of long haul. Chip says the owner is hard to get along with."

"What about Chip?" she asked.

"I can get along with him," I said.

James Albright

Flight Lessons 5: People

Flight Lesson: Masters of Ocean Flying Boats (The days before CRM)

Why pilots are called captains and first officers

The Wright Flyer, 1903 (The Library of Congress)

In the beginning there was the guy on his belly shifting his weight and manipulating strange levers to somehow manipulate a contraption that defied gravity. Before that there was the Greek word "pedon" which was the steering oar of a boat which became the Italian word "pedoto" which meant the person who steers the boat. So the guy defying gravity became a pilot.

The evolution of concern with crew factors must be considered in the historical context of flight. In the early years, the image of a pilot was of a single, stalwart individual, white scarf trailing, braving the elements in an open cockpit. This stereotype embraces a number of personality traits such as independence, machismo, bravery, and calmness under stress that are more associated with individual activity than with team effort. It is likely that, as with many stereotypes, this one may have a factual basis, as individuals with these attributes may have been disproportionately attracted to careers in aviation, and organizations may have been predisposed to select candidates reflecting this prototype. [Kanki et al., 2010, p. 5]

The addition of other pilots on the flight deck followed naturally as the size and complexities of aircraft increased. These additions had titles with variations of the word pilot in them, such as second pilots or copilots. All of this continued until Juan Trippe, the founder and CEO of Pan American World Airways, took to the skies with the flying boat.

The flying boat was born from the idea that two-thirds of the planet was covered in water and there were not many paved runways suitable for large aircraft. Besides, there was something comforting about being able to land just about anywhere if something went wrong.

> Juan Trippe, it was said, had a nautical fetish. On the walls of his home hung paintings of clipper ships, the fast full-rigged merchant vessels of the nineteenth century. It was Trippe's dream that his airline, Pan American, would become America's airborne maritime service. Pan Am flying boats would be the clipper ships of the twentieth century. So he called his flying boats Clippers. Aircraft speed was measured in knots. The pilots who commanded the clippers were given the rank of captain. Copilots became first officers. It wouldn't do for a Pan American pilot to look like the scruffy, leather-jacketed, silk-scarved airmail haulers of the domestic airlines. Instead, they wore naval-style double-breasted uniforms with officer's caps. When they boarded their flying boats, they marched up the ramp, two abreast, led, of course, by the captain. Trippe understood pilots, having been one himself. He knew they were prima donnas who loved the pomp and perquisites of command. The captains of the great oceangoing, four-motored behemoths like the China Clipper needed a suitable grand title. So he gave them one: Master of Ocean Flying Boats. Like commanders of ships at sea, the Masters of Ocean Flying Boats were a law unto themselves. While under way they exercised absolute authority over their aircraft and all its occupants. And with such authority went, inevitably, arrogance. [Gandt, 1995, p. 19]

Flight Lessons 5: People

How Pan American World Airways got it so wrong, and then so right

Juan Trippe was a visionary in many ways; he foresaw profitable international airline service before anyone else thought it even possible. He pushed aircraft manufacturers into bigger, faster, longer. You can argue that he was the driving force behind the Boeing 707 and 747 programs. Pan American World Airways and the Boeing 707 have a linked history, and that history shows just how important Crew Resource Management is in an airplane with more than one pilot.

During its lifespan, nobody crashed more Boeing 707s than Pan American World Airways. In fact, the accident rate in their first real transoceanic jet was going up while the rate for the rest of the industry was going down. There are lessons here.

Note: this list does not include aircraft involved with hijackings (24 Nov 1968, 22 Jun 1970, 29 May 1971, 17 Dec 1973).

3 Feb 1959 — Pan Am 115 — An inept copilot made several mistakes that plunged the aircraft into a spiraling dive. While the captain was able to recover, the question that should have been asked but wasn't is this: What trait of the Pan Am culture allowed such a pilot into the seat of their flagship aircraft? PILOT ERROR

8 Dec 1963 — Pan Am 214 — A lightning strike ignited fuel in a wing tank, causing that portion of the wing to separate; the pilots were unable to recover.

7 Apr 1964 — Pan Am 212 — The captain deviated from the ILS glide slope and ended up landing too long to stop on the runway. While nobody was killed, the aircraft was damaged beyond repair. PILOT ERROR

28 Jun 1965 — Pan Am 843 — An engine turbine disintegration caused a fire; the crew made a successful emergency landing.

17 Sep 1965 — Pan Am 292 — After the captain deviated from weather visu-

ally, the crew lost position awareness and descended too early into the terrain. PILOT ERROR

12 Jun 1968 — Pan Am 001 — The crew misset their altimeters on approach (millibars versus inches) and flew too low on approach. PILOT ERROR

12 Dec 1968 — Pan Am 217 — The crew flew into the ocean during approach, perhaps because of the visual illusion of the dark ocean against a dark sky. PILOT ERROR

26 Dec 1968 — Pan Am 799 — The crew attempted to takeoff without the flaps set. PILOT ERROR

25 Jul 1971 — Pan Am 6005 — The captain flew the approach improperly and impacted a mountain short of the runway. PILOT ERROR

22 Jul 1973 — Pan Am 816 — An instrument failure may have distracted the crew after takeoff; they flew a descending turn into the ocean. PILOT ERROR

3 Nov 1973 — Pan Am 160 — Uncontrollable smoke in the cockpit contributed to a number of CRM errors that left the aircraft unflyable. PILOT ERROR

30 Jan 1974 — Pan Am 806 — The crew failed to recognize an excessive descent rate caused by a recoverable windshear. PILOT ERROR

22 Apr 1974 — Pan Am 812 — The crew turned and descended 30 nautical miles early, opting to bet their lives on one ADF needle that had swung (indicating station passage) while the other remained steady, pointing ahead. PILOT ERROR

Note: Links to the case studies are provided in the references section of this book.

By the close of 1973, Pan American World Airways had lost ten Boeing 707s, not including one lost in a hijacking. (The 3 Feb 1959 aircraft was repaired *and returned to service.) As Robert Gandt [1995] put it, "Pan Am was littering the islands of the Pacific with the hulks of Boeing jetliners." Pan Am initiated a study to figure out what was wrong. As the study was being conducted, Pan Am crashed two more. [p. 112]*

> Something had to be done. Before the smoke subsided from the burning wreckage on Mount Patas in Bali, the probe of Pan American's flight operations had begun. Inspectors from the Federal Aviation Administration climbed aboard Pan Am Clippers all over the world. FAA men rode in cockpits, pored through maintenance records, asked questions, observed check rides and training flights. [Gandt, 1995, p. 115]

The FAA's findings confirmed what the airline's own review had already concluded: Pan Am was crashing airplanes at three times the average rate of the United States airlines and their rate was increasing. The FAA let Pan Am know that they would either have to straighten up or be shut down.

But the most profound change was still coming. It was an invisible transformation and it had more to do with philosophy than with procedure. Pan Am was forced to peer into its own soul and answer previously unasked questions. Instead of What's wrong with the way we fly airplanes? the question became What's wrong with the way we manage our cockpits? A new term was coming into play: crew concept. The idea was that crews were supposed to function as management teams, not autocracies with a supreme captain and two or three minions. It meant the captain was still the captain, but he no longer had the divine license to crash his airplane without the consent of his crew. Copilots and flight engineers-lowly new hires-were now empowered to speak up. Their opinions actually counted for something. [Gandt, 1995, pp. 117-119]

The airline also instituted standardization so that cockpits were no longer managed according to the edicts of the captain, but by the airline itself. The changes took hold and the airline was transformed. After the Bali crash in 1974, they never crashed another Boeing 707. In fact, the airline established a safety record that was the envy of the airline world. It was two Boeing 747 crashes that had nothing to do with the pilots that killed the airline for good.

James Albright

The first was in 1977 at Tenerife, where a KLM 747 took off in heavy fog and collided with a Pan Am 747 trying to exit the runway. The second was the terrorist bombing of Pan Am Flight 103 over Lockerbie, Scottland in 1988. These two accidents were too much for the already struggling airline to handle and sealed the ariline's fate forever.

Part Two

The Captain

7: The Regal Captain Returns to Earth

March, 2004

Gulfstream GV, Stuttgart, Germany (Photo: JetPix)

It was only my second serious job interview since leaving the Air Force. The Internet revealed that the owner, Gil Viceroy, Esquire, made his money years ago by buying big companies, breaking them into smaller companies, and selling the carcasses for a profit. Regulators finally caught up with him and shut him down, but by then his wealth was measured in billions. He didn't like crowds, so having his own Gulfstream GV allowed him to bypass the traveling public when he needed to be somewhere outside Massachusetts. But when he didn't need the airplane, he gave it to Bravo Zulu to charter.

He maintained an office in a small business block in Lincoln, Massachusetts where he showed up twice a week. The first-floor directory pointed me to the fifth floor to Viceroy, LLC. I approached the office thinking I had made a mistake, the only adornment on the smoky gray glass-paned door was the office number. I opened the door to see a brown-haired lady behind a desk look up. The walls were paneled in dark wood and the carpet was a plush, dark gray. The lady looked up from a keyboard but didn't speak.

"I'm Eddie Haskel," I said.

"Right on time," she said. "I'm Gail. Have a seat."

I picked the middle of three chairs on the wall adjacent to her desk and underneath a painting of a white rhino in the African grasslands. As I sat, I spotted for the first time the head of another rhino hanging from the opposite wall. I resisted the urge to examine the painting closely; perhaps it was the same rhino.

"He'll see you now," she said.

She held the door open for me and I entered a very large office. I walked in and was greeted by a lion's head on the floor, staring right at me. The head was attached to the rest of him, ten feet of pelt leading to a desk. The pelt was bordered by two chairs on either side, the legs of each chair only six inches from the pelt. Mr. Viceroy stood from behind the desk and extended a hand.

"Have a seat, Eddie," he said.

I approached the desk and stepped to the right side of the lion's head and shook Mr. Viceroy's hand. I picked the seat closest and to Mr. Viceroy's left. My leather shoes rested on the lion's pelt. Gail took the seat opposite, her heels also on the lion. Mr. Viceroy read my resume, looking up a few times. His skin was pasty white, accented with spots and wrinkled with age. Seventy, I guessed. His scalp was completely covered by white hair, but it was thin enough so the age spots showed through. He was thicker than I had come to expect from most men his age. He was about my height and weight.

"What was flying Air Force One like?" he asked.

"I flew the backup aircraft for many years," I said. "But never with the President on board. Being a backup pilot isn't a glamourous job."

"But you have flown Boeing 747s and Gulfstreams," he said. "So that's something. Backup or not, it is pretty impressive. Why should I hire you?"

"I have all the experience your charter operation needs," I said. "I've been doing the same kind of flying for the Air Force and as a civilian. I work and play well with others. I already live here and I am a check airman with Bravo Zulu Aviation. Besides, I am incredibly good looking."

Flight Lessons 5: People

Mr. Viceroy laughed, Gail followed on cue, and I felt a bit of relief that my risky joke paid off. "You know Chip, I take it," he said.

"Yes, sir," I said.

"What do you think?" he asked.

"I can get along with him," I said.

"Not everyone does," he said.

"I can," I said.

"When can you start?" he asked.

"One month from today," I said.

We shook hands and I followed Gail to her office for the paperwork. After an hour of that I drove home. *The Lovely Mrs. Haskel* was pleased that her children wouldn't be uprooted. "Postmortem?" she asked.

"Gary was a f...," I stopped myself, my mind racing to recover.

"Eddie!" she said.

I had started to say *Foe,* which he definitely was. *The Lovely Mrs. Haskel* had never heard me use the term and evidently thought I was going to issue my very first F-bomb, something I hadn't done since we first met, thirty years ago. "Gary was a full-fledged disaster of a boss," I said. Yeah, that should work. "I think if I had figured that out earlier, I could have treated him more like a general officer and maneuvered him into doing the right thing despite himself."

"But instead you seemed to enjoy making sport of him," she said, "even to his face."

"I guess I did," I admitted. "But in the end, it didn't matter. Q-Tron was going to fold. They say the average corporate job lasts two to three years; we got five out of it. And having a leadership position in Bravo Zulu certainly helped. I will end up with only a month without a paycheck."

"What about the flight department, itself?" she asked.

"That does bother me," I said. "I can understand being at war with Gary Storm, he deserved every bit of the battle. I don't understand why the pilots refused to speak up to him or me. We are all taught to speak up in the cockpit and none of those guys were novices. Now I'm going from a large flight department to a small one. Maybe I can figure it out with a smaller population."

"Always the engineer," she said.

"Now I have to call the new boss," I said. Dawson's number was already in my phone from his position at Bravo Zulu Aviation.

"Chip Dawson, chief cook and bottle washer," he said, picking up on the second ring.

"It's Eddie," I said. "I guess I work for you now."

"I just got off the phone with Gail," he said. "This is good. You must have walked on the lion's back."

"I did," I said.

"Good," he said. "I was told you start one month from today. As it turns out, there is a Gulfstream GV class starting one month from tomorrow. Get yourself to Savannah and try to forget everything you ever knew about the Challenger."

"The ram dump of knowledge has already started," I said.

The Lovely Mrs. Haskel and I kept news of the job turmoil a secret from the children, deciding it better to delay any bad news until if and when it was certain. As the events unfolded, they were none the wiser until realizing that I was going to be gone for a month. It was my first training event at the Savannah FlightSafety International center since 1994, when I attended a recurrent GIII course there as an Air Force pilot.

Everything about the training center was new and improved. The GV was so new that FlightSafety didn't have a chance to write their own manuals, so we were loaned our very own Gulfstream manuals. The ground school instructors were retired Army helicopter pilots who did nothing but teach the airplane, and they were quite good.

"Memorize this and I'll explain it as we go," Warrant Officer Steve Howell, U.S. Army (retired), said during the first hour of our first day. "Left before right and essential before main."

The GV's systems were well thought out and full of redundancies. Many of the electrical systems were divided left and right, with a further subdivision between essential and main portions. Backup electrical systems were designed to step in automatically in case of a failure, ensuring that the left-essential bus was top priority.

The aircraft systems were the easiest to understand that I had ever seen, and Steve Howell's classroom method made it all easy to absorb. Chip recommended the hotel at the airport, bypassing Savannah's Historic District and the best food on earth. "Too many distractions downtown," he said. "It's the toughest aircraft qualification course you have ever taken and you will need to focus. Heck, even I struggled!"

It was the easiest aircraft qualification course I had ever taken, mostly because of Steve Howell's instruction. Each day started with a recap of the previous and each lesson built upon the previous. I started taking notes about how to be a good instructor as well as how to fly a Gulfstream GV. But, as the knowledge poured in effortlessly, my boredom level started to rise.

I was learning a lot in class, but not enough to fill another volume of my notes. I now had two complete sets, one for use and one for backup. I wondered about a backup to the backup. No, that would be silly.

"Eddie!" Kari answered as I called at the precise moment I thought he would start his day at his White Plains office. "We were just talking about how nice it is going to be to have you on this account. Other than Chip, no pilot has ever lasted more than a year. We are putting our money on you going the distance. They treating you well in school?"

"They are," I said. "I was wondering how much that lady in Connecticut charges us for the International Operations Manual?"

"I think it is two thousand per pilot," he said. "Highway robbery if you ask me. But it is the going rate."

"If I rewrote it cover-to-cover would you fire her?" I asked.

"In a heartbeat," he said. "But wait till you get back from school, okay?"

I promised I would, knowing that I would not.

After two weeks of ground school I was paired with a retired airline captain to face the simulator as a team. He had been seated at the opposite end of our ground school class and we never had the chance for introductions. I knew him from his frequent questions, however. "Was that left before essential?" he managed to ask three times. Now he and I would be crewed for eight lessons in the simulator followed by a check ride.

"Thirty-five years in the left seat," Adrian Metzger said as we met for the first time.

"That's impressive," I said. "What types?"

"Every Boeing Northwest has," he said. "You are a Boeing guy too, I heard."

"Just the seven-oh and seven-four," I said. "This is my second Gulfstream."

"We are going to do great," he said. "I've been a captain for many years, you know."

"Thirty-five years," I said.

After the first day I thought, maybe, Adrian was going to be great, just as he predicted. His instrument work was precise, and he managed to learn the many normal procedures checklists quickly. Sim One was a chance to get to know the airplane without any malfunctions and was quite easy. I did find some of his chatter annoying but kept that to myself.

"Let's go flying," he would say prior to every takeoff.

"Let's," I said.

"Are you comfortable?" he would say prior to every landing.

Our Sim One debrief went well and Adrian was all smiles during dinner. "I like your style, Eddie," he said while devouring a plate of ribs. "Too many pilots take it all too seriously."

"I take it all too seriously," I said.

"And I really like your dry sense of humor," he said. "We are here to learn a new airplane. Why can't we have some fun while doing it?"

Adrian answered his own question the next day during the first half of Sim Two, our introduction to emergency procedures. It was my first takeoff of the day and the number two engine fire switch lit up just a few seconds after decision speed. I fed in left rudder and kept the nose pointed down the runway. A pop-up checklist appeared on Adrian's navigation display just as we got to rotation speed.

"What the . . ." Adrian said as rotation speed came and went. I pulled back on the yoke and we started to climb.

"Gear up, please," I said. I looked to my right and saw Adrian fumbling with the automatic checklist switches.

"Adrian," I said. "Adrian, I need you to raise the gear."

"Oh!" he said. I continued the climb. He managed to scroll the pop-up checklist and read the second item. "You want me to pull the throttle back?"

"No," I said. "That can wait." A few seconds later he placed his left hand on the left throttle.

"Adrian, please wait," I said.

"But it's on fire," he said.

"It isn't going to do us any good if you pull back the wrong throttle," I said. He pulled back the wrong throttle. Within a second, we were inverted; I was surprised enough that I forgot to relax rudder pressure and dove for the throttle instead. By the time the engine spooled back up we were both in simulator hell.

"Well I've never seen that before," the instructor said. "How soon after takeoff did Northwest allow you to pull back a throttle?"

"It was the captain's discretion," Adrian said. "In thirty-five years as a captain, I've never made that mistake."

"Oh well," I said. "We'll do better next time. But between you and me, Adrian, the only thing Gulfstream wants you to do below 400 feet is rotate and retract the gear. And with me in the left seat, the new rule is 1,500 feet. Okay?"

He nodded meekly. He did better for the rest of his right seat time on Sim Two. After a break we swapped seats and it was my turn as the trusty copilot. Just prior to rotation one of the engines simply quit but was still windmilling freely. Adrian rotated competently and started talking rapid fire. The instructor impressed on us both that there was no need to shut engines down or do anything else we might regret until 1,500 feet. But he didn't say Adrian couldn't talk.

"And let's get vectors for a single-engine ILS and put this puppy back on the ground," he said. "Do you concur?"

"Maybe we should try relighting the engine," I said.

"What?" he asked.

"Your call captain," I said. "But I don't see any signs of engine damage and we haven't heard any from tower. Maybe we can relight it."

"I already said we are going to land single engine," he said.

"Okay," I said.

That was, of course, the wrong answer. I'm not sure it was Adrian's fault. Part of the FlightSafety way of doing things was we had to demonstrate an engine relight at least once. The fact the engine was not on fire and continued to spin in the wind told me it was a relight situation. After we landed the instructor listed the reasons for and against a relight and recommended we try the relight in the future.

"We were a little rusty with the E.P. today, Eddie," he said that night at the bar. "But we'll get it. We both have what it takes in the old C, R, M department."

"I think so too," I said. "We just need to brush up on more of the emergency procedures. I do have a suggestion for your Crew Resource Management, however."

"Really?" he said. "At Northwest all my first officers had nothing but praise for my CRM."

"This is just a minor quibble, I suppose," I said. "But instead of asking 'do you concur?' after every decision, you might consider 'anything to add?' or 'what am I forgetting?' instead."

"What's the difference?" he asked.

"If you ask for concurrence you are asking for a yes or no answer," I said. "Some first officers are reluctant to challenge the captain and saying 'no, I do not concur' poses a challenge. But asking 'anything to add?' is more open ended. But the best part of this is that we, as captains, don't know everything. This way a sharp first officer can help us when we need it."

"But we have to take a check ride," he said. "Won't the evaluator see that as a sign of an incompetent captain?"

"Not at all," I said. "It is a crew airplane. We pass together or we fail together. I would rather pass together."

Adrian was a competent pilot until things went wrong. At that point, he often fell apart. Sim Three and Sim Four were repeats of Sim Two. The yelling started during Sim Five. He was yelling at himself, but it was still unnerving. "Why can't I get this?"

We followed each simulator session with dinner and a pep talk. "You can do this, Adrian. You just need to calm down."

"That's easy for you to say, Eddie," he said. "You have a job that is paying for this. Northwest forced me to retire at 60 and I used every bit of savings I had to pay for this type rating. Sixty-five thousand dollars! If I fail the type, I am truly and entirely screwed."

"You aren't going to fail," I said. "How can someone with thirty-five years as an airline captain fail?"

Sim Six was his best. From the left seat his stick and rudder skills were quite good, though he still had problems getting the rudder in smoothly anytime an engine failed. From the right seat he managed to get that pesky pop-up checklist on his first try. But he followed that with his worst performance ever during Sim Seven. We finished the post simulator dinner with him crying in his seat.

"Is the GV that much harder than what he flew for the airlines?" *The Lovely Mrs. Haskel* asked that night during our daily catch up with life call.

"No, not at all," I said. "In fact, in many ways it is easier. But I think as a thirty-five-year captain, he may have been coddled. The airlines are good about standardizing one airplane to the next, and since Adrian flew nothing but Boeings, the transition was probably easier. I've never flown with someone who can get so upset, so quickly. He can go from a big, happy smile to tears in no time flat. Schizophrenic."

"Bipolar, actually," she said. "Why is he so worried?"

"It sounds like he ended those thirty-five years with nothing saved," I said. "He had a couple of marriages, has kids all over the place, and has bills to pay. He thinks busting this check ride leaves him with nothing."

"Is that true?" she asked.

"I don't think so," I said. "FlightSafety rarely does that to pilots and even when they do, there are retraining options. They want him to pass so he comes back for recurrent training."

"Maybe he doesn't know that," she said. "If he fails, what does that mean for you?"

"It is a crew airplane," I said. "If one pilot fails, it can easily mean both fail. But not always."

"Maybe he is worried that he is going to take you out too," she said.

Adrian started Sim Eight in the right seat and seemed to do better with everything, even his Achilles Heel, the engine fire checklist. It was fairly complicated, but it wasn't a problem when he took his time with it. But if he skipped or misread a step, things usually deteriorated rapidly. His left seat performance was worthy of a pass until he had to execute a missed approach with an engine failed.

Flight Lessons 5: People

"Bank angle, bank angle," a synthetic voice boomed.

"Smaller corrections," I said from the right seat.

"Tell that to the airplane!" he yelled.

Our Sim Eight debrief was unpleasant, but the instructor tried to paint a rosy picture. "We all have good days and bad days, Adrian," he said. "You tend to alternate so it is actually a good sign that you are having a bad day just before the check. You'll do fine. I'd like you to review the engine fire checklist for a minute. Eddie and I are going to get a coffee."

We left Adrian with his checklist. As soon as we were alone at the coffee-maker, the instructor turned to me and lowered his voice. "Eddie you have to talk to him," he said. "He's going to take you both out if he doesn't learn to calm down."

That evening, as we drove to our favorite restaurant, I thought about *The Lovely Mrs. Haskel's* advice. The tongue in cheek Air Force answer to these situations was to instruct using fear, sarcasm, and ridicule. It was a joke, of course. But I would add to those three, "when all else fails, use empathy."

"What happened at Northwest if a pilot busted a check ride?" I asked.

"That was pretty rare," Adrian said. "But the airline knows they hired a good pilot to start with and that meant it was cheaper to spend whatever it took to retrain than to fire."

"So, they had a vested interest in seeing the pilot pass," I said.

"Exactly," he said. "Unlike FlightSafety."

"Why do you think that?" I asked.

"I already wrote them a check," he said. "No matter how I do tomorrow, they've got my money."

"But if you don't get your type rating, you won't come back," I said. "They want you to pass so they can see you in another six months." I pulled into an empty parking spot right in front of the Outback Steakhouse, it was an auspicious sign. We filed into our usual booth and ordered our usual beers.

"Have you seen anyone bust a check ride at FlightSafety?" he asked.

"Two or three," I said. Adrian's jowls slumped; it wasn't the answer he wanted. "But I've been coming here since 1992. And in each of those cases all that was needed was another training ride and a recheck."

"Really?" he said. "Who pays for that?"

"I suppose the pilot does," I said. "But isn't that worth it when in the end you get your type rating? I heard the going contract rate for a GV pilot is fifteen hundred a day. The world is your oyster." His jowls tightened.

"I guess that makes sense," he said.

"Besides," I said, "you aren't going to fail. We can make this work."

"A check ride strategy!" he said. "We should have a strategy."

As we dissected the Bloomin' Onion between us, we decided I would go first to put the check airman in a good mood. If Adrian felt at a loss anytime during the ride, he would say "Ah, just a minute," and I would try to help him out.

"Most important," I said as we each finished the last morsel on our plates, "don't worry about making mistakes. I have never had a perfect check ride. Nobody does. You will make mistakes. So will I. But when you make a mistake, turn the page and move on."

The normal sequence in a FlightSafety simulator check ride is for both pilots to undergo an oral exam, followed by two, two-hour simulator sessions. One pilot occupies the left seat and the other the right seat for the first session, and then the roles are reversed. Since each pilot is being evaluated in both seats, nobody gets a debrief until both simulator sessions are completed. That's not what happened the next day.

The first session went very well, and Adrian's performance was his best ever. He got the pop-up checklist on his first try and only fumbled with two of the procedures. But in both cases, he recovered without so much as a whimper. I rotated too aggressively during a takeoff with an engine fire and we got a little slow. "A little slow," he said quietly enough to escape the check airman's notice. "Thanks," I said.

"Let's debrief you now, Eddie," the check airman said as we climbed the stairs after the first session. "It makes things easier."

Flight Lessons 5: People

The check airman was full-on praise for us both. "You two work very well as a team," he said. "It is such a pleasure when a check ride goes so effortlessly." The check airman handed me my temporary license with the Gulfstream GV type added. "Let's take a break."

"I'm really happy for you, Eddie," Adrian said over our mid-session coffees. "The last thing I wanted to do was cause you to fail."

"Well you did me a favor by doing such a good job in the right seat," I said. "I just hope I can do as good a job as your copilot, captain." Adrian was as relaxed as I had ever seen him as we started the next session.

It was easily Adrian's best performance, in fact, it was a very good performance by any measure. His aircraft control was precise and his instrument procedures were very good. I checked my watch and realized we only had thirty minutes to go, but we still had the maneuver Adrian struggled with the most. The GV is an overpowered airplane which meant it needed a very large vertical fin and rudder to tame the adverse yaw of an engine failure. Going missed approach with only one engine required the pilot to push the rudder at the same rate the operating engine spooled up. Adrian struggled to get it right and rarely flew the maneuver without the airplane issuing its "bank angle!" complaint. After Sim Seven I recommended he put in half the rudder and freeze his feet until the engine caught up, and then go for all the rudder remaining. And that's precisely what he did during Sim Nine.

In fact, I was amazed at how well he was doing as we climbed to the missed approach holding pattern until I spotted the problem. Adrian forgot to disengage the auto-throttles. Doing the missed approach single engine using auto-throttles was against the airplane's limitations and would warrant a check ride bust. I glanced backward to the instructor console and saw the check airman was facing sideways, filling out paperwork. I thought for a moment I could disengage the auto-throttles but that would cause a warning chime to sound and it might upset Adrian. Perhaps the check airman didn't catch it.

He didn't. Adrian's debrief was a replay of mine and we both walked out of the training facility as newly typed Gulfstream GV pilots. We decided to return to the Outback Steakhouse in celebration. Adrian looked at his temporary pilot's license throughout dinner.

"We really did great, you and me!" he said. "I've been taking check rides for forty years, thirty-five as a captain. And I've never seen a perfect check ride. Until tonight. We were perfect!"

8: Everybody is a Captain, Nobody is Crew

June 2004

Not Alone in the North Atlantic (Photo: Ivan Luciani)

"Amazing," I said from the right seat of our Gulfstream GV cruising at 45,000 feet heading for Switzerland. As a tenant at Hanscom Field, Bedford, Massachusetts, we paid just under $3.00 per gallon for Jet-A. We loaded up with just over 3,700 gallons of fuel which put us at 75,000 lbs. for our departure, but still light enough to land at Teterboro Airport, New Jersey where the fuel was twice as expensive. We were then able to takeoff with our passengers bound for Geneva, bypassing the more expensive fuel. Cruising at Mach 0.83, our flight time was just over six hours. "Just amazing," I repeated.

"She is that," Chip said from the left seat. "So, I guess you aren't tempted to go back to the Challenger."

"Not at all," I said. The avionics made my navigation chores easier and I got our coast out navigation accuracy check done with a minimum of fuss. Chip sat quietly as I finished the first position report.

"Bravo Zulu Fife One checks fife fife north, zero fife zero west one three two one zulu flight level four fife zero, estimates fife eight north zero four zero west one four zero eight, fife nine north zero tree zero west next, over."

Gander Radio repeated my position report and asked me to call back at 58° North, 40° West.

"I wish you could teach Nigel how to do that," Chip said. "For a so-called international expert from United Airlines, he doesn't know the first thing about position reports."

I sat quietly and wondered about the novelty of it all. Chip Dawson was the Client Aviation Manager, the CAM, for a three-pilot and one-mechanic operation; he was the boss. I was the newest pilot on my very first trip and he was badmouthing the number two pilot to the number three pilot. But I made the mistake of stoking the fire.

"I think the airlines have got it down to a science where all you have to do is follow a cookie-cutter recipe for each city pair," I said.

"He can't even do that," Chip said. "He was an ERP. You know what an ERP is?"

"No," I said.

"He was an extended relief pilot," Chip said. "They put him as the third wheel of a two-pilot crew, just so they could fly longer trips. And he did that from San Francisco to Honolulu and back. That hardly makes you an international expert. It's more like riding a bike with training wheels."

The oceanic routes from California to Hawaii were among the easiest to navigate in the world. The tracks never changed, the weather was almost always good, and sometimes you could just follow the contrails of the airplane in front of you. But it was hardly child's play. I started to sympathize with Nigel even though I had never met him. Here was the boss attempting to pit subordinate against subordinate. When the boss is captain, what chance does the subordinate crew have? I let the subject drop.

"There goes YQX," Chip said pointing to the Radio Magnetic Indicator and the missing navigation needle. Moments before it was displaying an arrow pointing to the Gander Very High Frequency Omnidirectional Range, or VOR. "Now you have to plot."

Flight Lessons 5: People

I already had the plotting chart out and made all the needed entries so far in our 3,000 nautical mile journey. I remember he made that statement during our international procedures training, but I didn't challenge him then because I wasn't sure. Now I was sure. "What does losing YQX have to do with anything?" I asked.

"I thought you knew these things," Chip said. "The rule says the second you lose the VOR, you have to plot. Don't you know anything?"

"Where does it say that?" I asked.

Chip reached behind the throttle console and opened a below deck compartment and pulled out our thickest publications binder, produced by the Jeppesen Company. It was thousands of pages written in very small print on onion skin paper. "In here," he said, handing me the binder.

"I don't think that's right," I said, taking the binder.

"Wanna bet a quarter?" he asked.

"Okay," I said.

I knew the answer was that plotting was required for a turbojet once 725 nautical miles from the "service volume" of a qualified navigation aid. The service volume could be thought of as the reasonable range of a VOR or other navigation aid. That was usually around 100 nautical miles so the rule of thumb was that you had to plot about 800 nautical miles away from a VOR. For our trip to Switzerland it was an academic point, we had to plot. But for other trips it was a distinction worth knowing.

I knew also that the exact reference was sitting in my trusty leather binder but didn't want to retrieve it, lest it find legs again.

"You boys want some water?" the flight attendant asked.

"Not unless it has 100 milligrams of caffeine and is heated to 200 degrees Fahrenheit," Chip said.

"What?" she said.

"I think the captain is asking for coffee," I said. Our flight department didn't have a permanently assigned flight attendant, but we had several we used on a contract basis. Sarah Thomason was an experienced flight attendant but new to us. She rolled her eyes and headed to the galley for the coffee. Chip smiled confidently in his seat, thinking he had impressed the young lady. I thought back to his boast about building his own house. A pattern was developing.

I made the next position report and completed my other duties as Chip sat quietly, staring blankly at the horizon. I thumbed through the Jeppesen binder between cockpit chores. Just before my last position report, at 59° North, 20° West, I found it. "I think you owe me a quarter," I said, handing the Jeppesen binder cross-cockpit. He read the page twice.

"Good golly," he said. "I've been telling pilots this for twenty odd years and you're the first person to tell me otherwise. Now I got to find something else to beat up on them with."

"No beatings in the cockpit are allowed," I said. "It isn't good for morale."

For the next few hours he would ask questions starting with, "Do you know . . ." and I would answer, "Yes," and provide the answer. After a while he would stop waiting for the answer and just say, "Okay, okay." There are two types of oceanic pilots: those who let the time pass quietly while accomplishing their navigation and communications chores and those who want to fill every moment with chatter. I am of the former, Chip was of the latter. The strange thing about this dichotomy is that each type of pilot makes the other uncomfortable.

We ended up on the ILS to Runway 04 at Geneva, surrounded by terrain, fully configured to land but still in a thick cloud deck when Chip said, "Mind if I get in on some of this fun?"

"What?" I asked. He disengaged the autopilot and hand flew the approach from that point on. All of that is perfectly legal and safe, provided the pilot doing the flying does a good job of it. I don't normally do that in the weather because it increases everyone's workload.

"Drifting high," I said, watching the glide slope indicator slip below us. "And left," I added. The altimeter continued its unwinding; we had about 500 feet to go when we broke out. The runway was to our right and we were higher than we should have been.

Flight Lessons 5: People

"Well I may be too high," he said with a chuckle, "but at least I'm left of course." He pushed the nose down and dipped the right wing. We met the runway unceremoniously three thousand feet down, but we still had more than enough left over.

"Let's never do that again," I said.

"Ah come on," he said. "I've done worse and bragged about it."

Based on one flight I came to the conclusion Chip was an average pilot, at best, with above average knowledge, but a little lacking in the discipline department. During our three days off in Geneva he turned out to be well above average in his desire to tour the city but slightly below average in the consumption of alcohol and well below average in the social skills department.

"Never on a weekday," he said after I ordered my first beer. "But you go ahead."

I sipped on my beer and Sarah, seated to my right, nursed a white wine. Chip sat opposite us and stared vacantly at the space between us. He just sat with that vacant stare as Sarah and I made idle chatter. It could have been a few minutes, but it felt like ten. Once dinner was ordered and the first plates of food appeared on the table, everything returned to normal. After we returned to the hotel Chip announced our next scheduled event was breakfast at eight. Sarah said she would be there. "I think I'll skip," I said. "On second thought," she said, "I'll skip too."

I took the left seat for the flight home and everything was fairly routine. Chip's performance on the radio was okay, but a little too folksy for my taste and his report items were out of order. If I was the instructor and he were the student, I would have explained the layout of the radio operator's computer console and the importance of adhering to the standard format. But he was my boss and this was our first trip. The critique would have to wait. Once the airplane was tucked away in the hangar, Chip retreated to his office while Sarah and I busied ourselves with the galley. Once that was done, she wasted no time getting to her car and leaving.

Our hangar office was nothing more than four rooms, the main one being his, the second shared between the other pilot and me, the third for the mechanic, and finally a kitchen. I sat at my desk, filling out the company's expense report form when Chip handed me a quarter and a letter.

"This is the last quarter you are ever going to get from me," he said. "Sign this form and I'll send it to Bravo Zulu." The form signified that I was a Gulfstream GV international captain, a rite of passage at Bravo Zulu Aviation. I signed it.

I placed the quarter on the chair rail behind me. "I'll leave this here in case I ever have to give it back," I said. "Or maybe I'll start a collection."

"It sure will be nice to have the airplane go on trips without me," he said. "It hasn't done that in over a year."

"Why is that?" I asked.

"Because I like to eat," he said. "None of the other pilots stuck around long enough to upgrade. Kari Owens said you could upgrade as soon as I deemed you competent. I so deem. Have a good time in Kona."

I checked my email and was delighted to see that our Q-Tron dispatcher was now handling Viceroy LLC. I selected her name from my cellphone and hit the green button.

"This is Linda, still your dispatcher," she said.

"This is Eddie, still your pilot," I said.

"It is you as PIC and Nigel as SIC," she said. "Monday to Wilmington, Delaware empty. Your flight attendant for this trip is Claudia Lincoln, she'll meet you there. Tuesday morning it is off to Kona for five days, and then back the way you came."

Other than the fact we could fly from Delaware to Hawaii nonstop, it was a routine trip for me. I had been to both airports and was already comfortable in the airplane. The only unknown would be the other pilot.

I met him for the first time on Monday, just prior to our deadhead flight. "Nigel May," he said, extending a hand. "I got here three months ago."

"My pleasure to fly with a Brit," I said.

"I've been in the states for fifteen years now," he said. "I got my U.S. citizenship five years ago. I have a wife and two kids and a dog."

Flight Lessons 5: People

"As American as apple pie, then," I said.

I thought we were getting off to a great start, but Nigel seemed unsure of his role as the second in command for our trip. He made no effort to begin the preflight of the airplane until I asked, and then seemed a bit put off by my request. "You want the legs going west or east?" I asked once the airplane was fueled. Again, he seemed bothered by the question, but chose the left seat for our flights to Delaware and Hawaii.

The only thing that seemed to lift his spirits was Claudia. Whenever she appeared in the cockpit he smiled brightly and became talkative. It was my first trip with Nigel and I wasn't sure if this was his normal routine with flight attendants, but I thought he was bordering on pandering or perhaps worse. But it was still too early to say.

As we left the western shores of California behind, I started plotting our position passing each waypoint. I showed Nigel my plotted position about ten minutes after each waypoint and he simply said, "Okay." Once we were on the ground, every task seemed to be a nuisance.

"Nigel, am I being too bossy?" I asked.

"I was just wondering why you are calling all the shots when I am the senior pilot," he said.

"Because I am the pilot in command on the trip orders," I said. "It isn't a big deal to me; I assume we'll trade positions on the next trip. But right now, it's me."

Nigel rifled through his brief case and pulled out the trip orders. "Oh," he said. "Okay."

The next few days on the ground were fairly easy going. Nigel liked to walk and visit tourist sites. He enjoyed a good meal and didn't have a "no drinks on weekdays" rule. Claudia was fascinated by his British accent and hung on to each of his words. Nigel and Claudia had much in common and during our meals I became the silent third party. The day before our return I got a call from my favorite dispatcher.

"This is Eddie, your pilot," I answered.

"I just thought you should know Nigel is pretty upset," she said. "He wants to know why you are already a captain when you just showed up and he is still a first officer."

"I was wondering the same thing," I said.

"I told him it was because you have been with Bravo Zulu for many years and he just started," she said. "But he said he's been an international airline pilot for years and that should count for something."

"Well I will tread lightly then," I said.

With Nigel in the right seat it was obvious he had no intentions of plotting, so I pulled out a plotting chart and did so, from the left seat.

"That isn't required on a fixed track," he said.

"Let me show you something," I said, reaching to the cabinet behind the throttle quadrant. I found the appropriate reference and read the requirement.

"That's not how we did it in the mainline," he said.

"What's the mainline?" I asked.

"The main airline," he said. "You have regionals and you have the mainline. United didn't make us plot between California and Hawaii."

"I guess you airline pilots had different rules," I said. "But in our world, we are supposed to plot."

Nigel took the plotting chart and did so. His radio procedures were excellent, and his plotting was pretty good. I knew that the airline rules for plotting were the same as ours, but also that many pilots arbitrarily decided not to plot the Hawaii routes because of sheer laziness.

Over the next year I would learn that Nigel knew next to nothing about international flying in Europe, Asia, the Middle East, South America, and Africa; and was defensive about anything he didn't know. (Which meant he was often defensive.)

Chip, on the other hand, thought he knew just about everything there was to know about flying all over the world, but was wrong about half the time. (And he was too lazy to look things up.) I was lining up quarters on the

Flight Lessons 5: People

chair rail, but Chip never stopped betting quarters whenever I challenged his knowledge. Every surrendered quarter was delivered with a smile.

My knowledge came up short south of the equator, but I was learning. (And looking things up.) We usually flew as a crew of two and rotated two on, one off. That meant those who chose to gossip about the pilot who was off had ample opportunity.

"Chip is a jerk to all flight attendants," Nigel would say.

"How so?" I would ask.

"He sits at dinner and just stares at them, not saying anything," he said. "Or he says something in that fake professor tone of voice to make them feel stupid." I had noticed both traits but dismissed it as his strange sense of humor. But Nigel had a point.

"Nigel thinks he's a world class pilot but he's not," Chip would say. "You can't teach him anything because he thinks he already knows it."

"Example?" I would ask.

"We were in the middle of Africa this last trip and he didn't know the first thing about broadcast-in-the-blind procedures," he said. Chip had a point.

Of course, you can't expect any pilot to have the procedures for every country in the world memorized, which is why pilots charged with doing so need to spend so much time in the books. But Mr. Viceroy would only pay for one set of books and they had to stay on the airplane. Chip lived three hours away in Vermont and Nigel lived three hours away in Maine. Neither wanted to spend any more time at the hangar than absolutely necessary. I had a distinct advantage, living only 30 minutes from the airport. Of course, I also had one of the best collection of notes on the planet. I was starting to treat their existence as a national security secret, but the secret was poorly kept.

"Do you still keep that book of notes of yours?" a friend once asked.

The friend in question mattered and determined my answer. He was an ex-Air Force squadronmate whom I had flown into combat with. We were standing in the middle of an airline terminal somewhere in the world and did a five-minute catch up on each other's lives. He was an airline captain now, as were the majority of all my Air Force pilot peers. It was an odd request, but for him, anything. "Sure," I said. I rifled through my bag and pulled out my current primary notebook. "Maybe you can copy the whole thing and send it back to me."

"Sure thing," he said, taking the notebook forever.

That night I fired up the World Wide Web and learned how to create a website. Programming in raw Hypertext Transfer Protocol – the "HTTP" you see in many web addresses – was easier than the computer languages of my past. My website would be private; just for me and whoever asked for a copy of my notes in the future. I chose the name www.knownprocedures.com, from a favorite saying of mine: "Known procedures produce known outcomes." I had a renewed purpose in life.

I was planning a trip to Australia for a charter client the following week and wanted to do some research. Chip and Nigel were returning with the airplane from Europe about midday and it would be a good opportunity to watch the arrival operation as a fly on the wall before getting into the books stored on the airplane. I showed up at the hangar an hour before their scheduled return and parked my truck next to the mechanic's.

My truck is one of those you can be forgiven for thinking belongs to a "yuppie" who wants a truck but doesn't need one. It has a comfortable cab and the bed in back is barely big enough to haul a four-by-eight sheet of plywood. It is ten years old but looks new. Our mechanic's truck is one you would think is for a rough and tumble outdoorsman, covered in mud. There are scratches and dents from front to back. While the bed of my truck was topped by a pristine black cover, his was open with the bottom half of a V-8 engine. Chevy 357, by the look of it. My plate was generic, his said "DRJONES." Donald Robert Jones, mechanic. Beyond our two trucks were two, very nice, German sedans. Chip and Nigel both had expensive tastes in cars.

I walked into the office area, which was empty. Looking into the hangar, Doctor Jones was nowhere to be found but the hangar door was open wide enough for a person, even a person of Jones's girth, to fit through. I made my way outside.

"Hey, Eddie," he said as I approached. He was kneeling on the ground, holding what looked like an acetylene torch and the grate of a very large barbeque grill.

"Making a barbeque pit?" I asked.

"Yeah," he said. "It's going to be great."

I retreated to the hangar, being careful not to trip over a cargo pallet left near the entrance. Looking around in the unlit hangar I realized I didn't know how to turn the lights on but I did know how to open the door. "Mind if I open up?" I yelled to Jones.

"Go ahead," he said. "It's about that time."

Opening the door meant holding a switch down and walking along as the door slowly moved its one-hundred and twenty or so feet. The trip would take about a minute and gave me time to survey the inside. It was filthy. The floor needed to be swept and there was junk all over the place.

"What's in those barrels?" I asked, pointing to three 50-gallon drums, each painted a different color but made somehow uniform by rust.

"Old gas," he said. "I have to drain the EPA tanks on the airplane now and then and the gas has to go somewhere. I'll take those home one of these days to fill my lawn tractor."

Most of our trips were charters starting from another location and the passengers would never see our pigsty of a hangar. Even the charters leaving Bedford and our owner's trips departed from a local FBO, so nobody was the wiser that our beautiful airplane spent its nights at home in squalor. I was still relatively new and trying to fit in. But messy hangars rubbed me the wrong way.

The Rolls-Royce engines on the GV have a distinctive growl to them, a very nice audio signature. Many jet engines tend to whine on the ground, not so the GV's. I heard the pleasant rumble at the end of the taxiway and decided to hide in a corner, playing my proverbial fly on the wall. Chip was in the left seat and taxiing at a moderate rate. He pulled right up to the hangar with the nose gear straddling the hangar door tracks. In no time the engines were shut off and the main cabin door opened. As he disembarked he spotted me.

"More study time," he guessed.

"Yup," I said. "I haven't been to Australia in a while, I need to brush up on a few things."

"Maybe I should take that leg," he said. "If you don't know how to fly down under."

"Your call," I said. Chip laughed and disappeared into the office.

I walked to the airplane but stopped at the stairs as Nigel rushed down. "I don't know how you put up with him," he said, heading for the office. I took the stairs by twos and turned right to see a flight attendant I didn't recognize.

"I'm Eddie," I said. "I'm the third string pilot around here. Can I help you with the dishes or anything else?"

"Absolutely!" she said. On my second trip from the airplane to the hangar kitchen with a load of dishes for the dishwasher, I noticed Nigel's car pull out of our driveway. On my third trip Chip was waiting with a stack of papers.

"You mind dropping my paperwork off at the office?" he asked.

"I can do that," I said.

"Good," he said. "See you in Hawaii."

I was going to airline to Hawaii and spend a night as he and a contract pilot flew our passengers from Washington, D.C. In Hawaii, Nigel and I would take over and fly to Sydney. I knew his earlier threat to take the Australia leg was idle. Chip was an avid photographer and wanted five days off in Hawaii while Nigel and I did the long legs to and from the Land of Oz.

On my fourth and final trip, I spotted Dr. Jones carrying his makeshift barbeque grate to his truck. "You mind closing up, Eddie?"

"Not at all," I said. "I thought I could help you with the postflight."

"Done," he said.

Flight Lessons 5: People

"Really?" I asked. "I was going to run the switches as you checked each light."

"I did that as they taxied in," he said. "You gotta learn to be efficient."

"How did you check the landing lights?" I asked.

"Listen, pilot man," he said. "You don't tell me how to do my job and I won't tell you how to do yours!" He chuckled, grinned, and slapped me on the back. I wasn't being so much rebuked, I guess, as being warned.

"I don't know how you do it," I said. "I couldn't face another ten hours in a hollow aluminum tube, especially as an airline passenger. I'm having dinner with my parents tonight, you are invited."

"No thanks," Nigel said. "The key to flying as an airline pilot is to count the number of days at home. He who has the most nights at home at the end wins. Besides, I have another trip next week while you and Chip are off to another standards boondoggle."

That was true, but Chip and I would actually be gone about the same number of days. While Nigel would be doing a domestic trip to the West Coast, Chip and I would be in Dallas again for a Bravo Zulu Aviation standards meeting.

I let the subject drop. Nigel and I had spent the last six days together and it was actually pleasant. Day One was on the airline, the mainline as he would say. He insisted on a Luau for our night in Honolulu, something I could have done without. Day Two was flying to Sydney. Days Three, Four, and Five were as tourists Down Under. We were living Day Six in the forward most seats of our airplane. I was spending the night in Hawaii before crawling into an airline passenger's seat headed home.

The standards group had grown again, and this time the room was filled to capacity. I knew Bravo Zulu Aviation USA had doubled in size since I joined, but the number of standards pilots was only a third higher. Of the many training and other meetings, I enjoyed the annual standards group the most, but still wondered if it was worth three days of my time. Over the course of a year every BZA pilot had to attend two aircraft recurrent training sessions, each a weeklong. Then there was a three-day BZA recurrent, a one-day international procedures recurrent, and another one-day first aid class. My only goal for this conference was to escape any additional duties. A white dry erase board had an agenda in neat, block letters, and the third item was: "Standards Pilots Work Distribution." Not a good sign.

Kari's opening pitch was his normal one: the company is doing great, we in the standards group are doing great, and we have challenges ahead of us. The second item was an itinerary of sorts, what we had in front of us for the next three days. Item three required a slide change and revealed a table I had never seen before. It was a list of all 38 standards pilots listed with their base location and a number. The list was in order of those numbers, from highest to lowest, my name was third from the top with BED denoting Bedford, Massachusetts and the number 15. Above me was a 16 and an 18, both from SFO. We were the only three in double digits, the majority hovered between 4 and 8. I noticed Chip Dawson was one from the bottom with the number 1.

"Any guesses?" Kari asked.

"Check rides," someone offered.

"Yes," he said. "These are the numbers of check rides administered by each of you in the last twelve months. Bravo Zulu Aviation USA now has 250 pilots, give or take. With 38 of you guys and gals, that means each of you need to average 7 check rides a year."

There was a collective groan and a few complaints. "We all have other jobs, you know!"

"Yes, yes," Kari agreed. "I said average. We have three standards pilots who give much more than the average." He pointed my way and to the two San Francisco pilots. "Plus being based in San Francisco, Bedford, or White Plains means you are closer to the action. If you can't get out into the sys-

Flight Lessons 5: People

tem for check rides, all I am asking is that you find another way to contribute. We have a lot of work to do and it would be nice for the workload to be spread out a little more."

Chip shifted nervously in his seat. It was his third year as a standards pilot and he never gave a check ride until the most recent year. The pilots he checked complained loudly about Chip's conduct in front of their passengers and the harshness of his critiques. Chip decided he would never give another check ride.

"I have a list of twenty projects we need completed in the next twelve months," he said. "I expect anyone with fewer than 7 check rides in the last year to volunteer for one project, first come, first served."

I scanned the list of pilots and counted, there were exactly 20 pilots in the less than 7 category. Kari was a master at this. So Item Three worked to my advantage, no additional work received. Item Four was "New International Operations Manual." Kari's secretary walked behind our seats and presented us each with our own copies. It was a glossy five-ring binder, sized to fit a standard pilot's book bag. There were 387 pages, I knew.

Pilots around the table quickly thumbed through the contents. Chip, seated to my left, dove right for the Table of Contents and then browsed various sections at random. I looked at the cover page to confirm it read "Version 1.00" and, satisfied, closed it.

"Aren't you interested in this?" Chip asked. "Or have you already got it memorized?"

"Of course he does," Kari said, still standing at the head of the table. "He wrote it."

All heads turned my way. "In fact, he wrote it while going through GV initial."

Now I was fully embarrassed. I never asked Kari to keep the new manual's author a secret, but I should have realized Kari would broadcast it to the world. He enjoyed singing the praises of others and I imagine he thought this would encourage the others to volunteer for a project of their own. Kari's intentions were good, I knew. He had long ago gravitated fully to the *Friend* category.

In the next few days I got more praise than I deserved about the manual, as well as a few complaints about how they now had to become experts on something entirely new. Our old manual, written by Ms. Rebecca L. Cherbourg, was useless but had been with our company for years. Our pilots hated the book because they had to lug it around in each cockpit but never used it. Bravo Zulu hated the book because it was expensive. So the growing consensus was that anything was better than what we had.

On the third and final day, Kari pulled me to one side when he found a quiet moment with no other witnesses. "Chip has volunteered to take on our polar operations authorization."

"That's a big bite," I said. "I wonder if he can handle it."

"He tells me he's flown polar more times than a penguin," Kari said.

"Can penguins fly?" I asked.

"No," Kari said, without laughing. "Please give him some help, without making it obvious that we think he needs help."

"Sure," I said. It seemed that I had not escaped without any additional work after all.

9: The Oblivious Captain
January 2005

The Great Wall of China (Eddie photo)

The vast majority of our GV trips were flying charter all over the world with passengers who were flying there to be tourists, which meant we got to be tourists too. Flying for ten or twelve hours may seem to be too many hours trapped in a hollow aluminum tube, as many short-range pilots will tell you, but we had distinct advantages over our smaller charter siblings. They could be gone for a week after having flown three or four times a day. We might be gone for a week with only the first and last day spent flying, and everything in the middle was time off as tourists. It was a good way to make a living.

But then came the other part of our flying, that part devoted to flying the owner. Mr. Viceroy was primarily interested in New York City and Washington, D.C. for business. He also was a frequent visitor to Denver and Omaha where he had family. Owner trips were without a flight attendant, so it was up to the copilot du jour to stop by a sandwich shop for lunch and to make sure Mr. Viceroy's gin bottle was full. He usually showed up for the Bedford departure on time and the return trips early. He was an easy passenger.

"I hate this part of the job," Chip said as he poured from a 1.75-liter bottle of Beefeater gin from our kitchen into the smaller 0.75-liter bottle on the airplane. "Who does he think he's fooling? He'll drain this bottle before we get to Omaha and yell at us because it's empty on the way back."

"We should carry another three-quarter liter bottle in the baggage compartment," I said, "and then swap them in Omaha."

Chip looked at me, eyes blank and mouth agape. "Yeah," he finally said, "I guess that could work."

True to form, Mr. Viceroy showed up on time, parked his car on our left wingtip, ran up the stairs carrying his overnight bag, and yelled, "Go, go, go!" When we got to Omaha, his rental car was waiting for him, engine running. He darted off the airplane with a quick, "See ya!" and sped off in the rental.

As I returned to the cabin Chip held up the empty gin bottle. "How on earth can he drive after putting away this much gin?"

The other drawback of flying the owner versus the high-paying charter clients was we were no longer reimbursed for our expenses but given a flat seventy-five dollars a day for food. Chip favored the Cracker Barrel genre of fine dining establishments, since they filled him up and left him some pocket money. He didn't need any alcohol, just a table where he could sit and talk. He was a different person without a flight attendant present, where his conversations were marked by short sentences and long polysyllabic words. With just me as an audience, he usually had a topic in mind.

"Why does everyone use PowerPoint," he began for our dinner in Omaha. "When there are so many better programs out there."

"Name three," I said.

"I don't know," he said, "there has to be. Kari is expecting my first presentation on polar operations to be on a Powerpoint."

"Draw me pictures of what you want each slide to look like and I'll show you how to turn those into Powerpoints," I said. "It isn't too hard."

"I can't draw," he said.

"Anyone can draw," I said. Somehow rebuffed, Chip resigned himself to his steak.

"Bravo Zulu gave me a copy of PowerPoint for free," he finally said. "Maybe tomorrow, before you go home, you show me how to get started?"

"I can do that," I said. "But I need to get to our town hall before 7 p.m. so I can vote."

"Don't bother," he said. "The election isn't going to be close. The last poll I saw had your guy behind by twenty percent!"

"The polls have it wrong," I said. "It looks like a losing battle, but it will be closer than that."

"What?" he said. "How can they be wrong. Don't you know how polling works?"

"Okay," I said, "tell me how polling works." I didn't often invite a Chip Dawson debate, but dinner was only half over, and it was a chance to add a quarter to the chair rail of my office. Chip chuckled, his poker face tell told me he thought he was about to humiliate my lack of knowledge.

"Well obviously if you wanted to predict how a population is going to vote, the best way is to ask a hundred percent of them ahead of time," he said. "But you can't do that. So you pick a random sample of them. We can predict how Vermont is going to vote if we run through a Burlington phone book, pick a large enough sample of people and ask. It is all very scientific. How can you have a problem with science?"

"What is that minimum sample size?" I asked.

"I think it is about a thousand," he said. "At least that's what most polls use."

"You usually see 1,004 polled produces a 3 percent margin of error," I offered.

"Yes!" he said, taking the bait. "I do remember that. So as long as you ask 1,004 people you are guaranteed to get it right, as long as the results are at least 53 percent to 47 percent. Your guy is behind by 20 percent! You might as well skip the election."

"I think my guy is going to lose," I agreed. "But it isn't going to be by 20 percent."

"Wanna bet?" he said. "A quarter?"

"Sure," I said. The chair rail had seven of Chip's surrendered quarters on it. I had them arranged in a group of three and another of four. Two groups of four would be more impressive. I knew the election was a loser but I also knew that national polls tended to push an agenda until just a week prior to the election. Then they tended to wander into reality so as to be able to say they got it right. The last poll I saw had our side down by ten percent.

Our return flight to Bedford was in many ways a replay of the day prior, including the empty bottle of gin. Dr. Jones had Mr. Viceroy's car warmed up and ready to go. Mr. Viceroy sped off in an instant, spared having to look at our filthy hangar.

"You say the word," I said to Chip once we were inside the hangar offices, "and I will go through that hangar like a tornado. I just need a thirty-yard dumpster for all the trash."

"Leave it alone," he said. "I learned a long time ago you don't want to upset Don Jones. Besides, we have China to plan for."

I showed Chip how to type words onto a PowerPoint slide and how to import photos and he was satisfied enough to allow me to run home and cast a vote. My guy lost by seven percent.

The passenger was from Hawaii and needed a ride to Beijing, China, for a few days there, and then a ride back. The fact we had to fly empty from Bedford to Honolulu and then back again was of no concern to the passenger. It was a lucrative contract for us except for the fact we would need three pilots for the two legs that would be longer than ten hours. It would be our first opportunity to fly as a crew of three.

Chip showed up a few minutes after me. He passed me in the outer office, ran into his office, and came out with a quarter. Wordlessly he placed the quarter on my desk and returned to his office. I could see Nigel's wide grin, but he too kept quiet. I rearranged my three/four row of quarters to four/

Flight Lessons 5: People

four and said, "Pretty soon I can retire."

I flew the first half of the trip out of Honolulu and sat in the jump seat with Chip in the left and Nigel in the right for the approach into Beijing. All of this was fairly routine except for one complication. China, at the time, insisted on using metric altitudes for all its airports and that meant the rest of the world had to convert from feet to meters when deciding what altitude to fly.

I wasn't a stranger to metric altitudes, having spent many years flying through Russia while in the Air Force, years before they agreed to do anything Western in nature. But that was a long time ago and I dutifully studied everything we had on the subject during our week between trips. None of this was complicated, I knew, but in the heat of the moment people tended to revert to old habits. Getting meters confused with feet could kill you. I offered to teach a class to Chip and Nigel, but both declined.

"What else do you have to do in the five hours?" I asked after relinquishing the pilot's seat.

"You make everything more complicated than it needs to be, Eddie," Nigel said.

"I bet I have more time flying metric than you do," Chip said.

The GV had a big advantage over every airplane I had ever flown when it came to flying metric altitudes. The airplane's avionics did the conversion for us, so there was no need to fly with a conversion table taped to the instrument panel. But there was a flaw in the system. We used the autopilot for almost all of our flying; we in the front two seats spent more time programming the computers than hand-flying the airplane. While the airplane's FMS understood meters, the autopilot's altitude select function did not. This too wasn't a problem, if the pilots remembered the correct procedure.

"I know you both don't want to hear this, but let's go over it before we go 'feet dry' in China," I said from the jump seat. They pretended to ignore me. Ever since I had discovered the flaw, I made a point of using the modified procedure at all times. Autopilot changes were made using the Altitude Select knob, called the ASEL. These changes were verified using the pilot's flight display, the PFD. "When you get an altitude assignment the right seater spins the ASEL while looking at his PFD. The left seater points to his PFD, not the ASEL, to verify. Since you've already changed the PFD to meters, this keeps you safe."

"We know that, Eddie," Nigel said.

"Not my first rodeo," Chip said.

Two hours later we were in Chinese airspace and made the switch from feet to meters by selecting it from a menu in one of the flight computers. Our initial descent into Beijing airspace was in meters.

"Bravo Zulu Fife," the controller said in a good, but somewhat Australian version of English, "descend to and maintain tree thousand tree hundred meters."

"Bravo Zulu Fife," Nigel answered, "down to tree thousand tree hundred meters." He looked down to his approach plate and saw that came to 10,830 feet. He spun 10,830 in the ASEL. Chip pointed to the ASEL and said, "here we go." I reminded myself to watch very carefully. Nigel could have spun the ASEL while watching the meters in his PFD, but his method worked.

The two pilot seats in many airplanes are jammed in front so as to give the pilot as clear a view outside the aircraft as possible. That position robs both of much of the periphery and requires a definite head movement to scan parts of the cockpit. From the jump seat, I had an unobstructed view of most of the cockpit. With a quick scan I could see the altitude select knob nearer the center of the cockpit and at eye level, it read 10830. I could also see both pilots' flight displays, slightly below eye level, reading 3300m, the "m" for meters. We were off to a good start.

The airport was covered by a thick overcast and based on the weather reports, we wouldn't be able to see the runway until a few hundred feet above it. Our step-down altitudes continued until speaking with Beijing approach control.

"Bravo Zulu Fife," the controller said in the best Chinese-English of the day, "descend to and maintain six hundred meters, cleared for the I-L-S approach, runway zero one."

Nigel repeated the instruction and dialed six hundred into the ASEL. Chip pointed to the ASEL and said, "Six hundred, here we go." He pushed the "Flight Level Change" button that would cause the throttles to come to idle and the autopilot to push the nose over while maintaining our selected airspeed. It would do so until we hit 600 feet or the ground, whichever came first.

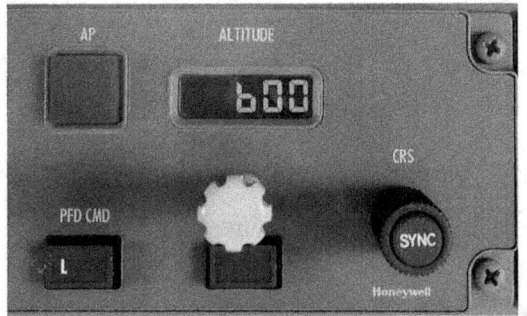

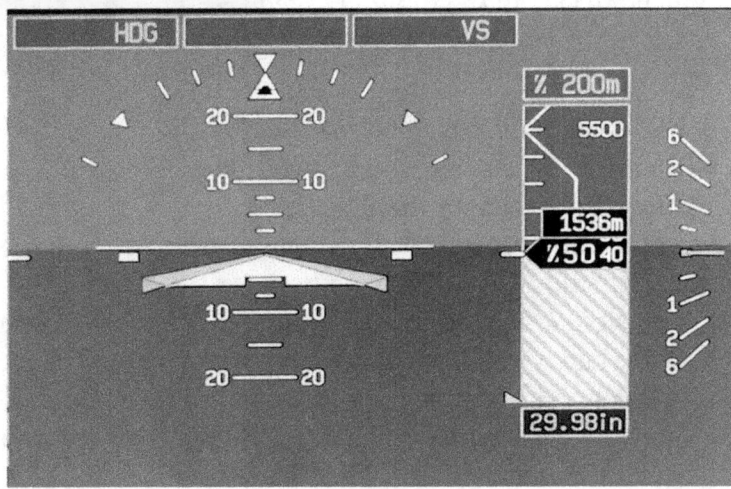

600 feet in the altitude select window (top) translates to 200 meters in the PFD (bottom)

"Meters!" I said. "Meters! That's way too low." There was a long pause until finally they recognized the error.

"Oh yeah," they both said. Nigel dialed the ASEL up until the PFD read "600m" which brought the ASEL up to 2,000 feet. We would have been nearly 1,400 feet below our assigned altitude. The only good thing about the approach was that in all the confusion Chip forgot his usual "Mind if I get in on some of this fun" routine. He kept the autopilot engaged until we broke out of the weather, just a hundred feet above our descent altitude and perfectly aligned with the runway.

After the passengers were whisked away in a limo I busied myself with the engine oils and installing the various covers required by the airplane for a week's ground time. Wheezing because of the thick Beijing smog, I made a mental note to check the windows and aircraft skin when we returned.

That night at the bar I brought a terrain chart with me and showed both pilots that descending to 600 feet would have put us in the middle of a town called Tongzhou, a business district with high office buildings.

"So what?" Nigel said. "we would have caught it eventually."

"I guess we ought to use your PFD-not-ASEL technique whenever we are in China or Russia," Chip said.

"Why not use it all the time?" I asked.

"Now you are being silly," Chip said.

I realized, too late, that I had made a mistake. Chip and Nigel tended to be defensive when critiqued. In fact, most pilots become defensive when challenged as a team. I should have approached both privately. They were my peers, but both were technically senior to me and one was also a fellow check airman. After flying with both for two years, I had long ago come to a conclusion about their fitness for flight. Chip was a competent, but lazy pilot. He had poor stick and rudder skills, but he was overconfident about his abilities. Nigel was a better stick and rudder pilot but was lacking in knowledge. He listened well and learned quickly but refused to do so if the instruction came from Chip or in Chip's presence. In my haste, it seemed I missed an opportunity to get the critique over with.

I replayed the approach in my head, over and over. If I wasn't in the jump seat, when would they have caught it? If I was in the pilot's seat, would I have made the same mistake? The approach would be a recurring nightmare for me; I knew it would haunt me for years to come. And yet, both my peers seem unfazed. Was I overreacting or were they underreacting?

Chip and Nigel were cordial during our ground time in China and, if anything, I was the odd man out. We had several days off with nothing to do and the best option seemed to be heading for the nearest thing we all had heard of. The cost of the tour bus for the two-hour drive to visit the Great Wall of China was a bit high, but everyone agreed and so off we went.

Flight Lessons 5: People

The toboggan ride at Mutianyu section of the Great Wall of China

The wall wasn't as impressive as I thought it would be, but how could it have lived up to the hype? I was surprised that most of it, as far as we could see, was covered by the surrounding forest. Another surprise was that it had become a bit of a theme park. You walked or took a chairlift on your way up the mountain; the former took about an hour the latter about ten minutes. Our group elected to walk, scoffing at those too lazy for the exercise. Then you could walk or ride a toboggan down.

It all seemed somehow sacrilegious, but Chip, Nigel, and our flight attendant lit up when they saw the toboggan. Chip and Nigel debated which of our foursome should be the first in our group. "I don't want you holding me back," one would say to the other. "I'll be in back," the flight attendant said. "No, it will be me," I said. Chip outweighed Nigel by almost 100 pounds, so the two agreed Chip should go first. At the tail end, I had a view of everything to come, much like I did from the jump seat during our approach. The gate keeper assigned each of us a sled and waited until we had at least sixty seconds delay after the preceding group. The only control we had was a hand-operated brake. Once given the thumbs up, Chip was off to the races, no brake in use.

From my perspective, Nigel was on Chip's tail right off the bat and was never further than a sled length behind. It would have made a good physics question. At our average slope, would Chip's extra downward force create more drag than it created forward gravitational propulsion? Either Chip was on the brake or was creating more friction than kinetic energy. But in the end it didn't matter. We caught up with the preceding group and soon it was Chip, Nigel, our flight attendant and I bunched together.

After a day of walking, touristing, and tobogganning, Nigel and the flight attendant fell fast asleep on the van ride back to our Beijing hotel. Chip was still hyped from the toboggan ride and in a mood to talk. "So what happened to the polls in that election? How did science get it wrong?"

"Polling isn't science," I said. "You ever hear about the statistics exercise of the Martian's attacking the earth?"

"No," he said. "Tell me."

"Let's say there is life on Mars and you are a Martian sent to Earth simply to observe from afar," I began. "Using your best surveillance cameras from low Earth orbit, you notice that there are males and females and that in general the males are larger. Your superiors back on Mars are considering an invasion and want to know the percentage of males versus females. They give you permission to land in a remote region of the most populous country of the world, and ask you to spy on a hospital newborn nursery for one day to report back on the percentage of male births versus female births."

"Makes sense," Chip said. "That should give them a good answer."

"You pick a small town in a remote region of China because you want to remain incognito," I continued. "The only hospital in town averages four births a day. You place your spy in a room adjacent to the nursery with a pad of paper. Your spy reports back 24 hours later that there were indeed four births that day, three males and one female. You report back to Mars that 75 percent of the population on Earth is male. The Martians are alarmed, recall their spies, and decide to cast their hopes of conquest on another planet. Earth is saved."

Flight Lessons 5: People

"Four is less than a thousand and four," Chip said.

"But it illustrates a few points," I said. "First, about the sample size. You cannot learn valid statistics when the sample size is too small to capture a sense of the entire population. The Martian hypothetical was an accurate statistic for that particular day and that particular hospital. But it gets worse."

"The sample source has to be right too," I continued. "You cannot extrapolate a population's behavior on a smaller sampling, unless that smaller sampling is representative of the population being examined. Let's say that particular rural town in China still has the one child per couple rule and many couples chose to abort females. Your statistics could very well be valid for that entire town, but certainly not for the entire world."

"But what if in an election we pick from the entire country, and not just one town?" Chip asked.

"You cannot learn from the answers to a question that does not relate to the purpose of the statistical analysis," I said. "Our Martian warlords were worried about whom they would have to fight in an invasion. The percentage of newborn babies may not necessarily reflect those who achieve warfighting adulthood. The framing of the question determines the answer and if you don't ask the right question the answer really doesn't matter. In modern warfare, male versus female isn't all that important."

Chip didn't have a rejoinder and the subject evaporated, never to be mentioned again. It was a typical conversation for us. If he had something to say I didn't know anything about, I was in receive mode. But if our positions were reversed, he more often than not let the subject drop.

Getting out of China was easier than getting in, and the only debate left to us was Nigel asking to airline home once we got into San Francisco. As usual for him, he didn't want to spend the night in San Francisco if he could get home a day earlier.

"You and Eddie can fly the airplane home," he argued. "Why should I spend another night away if I don't mind the red eye on an airline?"

"If the cost of the airline ticket is less than the hotel and a meal," Chip said, "then go ahead. Otherwise you are stuck with us."

Of course we knew a last minute airline ticket would be far more than a hotel reservation made weeks in advance, so Nigel's fate was cast. His approach into San Francisco International Airport was textbook perfect, and Chip remained a silent witness in the jump seat.

Once our passengers were gone, I spotted an FAA inspector approaching from the FBO's terminal. I got Chip's attention and pointed. "Let me handle this," Chip said. I followed him down the stairs. "You keep quiet," he said.

"I'm Captain Dawson," he said to the inspector, who showed us his FAA inspector's credential.

"Are you operating under fourteen CFR one-thirty-five, captain?" the inspector asked. That was a fancy way of asking if we were operating under Title 14 of the U.S. Code of Federal Regulations, Part 135, meaning commercial rules.

"Yes, sir, we are," Chip said.

"Who has operational control?" the inspector asked.

"Operational what?" Chip asked.

"Control," the inspector asked. "What entity is controlling this airplane?"

"Oh that," Chip said. "Bravo Zulu Aviation has operational control."

"Is that a U.S. entity?" the inspector asked.

"It is," Chip said.

"I see," the inspector said, holding out a clipboard. "Sign here to signify we had this talk." Chip read the short form, signed, and returned the clipboard. The inspector did an about-face and left.

"I told you I could handle it," Chip said as we returned to the airplane.

I called Kari that night and replayed the event with the FAA inspector. "We've got five or six other examples of that this week," he said. "Something odd is happening. I don't know what, but it isn't good. But I'm glad you called. We got a check ride for you tomorrow. We'll have Chip and Nigel fly your airplane home and we need you to airline to Houston so you can jump

Flight Lessons 5: People

seat on an RJ to Gunnison."

I had the night off in San Francisco, (panko crusted red snapper), a day on an airline Boeing 757, (mystery meat), and a night off in Houston (crawfish boil). My personal notes had matured to the point I could refer to them anywhere with an Internet connection and work on them anywhere I had access to my laptop. The HTML editor's green screen would elicit a, "Matrix, huh?" from whomever was seated next to me in an airliner or a passenger lounge. But for the most part my workflow when it came to the notes had become efficient. My notes about dealing with metric altitudes were okay and I left them alone. My notes about Crew Resource Management continued to be a mess.

I thought that a three-pilot operation with a dysfunctional leader would be a perfect laboratory for demonstrating how two subordinates could effect change from the bottom up. Nigel appeared to be a good pilot and able to listen to critique. But Chip brought out his demons. In fact, I realized, Chip brought out my worst demons. After a lifetime of not worrying about throwing daggers at the king, I was starting to modulate my criticisms. Nigel and I were having no impact on our boss and CRM is impossible when the captain is a boss who is blind to critique.

10: The Captain Has Gone Too Far
October 2005

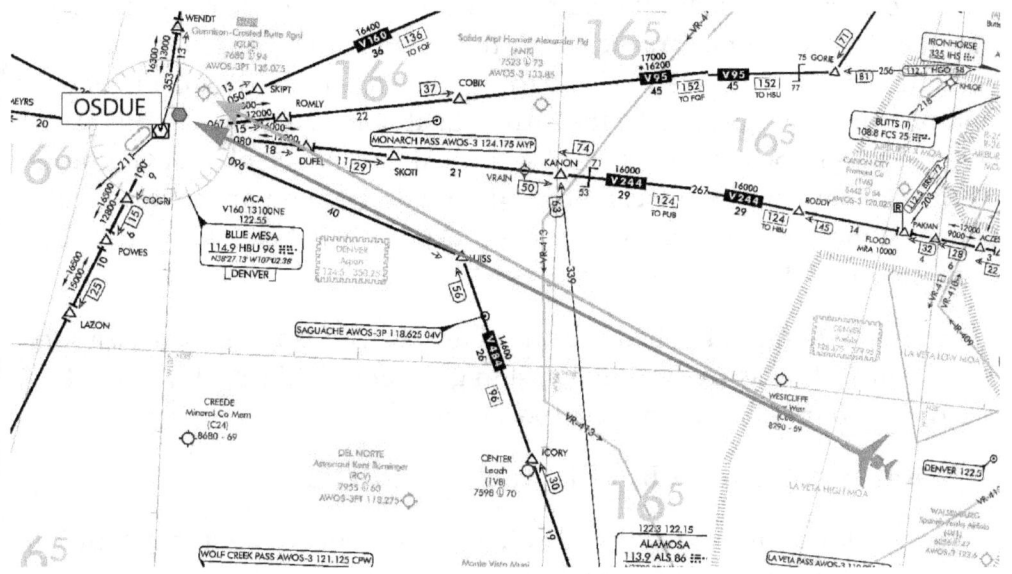

Gunnison Airport, from 100 miles out

I met the RJ crew at their Houston Intercontinental hangar and learned they would be flying the owner to his Colorado mountain home just outside of Gunnison. It was a trip they made almost every month and the weather was CAVU, ceiling and visibility unlimited. "A piece of cake," the pilot said.

Harvey Cochrane was a short, stumpy man with a jovial face underneath a perfectly shaped, bald head. His copilot was equally short, but thin with a full head of hair. They sat in the front of their Canadair RJ, a luxury version of the commuter airliner decked out with a stateroom, a conference table, and the largest galley I had ever seen in an airplane of its size. The two chatted easily about Texas college sports and Colorado ski resorts. I nodded my head quietly from the jump seat, clutching my notepad which was blissfully empty after an hour in the air.

"Cleared direct Gunnison," Denver Center said when we were just over 150 nautical miles to the southeast.

"Dye rect, roger that," the copilot said. I noted the sloppy radio procedures on my pad, happy I would have something to critique during what was shaping up to be a boring debrief. But then Harvey reached down and programmed his FMS to navigate directly to OSDUE, the final approach fix for one of the instrument approaches to Gunnison. I made another note.

Both pilots resumed their idle chatter while the aircraft closed our distance with the airport. Our clearance was to the airport, which meant the airport. Many pilots preferred to head to a point a few miles downwind of their landing runway, so as to make the turn to final more convenient. This wasn't possible at most busy airports, but I suspected it would be okay at Gunnison. But it was contrary to our clearance. I drew a diagram on my notepad and estimated that we were heading just a few degrees left of course. But as our distance closed that gap would increase.

At one hundred miles I pulled out one of my favorite examiner tricks, asking a question as if I was really asking, just to get them to think. "Hey guys," I asked, "was our clearance to the airport or the fix?"

"It doesn't matter," Harvey barked, "we always do it this way."

"If you want to go to the fix," I said politely, "you could request that. Otherwise your clearance is to the airfield."

The king of the airplane was not amused. "I am in command here and I told you this is perfectly okay. When we land, I'm going to give Kari Owens a call. This will be the last check ride you ever give to a Bravo Zulu crew!"

I listened quietly to the dressing down I was getting, while watching the angle between our course and our clearance grew. Captain Harvey Cochrane's practice of heading "dye rect" to an offset point was common. Common, but wrong. I was starting to wonder what my legal obligation was when Denver center called, "Bravo Zulu Four Fourteen, say heading?"

"Ah, three oh five," the copilot responded.

"I need you to turn right heading three two zero," Denver Center said. "Your clearance was direct the airport, wasn't it?"

"Ah, yes sir," the copilot said, meekly. "Sorry about that."

"I need you to give me a call when you land," the air traffic controller continued. "Advise when ready to copy my number."

Flight Lessons 5: People

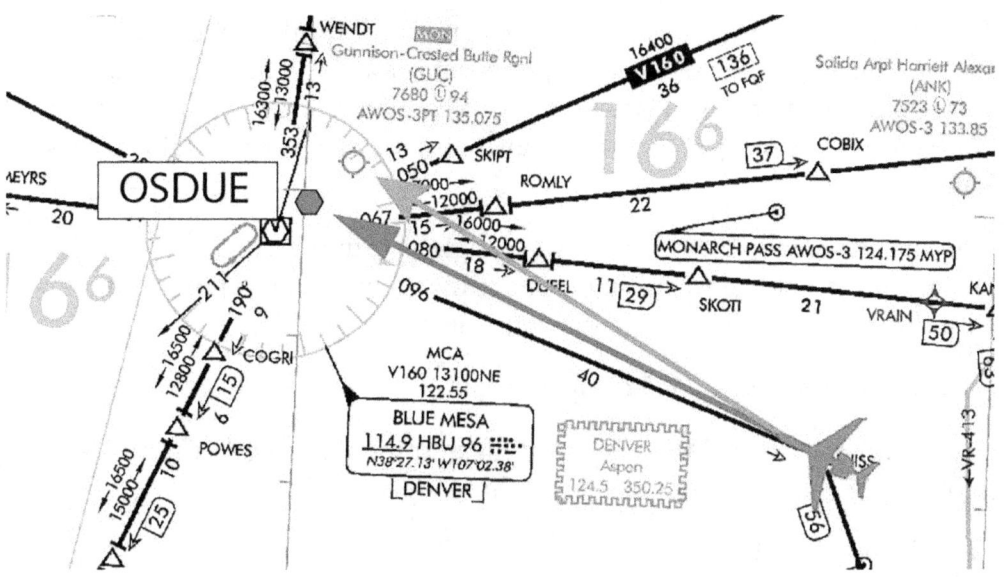

Gunnison Airport, from 40 miles out.

After we landed, Harvey called Denver Center and I called Kari. Harvey then called Kari to say I had distracted him in the cockpit and the blame, obviously, was mine. But Kari had already talked to the air traffic controller's supervisor and had made a deal. Kari got Harvey out of the violation provided Harvey retake the Bravo Zulu Crew Resource Management class and then spend an hour with a standards pilot to relearn basic instrument navigation procedures. Harvey, of course, was furious.

I rented a car and drove to Denver, about a four-hour drive, and reflected on what was one of the few adversarial check rides I had ever given. Failing a check ride, the so-called bust, was uncommon. Most check rides that don't go well result in additional training and perhaps a phone call or two. The Stefano Wayland crew bust was a rare one for me. In that case, an entire flight department and owner hated my guts. Having Harvey Cochrane as an enemy was minor, in the grand scheme of things.

"Making friends wherever you go," *The Lovely Mrs. Haskel* joked as I gave her the details on the phone, my first cell phone with unlimited domestic calling.

"I am thinking we should change all the locks," I said.

"Make sure you don't drive any predictable routes," she said.

Then my phone made a beep I didn't recognize. "I think I have another call, sorry I have to go." I looked at the phone and saw Kari's name. I pressed the wrong button and both calls went away. Negotiating the next intersection took both hands so I put the phone down only to hear it ring again. It was Kari.

"Hey, just wanted you to know how a couple of things turned out," he said. "First, Harvey said he was going to move his account to IFE but I chatted with the owner and he said they are staying put."

"I bet Harvey is not a happy camper," I said.

"He is not," Kari said. "We scheduled his training with another standards pilot so you won't have to put up with him any longer."

"Thank you," I said.

"And the big news is the congressional investigation ended up with a big fat zero. They threw it all out, so no action taken on any of those check rides you had to testify about."

"That's the impression I got during the deposition," I said. "They seemed to be searching for something but didn't know what. How did everyone else do?"

"The same," he said. "A few of our guys got dusted up a bit, but in the end the committee didn't issue any findings and we as a company have no action items to take."

"That is good news," I said. "Any idea what caused it all in the first place?"

"I have my suspicions," he said. "When I figure it all out, I'll let you know."

"We are now officially a Bravo Zulu Charter airplane when we fly commercially," Chip said at our first-ever flight department meeting. "The feds are saying that since Bravo Zulu Aviation is more than 51-percent foreign owned, they cannot have operational control of any commercial charters. So we now have two manuals, two crew badges, two of everything. When we fly Mr. Viceroy on a personal trip, we are with Bravo Zulu Aviation. But when we fly commercial trips, we belong to Bravo Zulu Charter. Got it?"

Nigel and I nodded our heads. The news was in all the trade publications. An unknown entity filed a complaint in federal court about BZA ownership jeopardizing public safety. In the thirty years since Monsieur Bertrand Zacherie founded Bravo Zulu Aviation, not a single airplane had ever been involved in an accident. We were the largest charter management company in the world. But no longer. The commercial half of BZA was broken off into BZC.

I looked at my new crew badges, one for BZA and the other for BZC, identical save one letter. It didn't make any sense, of course. But the BZA/BZC plan didn't make much sense either. We were flying the same trips on the same aircraft with the same crews. It was a paperwork game that ceded our position as the world's largest charter operator to our main competitor, International Flight Enterprises, IFE. The IFE philosophy was very different than ours at BZA, now BZC. Our aircraft were owned by individuals and companies, and when they weren't flying them, made available for charter by BZC. IFE owned most of their aircraft on behalf of various entities. A rich person could invest in a "share" of an airplane and have access to a fleet of airplanes instead. IFE crews had no direct ties to the aircraft owners and tended to fly as disinterested parties. Bravo Zulu crews knew their owners and tended to take care of the airplanes. IFE crews were little more than airline crews.

We often picked up IFE charters when their aircraft broke, or their crews ran out of legal flying time. Sometimes the reason for the charter made no sense at all.

"Why are we flying ten passengers from Rio to Geneva when they got here on an IFE Gulfstream two days ago?" I asked as Nigel and I sat on the ramp at the Rio de Janeiro airport, waiting for our passengers. I pointed to the IFE Gulfstream. "They flew in on that airplane three days ago with twelve passengers. Today they are taking two of the passengers to Geneva, leaving the other ten for us."

"I met the IFE pilot at breakfast this morning," Nigel said. "He told me they didn't have the fuel to make it with twelve passengers."

"But it's only a ten-hour flight on an airplane with fourteen-hour legs," I said. "We are doing the same trip with those ten passengers they are leaving behind and we aren't using anywhere near max gas. Something isn't adding up."

"I really don't care," Nigel said, staring at my name on our flight plan. "I should have been upgraded a year ago to international captain. It seems Chip wants to keep all the cookies for himself."

"I don't know," I said. "You get paid the same and we rotate through the schedule equally. I'm sure he'll upgrade you soon."

"It is never fair unless you are the guy in charge," Nigel said. I started to object but Nigel anticipated me. "The pilots at IFE upgrade according to seniority. At the mainline we had the union looking out for us. Here it all depends on the good will of our overlord, Master Chip Dawson."

Our passengers arrived fifteen minutes early and we made it off the ground before the IFE Gulfstream. As we settled in at 45,000 feet cruising at Mach 0.83, we started to hear our sister ship behind and below us. In less than an hour they passed us. They checked in with air traffic control at 35,000 feet. I pulled out my circular slide rule and timed their position reports. "They are doing Mach 0.86," I said to Nigel. "At 35,000 feet they must really be sucking down the gas."

"No wonder they didn't have the fuel for all twelve passengers," Nigel said. "The paperwork says this charter is costing them $300,000. Good news for Mr. Viceroy, bad news for the IFE passengers."

I feared the news for our passengers was even worse than a matter of the price. "Why is half the food uneaten?" I asked Claudia while helping to clean out the galley in Geneva.

"I didn't have time to serve it," she said. "There is only so much you can do with ten passengers on board."

"It was a ten-hour flight," I said. "We had breakfast right after takeoff, lunch a few hours after that, and then dinner about three hours before landing."

"I always make sure my boys up front get fed first," she said.

"In the future please put a priority on the passengers," I said.

Flight Lessons 5: People

Our passengers joined up with the rest of their party in Geneva. Nigel and I ended up at dinner with the IFE crew who didn't mind discussing altitude and speed selection. "We don't want to fly much higher than thirty-five or thirty-six thousand and the speed is up to the pilot."

"Even if that costs the passengers tens of thousands of dollars?" I asked.

"Doesn't matter," he said. "These are pilot decisions and the company would never question us about it."

The following week it was Nigel and Chip to Japan. I offered to sit down with Nigel to talk about Japanese air traffic control, but he declined. "I know about the Pacific," he said. The aircraft returned on a Saturday about 5 p.m. I had a trip with Nigel on Monday and needed to look at the navigation charts so I showed up around 6 p.m. I pulled into the parking lot and spotted Nigel closing the door to his car. The car shook. Nigel was beating the steering wheel with both fists, his face contorted in anger. I left the parking lot and circled the airport. When I returned Nigel was gone.

"How'd the trip go?" I asked Chip as I finally entered our hangar office.

"No problems," he said. "Nigel doesn't know the first thing about flying in Japan. But that is ops normal for him."

"I imagine you taught him quite a bit," I said.

"He doesn't want to learn anything from me," Chip said. "He'll never be an international captain, but he has a pulse, so we need him."

I drove home trying to make sense of it all. Chip was an average pilot with more confidence than talent, who didn't know how to instruct. Nigel was a good pilot without enough confidence to confront his boss, who didn't want to be instructed.

"Should I say something?" I asked *The Lovely Mrs. Haskel*. "I don't understand why two grown men choose to be unhappy when the solution is right in front of them."

"Be careful," she said. "You are in the middle of two strong personalities with fragile egos. Sometimes a pretend civility is better than no civility at all."

"Pleased to meet you," Chip said, bowing from the waist. "I hope you have a good time in Florida."

"Nice to meet you too," *The Lovely Mrs. Haskel* said while putting down her suitcase. "I'll try my best to stay out of the way."

It was one of our rare perks. Mr. Viceroy allowed us to put family members in the jump seat on his personal trips, so long as they didn't make eye contact with him and stayed out of the cabin. He rarely traveled for more than an overnight and we had yet to take him up on the standing invitation. But with two full days in Boca Raton and the chance to escape a bit of the Boston winter, *The Lovely Mrs. Haskel* and I decided it was too good to pass up.

Mr. Viceroy showed up in his normal rush and the "Go! Go! Go!" cheer as he ran into the cabin. Chip closed the main entrance door, and climbed into the right seat. I turned from the left seat to make sure *The Lovely Mrs. Haskel* was belted into the jump seat correctly. She was.

I flew us down to Boca Raton while Chip tried on all of his jokes that I had heard a few times. *The Lovely Mrs. Haskel* laughed politely at each and managed to ask a few questions about Chip's family and personal history. For every question, Chip had a long and detailed answer. I had never heard him talk so much.

After we shut down in Boca, Mr. Viceroy came forward, made eye contact with *The Lovely Mrs. Haskel* and stopped. "Hi," she said, "I am Ginnie, Eddie's wife. Thank you so much for letting me fly down with him."

"Oh, it is so good to meet you," he said. "I think the world of Eddie. You can fly with us anytime." And then he was off to the races.

"Well that's a first," Chip said. And that was true. I had witnessed Chip's and Nigel's wives on board with Mr. Viceroy paying them barely a nod of the head.

The next hurdle would be dinner, but Chip was in rare form. He never pulled the vacant stare into the flight attendant's eyes routine with *The Lovely Mrs. Haskel* and managed to hold a civil and polite conversation through the night. She asked him about my workload and all the projects I had going with Bravo Zulu.

"All of us standards pilots have high workloads," he said. "You can't run a company like this without a special cadre of experts, like me and Eddie."

"I thought so!" she said. "What's on the top of your inbox these days?"

Chip described his polar operations project in fine detail, covering everything from the temperature lapse rate of the tropopause to the limited number of alternate airports with medical facilities. He told us about his first flight near the north pole flying a DC-3 when one of the "jugs blew." That of course evolved into a discussion about what exactly a jug is and why a jet engine doesn't need one.

The next morning Chip showed up with his laptop computer at breakfast and gave us his presentation. There was a typo on the first slide, which we ignored, and a bit of grammar on the second. "It's temperature determines chance of clear air icing."

"There's no apostrophe in the it's," *The Lovely Mrs. Haskel* said.

"No that's not right," he said. "You need an apostrophe to show possession, everyone knows that."

"I believe this is an exception to that rule," she said.

"Wanna bet?" he asked.

"Can I put her quarter on the rail next to mine?" I interjected.

She had a shiny new quarter of her own before dinnertime. "I think I'll start my own collection," she said.

The flight home was routine except that Bedford was shrouded in fog and the closest airport to Mr. Viceroy's house with good enough weather and a runway we could use was in Nashua, New Hampshire. "It is right at minimums," I said from the right seat. "You need a half mile visibility and that's what you got. The runway is 5,500 feet long and 100 feet narrow. Manchester is a better option."

"That's an extra thirty minutes from the boss's house," Chip said. "I'll just have to put on a master class of my superior airmanship."

We had enough fuel for one approach into Nashua and then another at Manchester. I resigned myself to my fate, even though the entire contingent of my children's parents were on the airplane.

The approach into Nashua's Runway 14 is about as straight forward as they come. There are no obstacles other than the surrounding city and there are only three altitudes to worry about. You first level the airplane at 1,800 feet Mean Sea Level (MSL), which is 1,600 feet Above Ground Level (AGL). You then fly a 3-degree glide path to a decision altitude of 400 feet MSL, just 200 feet above the runway. If you see the runway, you land. If you don't, you execute a missed approach by climbing to 3,400 feet MSL. Easy.

Lateral guidance on the approach is provided by two radio signals shown as a single needle that moves left or right to show the airplane left or right of course. Vertical guidance comes from two more signals and another needle that shows if you above or below the 3-degree glide path. In some of my earlier airplanes, it was up to the pilot to center those needles. Later generations of automation had a flight director that showed the pilot the correct roll and pitch to make that happen. Our aircraft did all of that, plus the autopilot could do it all for us, leaving us to simply monitor it and take over if the automation made a mistake, which was rare. The hardest part of the upcoming approach would be to spot the necessary visual cues to be sure there was a runway in front of us while we were still 200 feet in the air, just 20 seconds from landing.

The autopilot did a fine job of getting us to 1,800 feet MSL, right on course. Once we approached the glide slope, Chip directed me to extend the landing gear and our last notch of flaps. At 1,500 feet MSL we were on speed, on course, and on glide path. "Stable," I said.

At 1,000 feet MSL we were 800 feet AGL, and things were good. I was so busy watching everything that I didn't expect what I could have predicted.

"Do you mind if I get in on some of this fun?" Chip said.

"I wish you wouldn't," I said just as I heard the "high low high" tone from the autopilot telling us it was no longer contributing in our effort to turn our aerospace vehicle into a ground vehicle without breaking anything or any-

Flight Lessons 5: People

one.

Now my chores had doubled. I was supposed to monitor the instruments to make sure we stayed on course and on glide path. I was supposed to monitor the altimeter to make sure we remained situationally aware of where the ground was as well as at what point the approach was no longer viable. And I had to look out the window to spot the runway environment.

"Drifting high," I said. The triangular needle indicating where the glide path was in relation to our airplane was starting to move below us. From the left seat there was only silence.

"A dot high, moving higher," I said. The scale given to that triangular needle was divided into a portion above and below, with two dots on either half. For most installations, each dot was worth 0.7 degrees. A dot high doesn't sound like much, but it can be the difference between never seeing the runway and hitting something other than a runway.

"One hundred feet above," I said, noting that we were at 500 feet MSL, 300 feet AGL, and ten seconds away from having to make a decision. I was forgetting something, but my eyes were moving faster than my brain.

"There she is," Chip said, spotting the runway, or what was left of it. He shoved the nose forward before I could react and, in an instant, we touched down, with about half the runway behind us. There are two reasons we walked away from the landing unscathed, for neither of which I can take credit for. First, the GV's approach speed is so slow, between 20 and 30 knots slower than most aircraft its size, that stopping it isn't as difficult. Second, the brakes are wonderfully good.

As he pulled off the runway I finally exhaled. "Let's never do that again," I said.

"Ah come on," he said, "don't embarrass me in front of your bride."

The Lovely Mrs. Haskel didn't say anything about it, other than to say Chip's landing was much harder than mine. We were so close to home we took a cab there, knowing I would have to take another cab to retrieve the airplane the next day when the weather improved. As I lay in bed that night I replayed the last sixty seconds of the flight, over and over again.

Was this a case for a Crew Resource Management study or was it more primal than that, just a case of two pilots who didn't know how to fly an instrument approach to minimums? From a CRM standpoint, I had made the correct calls. "Drifting high." "A dot high, moving higher." "One hundred feet above." What was missing? At some point I should have said, "Go around." But that was a call for when we got to decision altitude. When we got to that altitude, Chip spotted the runway.

After the third or fourth replay in my head it finally came to me. It was, as many things in aviation are, a matter of geometry. You can imagine the glide path of an airplane as a triangle, with the glide path as the hypotenuse. The point of the triangle is the desired aim point of the airplane. When Chip drifted high, the triangle changed so that the angle either had to become steeper, the end point had to move further down the runway, or a combination of those two. By the time we got to the decision altitude, we had already used up much of the runway.

My mistake, I realized, was not to call for the go around when we exceeded a dot high on the glide path. For the first time in a long time, maybe ever, I became angry. Chip had endangered our lives because he wanted to "get in on some of this fun." I had endangered our lives because I was so far behind the airplane I failed to remain situationally aware.

I had been on the fence about Chip's status among the many bosses I had over the years. But now there was no doubt. Chip was not a *Friend*. He was a *Foe*.

11: The Captain is Dead, Long Live the Captain

February 2006

Gulfstream GV landing (Photo: Steve "Slats" Denny)

The next week it was Nigel and me to Tanzania. I searched the hangar for the aircraft flight log in vain; it wasn't on Dr. Jones' desk as it normally was. I looked into Chip's empty office and saw it on his cluttered desk. I walked in to retrieve it and saw a name on a notepad that made my blood run cold: Gary Storm. The note had a phone number and a six-figure number with a dollar sign next to it. If it were a salary, it was double my current gross. I pushed the thought from my mind; I had a mission ahead of me.

The trip began from White Plains, New York where we could have used the Bravo Zulu terminal, but since this was an International Flight Enterprises charter, we used the FBO of their choice. Today that was Signature Flight Support, as proclaimed by the mat laid out at the foot of our aircraft stairs. I sat in the cockpit looking at the oceanic chart while Nigel completed the aircraft exterior inspection and the flight attendant stocked the galley. She had Beethoven playing on the aircraft sound system, telling me that she at least knew that much about the airplane's systems. It was going to be a good trip.

"Eddie," Nigel said from the aircraft doorway. "An FAA inspector wants to talk to you."

I straightened my tie and went downstairs. A trim gentleman of about my age extended one hand to shake mine and flashed an FAA Form 110A with the other. That form, often wielded like a sheriff's badge, meant he was interviewing me in an official capacity.

"Is this flight being conducted under 14 CFR 135, captain?" he asked.

"It is," I said. Part 135 meant we were being operated under commercial regulations, much like an airline.

"Who has operational control?" he asked.

"Bravo Zulu Charter," I said, careful to say charter and not aviation. Bravo Zulu Charter was one-hundred percent U.S. owned. I pointed up to the sign in the pilot's window that included our company's certificate number.

"I see," he said. Of course, he should have already known that. "May I see your company ID?"

I pulled off the lanyard around my neck and unclipped the laminated Bravo Zulu Charter identification card, being careful to cover the Bravo Zulu Aviation card that I had hidden in the middle of the stack of cards. It had become a minor nuisance, having to restack the IDs depending on the type of flight. But now that precaution was paying dividends. The inspector recorded the information and returned the card.

"If Bravo Zulu Charter has operational control of this flight, why does the mat at your steps say Signature?" he asked. I laughed. "Something funny, captain?"

"That's nuts," I said.

"I don't think you understand the gravity of this situation, captain," he said.

"I guess not," I said. "But I think you are nuts." He shook his head and walked away. I returned to the cockpit and retrieved my cell phone. It was past business hours, but he would want me to call.

"You are the second person without operational control of a floor mat today," Kari said. "It's nuts."

Flight Lessons 5: People

"That's what I said to the inspector," I said. Kari laughed.

"What did he say about that?" he asked.

"Nothing," I said. "He just turned around and left. I hope I didn't screw up by not kissing his ring."

"No you did fine," Kari said. "Whatever is happening is bigger than you and me both."

From the corner of my eye I spotted Linda "this is your dispatcher" waving at me from the fixed based operator that I had no operational control over. "I think my passengers are here, Kari. I got to go."

"Fly safe, buddy." It was typical for Linda to meet us for a White Plains departure. It was late at night and we didn't expect this kind of personal flight following from the other dispatchers. But with Linda, it was standard operating procedure.

"Your pax are en route," she said. "I think they are going to be a little early."

"Thanks," I said.

"Nigel says you are going to climb Mount Kilimanjaro," she said. "Please be careful."

"Of course!" I said.

The flight over the pond was south of the busiest part of the Atlantic and quiet. Once we had full radar and radio coverage things became routine. Nigel flew competently from the left seat and my challenges were minimal from the right.

Our passengers were doing a six-day safari on the Serengeti. Nigel and I hoped to climb Mount Kilimanjaro with no planning, no gear, and no idea what was required. We hadn't even mentioned it to our contract flight attendant, Sarah Thomason. I worried about that for a bit; but my worry was premature. The airport handler assured us that a climb to Mount Kilimanjaro was impossible, since only organized tours were allowed and none of these were allowed with less than seven days from start to finish. We managed to find a five-day safari on the Serengeti, but the cost exceeded our allotted hotel expense. It would mean an extra one-hundred dollars per day, per person, out of our own pockets.

"I'm in," Sarah said.

"Me too," Nigel said. "It beats staring at the hotel walls here."

"So, it's decided," I said. We spent the rest of the day raiding local ATMs which seemed to object to giving more than a hundred dollars in the local currency to any one person. After our fifth ATM we presented the safari company with the needed cash and anticipated the days to come. We met the next morning with our bags packed, anxious for the adventure to begin.

"They made an exception for us," I announced as we waited. "They usually have a four-person minimum but agreed to charter a vehicle with just us three."

"Well I wouldn't miss this for the world," Sarah said. "This is my first time to Africa and I doubt I'll ever have a chance like this again."

"You are lucky Chip Dawson isn't on the trip then," Nigel said. "He would never agree to spending a hundred dollars a day of his own money."

"Isn't he your boss?" she asked. "Why is he so cheap?"

"Because he likes to eat," Nigel and I said together.

It wasn't until we saw our Toyota Land Cruiser that it really hit us that we were about to go on safari. It was a large four-wheel drive truck with large tires, a raiseable roof, and an intake snorkel for crossing rivers. What it wasn't, was comfortable. It was about a six-hour, punishing drive to our campsite, most of that on dirt roads. I was wondering about spending a hundred dollars for all of this until we arrived at our "tents." We each had our own air-conditioned tent with a plush bed and wet bar. The only thing missing was a television. Dinner was worthy of any first-class restaurant. It was in the largest tent in the complex with a large fire in the middle, bordered by about ten tables. Each table except ours had four to six patrons, we had a table of our own.

"I just want to see a lion, up close," Nigel said. "I don't have a telephoto lens, so we need to get close."

"The driver said lions are rare this time of year," Sarah said. "But there will be lots to see."

"If I don't see a lion," Nigel said, "the week will have been a waste."

The next morning, we boarded our Toyota Landcruiser which had its top raised. I sat with Sarah as Nigel stood in back, searching in vain. The dust had become relentless and the driver stopped to lower the roof. We had seen and photographed giraffes, zebras, and a few elephants at a distance. Nigel kept his thoughts to himself, but I imagined his unhappiness would need to be vented sooner than later.

The dirt roads were pockmarked with holes and the driver had to come to a stop a few times to remove fallen branches from our path. After a while the driving became easier, until it became harder. I looked forward just in time to see us skidding sideways into a ditch. The driver spun the wheel opposite the skid, which only made matters worse. He reversed the front wheels at the last second so we hit the ditch with all four wheels on the ground. We ended up our right side at what I thought was about a 90° angle. The driver looked back and saw that the three of us were okay. We climbed out and inspected the damage to our vehicle.

Our Land Cruiser in a ditch

"A little polishing compound and we'll be as good as new!" Nigel said. I was a bit embarrassed to see the truck came to rest at no more than at a 45° angle, so the crash wasn't as bad as I had imagined.

"We have another Land Cruiser coming to tow us out," our driver said. "Please stay nearby." He held his rifle at his side, as if to emphasize his last instructions to us. That lasted for about 30 minutes until Nigel decided to walk in the tall grass towards a nearby rock formation. I followed, wondering about snakes and other creatures under the cloak of the grass. Nigel was doing the same as I bumped into him.

"Maybe we should head back," he said. I looked up and spotted them.

"Not before you take your photo," I said. He turned around and spotted them. There were two lions sunbathing on the top of the rocks, the larger of the two staring right at us. Nigel took his photo and we reversed course. "Try not to show any fear," I said.

"Like you?" he asked.

Nigel spots his lions

Flight Lessons 5: People

Our Land Cruiser was pulled from the ditch and we pressed on to see a few giraffes up close, a rhino, and lots and lots of zebras. Through it all, Nigel kept checking his digital camera to make sure his lion photo was still there.

That night for dinner I brought my laptop computer and made a copy of the precious photo. "I'll email this home first chance I get, Nigel." When dinner was ready, our table was served first. Maybe it was compensation for our time in the ditch.

"You guys have a great life," Sarah said, eying the tables opposite ours. "Most of these tourists saved up for a lifetime to do this. And you guys get paid to do it."

"That is true," I said. "Today was fun."

"And you get to do it with Bravo Zulu," she added. "You guys have the best airplane, flying the best trips, and you are flying for the best company. If you ever want a full-time flight attendant, please call me first!"

It was something we heard often, but after a day on the Serengeti, I realized more than ever how true her words were. I think they had the same impact on Nigel, who stopped his usual whining. The flight home was the best I ever had with Nigel.

After we returned to Bedford with the airplane tucked away in the hangar, and after everyone else had gone home, I sat at my desk with the last bits of paper that needed to be faxed. I added the cover page to ensure the stack ended up on our dispatcher's desk and fed everything into the machine. The connection to White Plains was instantaneous. I knew the machine opposite Linda's desk would be spitting out paper copies of everything, something she would be happy to see in the morning. My cell phone rang.

"It's terrible," she said.

"What happened to 'this is Linda your dispatcher?'" I asked. "And what are you doing up? It's past midnight."

"Haven't you heard?" she asked.

"What?" I asked.

"The FAA just shut us down," she said. "You may have had the last trip of a

Bravo Zulu aircraft."

I opened my laptop and started to read the emails I had missed since we left Africa. The list was long, but I skimmed quickly to find the one from Hank Callaghan. "I regret to inform everyone that talks with the FAA have broken down and we have been ordered to cease all operations effective immediately. Bravo Zulu Aviation and Bravo Zulu Charter have been deemed a danger to the flying public because of the uncertainty of our operational control under foreign management. It is a profound irony that we continue to have the best safety record in the industry. But we no longer have the financial resources to contest this. We will do our best to help our clients move on to other management companies. We will be in contact soon."

The FAA refused to reveal who had driven the effort to shut Bravo Zulu down and would not respond to questions about the conflict between Bravo Zulu's flawless safety record and the order's statement that said Bravo Zulu was a danger to the flying public. Bravo Zulu's largest competitor, International Flight Enterprises, was reaping the rewards. IFE was collecting four out of every five Bravo Zulu clients, including us.

"Beats me," Chip Dawson said as we flew our airplane to IFE headquarters in Kentucky. "Mr. Viceroy never asked, and his assistant told us we needed to fly to IFE so they could approve our airplane for charter."

It would take IFE two days to inspect our Gulfstream from nose to tail and two days to train us pilots to learn how to fly the IFE way. We filed into a classroom and recognized ten fellow Bravo Zulu expatriates. "This is our life now," Chip said. "No sense complaining about something you can't do nothing about."

We each had a large, 3" binder in front of us, with a photocopied cover that said, "International Flight Enterprises Indoctrination Class, 2006." I thumbed through and was immediately hit by the amateurishness of it all. Every page was a photocopy several generations old. Many of the pages were illegible. The instructor walked in a minute prior to our scheduled start time and asked us to be seated. "The director of operations will be here in a few seconds," he said. "Captain Storm is a very busy man so let's keep the questions to a minimum so we can get this over with quickly."

My face flushed with the realization. Page two of the indoc binder was Captain Gary Storm's biography. He was a current and qualified Challenger pilot, as well as the top IFE officer in charge of all flight operations. Scanning his job history, he was Q-Tron's chief pilot for five years. Okay: at least one fabrication.

The man himself walked in and the sight was breathtaking. Gary had put on at least a hundred pounds since the last time I saw him, about three years ago. His newly acquired girth was made all the more impressive by the way he wore his white shirt with four-bar epaulets and a black tie that only made it halfway down his chest. He took the chair at the head of the table and looked at a point on the opposite wall. He breathed heavily as he spoke.

"You may be wondering why I am wearing my pilot uniform on a day I am not flying," he began. "Well I've always considered myself on call and I am qualified in two types that we fly out of this very airport. In the last couple of years I've had to go fly twice, with minimal notice. So that's why. But you aren't here to listen to my dress code, you are here to become IFE pilots." He stopped in mid-sentence as his eyes met mine. "Ah, so …"

"And that's what Sam here is going to do for you," he said, recovering his chain of thought. "So, listen well, gentlemen. Welcome to IFE. I think you will find we are every bit as good as where you came from."

And with that, he was gone. Once everyone opened their binders the mood turned ugly. As the instructor unveiled just how different being IFE pilots would be, the complaints only intensified. I reminded myself that in a new environment the best technique is to shut up and listen, but it had just become too much.

"Are you saying that we cannot curtail our center of gravity?" I asked.

"Yes, that is what I am saying," the instructor answered. "We do not have the necessary letter of authorization to do that." At Bravo Zulu we had the necessary LOA. Every aircraft plays a balancing game with different weights to keep the airplane stable. Where you place fuel, baggage, cargo, and people will have an impact on that balance. Manufacturers publish center of gravity charts that show the largest limits available, based on precise placement of every pound of payload. That becomes a pilot's center of gravity envelope. Curtailing the envelope, making it smaller, means not having to weigh everyone and everything with precision. But the price for this convenience is you need an LOA that attests that you know what you are doing. IFE didn't have the LOA.

"Well then just get it," someone else offered.

"It isn't as easy as that," he said.

"So that means we have to ask every passenger how much they weigh, and we have to put every bag on a scale," I said. "You can't be serious!"

"That's how we do it at IFE," he said. "You will just have to get used to it."

"That's BS!" someone shouted. The class erupted and the instructor fled. I felt embarrassed to have started the insurrection and Chip shook his head in disapproval. "There's nothing to be done about it," he said.

The instructor returned, flanked by a gentleman in a coat and tie. "Please everyone be seated," the instructor said. "I've brought in the chief pilot to settle this."

"Good morning," he said. "And it is a good morning. I'm Captain Ray Ford, the IFE chief pilot. I'm also a Gulfstream pilot so I have something in common with many of you Bravo Zulu pilots. Sam tells me you guys have a problem with having to ask your passengers for weight information." We all nodded, a few grunted. Captain Ford was of medium build, his face pockmarked with evidence of an earlier life dealing with acne and later with age spots. He looked to be in his late sixties.

"Well it isn't that hard. We know we have to ID our passengers too. So, I ask to see their passports, I check to see they are who they say they are, and I quickly scan the passport and memorize their weights. So, I get the job done without having to ask."

I thought about that and reached into my briefcase to fetch my passport. "My passport doesn't have my weight on it," I said.

Captain Ford's face flushed beet red, but then he smiled. "Oh, did I say passport? I meant driver's license."

Flight Lessons 5: People

"Why don't we just get LOA A097 and be done with it?" I asked.

"That's easier said than done," Captain Ford said. "There is a lot of math needed and you just can't sit down in an hour or two and draft the application."

That night, I sat down and in an hour or two, drafted the application. The next morning, I found Captain Ford's office and presented the completed application. "We can't submit this," he said. "It wouldn't be fair."

"What do you mean fair?" I asked.

"How can we allow your airplane to have this and everyone else has to stick with asking for weights?" he asked. "I am not going to have one set of rules for one set of airplanes and another set of rules for everyone else."

"Do you allow all your aircraft to fly outside of gliding distance from land?" I asked.

"No, of course not," he said.

"So you have one set of rules for one set of aircraft, and . . ."

"I'm done talking to you," he said. "You have a class to go to."

I showed up to the classroom and saw that the tables were arranged with three or four chairs on each. The lady at the front of the class introduced herself as Suzy and explained we would be doing group dynamic exercises in CRM. "Now who can tell me what CRM stands for?"

The class remained silent; it was such a ridiculous question. "Come on now, you all look like very smart pilots."

"Crew Resource Management," Chip offered.

"Yes!" she said. "Very good!" She explained that since our class was all pilots, some of us would have to role play as flight attendants and mechanics. We were to learn how all decisions were to be achieved through consensus. "We are all part of the crew!" she said.

It was a painful four hours, with each of us having to play the role of a non-pilot and learning to assert ourselves. "Next time you lose an engine during takeoff, Eddie," Nigel said. "You better not decide which rudder to press without ringing the cabin first."

The near unanimous consensus of our class of former Bravo Zulu pilots was that flying for IFE was a step backwards in every conceivable way. The lone dissenter to our gloomy outlook was Chip Dawson. "I think it's going to be even better than Bravo Zulu. Sure, they have a few problems, but it is up to us to fix them."

Nigel and Chip observed the first rule of getting along as new pilots in an organization. They listened patiently and agreed to ignore the rules they didn't agree with. I insisted following each rule, to include asking every passenger how much they weighed while Nigel and Chip pretended they didn't know me. IFE didn't have the authorizations that allowed us to fly several types of instrument approaches in Europe or to allow us to use some of our aircraft's vertical navigation capabilities in the U.S. We were starting to get comfortable deviating from the company's rules.

But I never failed to ask a passenger how much they weighed.

"I think you like provoking them," *The Lovely Mrs. Haskel* said. "I know the rules are important to you, but it seems that rule is one you are trying to stir the pot with."

"Oh, I don't know," I said. "You might be right."

The next week we picked up a former Prime Minister of Canada and his wife from Miami, then flew to another airport in Ohio to pick up two members of British Royalty, and then on to Canada. Chip pretended he was busy that day and scheduled Nigel and me for the duty.

"You are asking my wife what?" the distinguished gentleman asked. I explained that company rules required it. His wife blushed and whispered her weight, which I recorded. At our next stop the Canadian couple warmly greeted the British couple and there were smiles all around until I approached.

"You won't believe what this dreadful man is going to ask you," the wife of the

Flight Lessons 5: People

former Prime Minister said."

But I asked, and The Lady answered. The IFE Chief Pilot, of course, was not amused. He signed off Nigel's upgrade orders and I found myself scheduled only as a first officer. Nigel was as happy as I had ever seen him. I was still unhappy with having to ask passengers about their weight and the poorly written manuals. But being a first officer was the least of my complaints. A month later, Captain Ford suffered a stroke and was forced to retire. A week later, IFE announced that Captain Chip Dawson had agreed to take his place.

"Because I like to eat," Chip said when Nigel and I asked. "Mr. Viceroy is going to interview you both to decide who takes my place."

"I don't want the job," I said. "Nigel will do a better job working with IFE."

"Does it pay more?" Nigel asked.

"Of course," Chip said.

"Then count me in," Nigel said.

"Well we got that settled," I said.

"Doesn't matter," Chip said. Mr. Viceroy wants to meet with you both.

"You have to take the job," *The Lovely Mrs. Haskel* said that night. "The economy is in the tank and there are lots of pilots on the streets these days."

"I'm not taking the base manager's position," I said. "Nigel wants it. This way we'll both be happy."

The Lovely Mrs. Haskel gave me the look I didn't see often, but often enough to read her thoughts. She didn't agree but realized my mind was made up. The next day, Mr. Viceroy met with Nigel at 9 a.m. At 10 a.m. his assistant called and asked that I come in as soon as possible. I managed to make it by noon.

"Why don't you want the job?" Mr. Viceroy asked. "You have the necessary experience. You've done this before in the Air Force, after all."

"This is something Nigel has wanted all his career," I said. "I can work for Nigel."

"There is more pay," Mr. Viceroy said.

"Give it to Nigel," I said. "I'll mentor him as best I can."

"Let me give you some advice, Eddie," he said. "People who do not want power leave a vacuum; people who do, fill the vacuum. My best interests are served by putting you in charge. You may not want the position, but you've got it. You don't have a choice in the matter."

I was seated at our kitchen table staring at my HTML editor and the page reserved for all things crew resource management. "It has to come from the top down," one version of the notes said. Gary Storm nuked that. "It has to come from the bottom up," version two point oh said. Then came Chip Dawson who somehow ran a pilot mill where he outlasted any of his crews' attempts at change. Although published on the World Wide Web, the notes were just for me. At most, twenty friends were using them too and I always started pages like this with the warning, "These notes are a work in progress." I only erased the warning once I was happy with the article. The CRM article was nowhere near that point.

The Lovely Mrs. Haskel appeared at the table with a fresh pot of coffee and her ever present smile. She was pleased about Chip's departure and about the pay raise. "This may be our last postmortem on a boss," she said.

"Everyone's got a boss," I said.

"So what went wrong with Chip?" she asked.

"I don't know," I said. "He seemed to be a barely competent pilot who gravitated to the top because he outlasted the competition. Once he was on top, he chased all the competition out because, well, I don't know the because."

I thought back to Nigel beating his steering wheel with both fists, his face contorted in anger.

"Good riddance," she said.

Flight Lessons 5: People

"Not really," I said. "In a way I'll still be working for him. He's now the IFE chief pilot, after all."

"And now you are the boss of this flight department," she said. "I don't know why you keep turning down these opportunities. This is what you were meant to do."

"Well right now it is just a flight department of three," I said. "I think I can improve things with Nigel. I'm not so sure about the mechanic."

Flight Lessons 5: People

Flight Lessons: The Captain (First Generation CRM)

By 1973, when "Pan Am was littering the islands of the Pacific with the hulks of Boeing jetliners," other airlines were having their own problems and it became apparent that was happening even when crews appeared to get along.

How two light bulbs forced a wakeup call

Artist's depiction of Eastern Airlines Flight 401, (Creative Commons)

In 1972, a Lockheed L-1011 operating as Eastern Airlines Flight 401 flew into the Everglades in Florida as all members of the flight deck crew were focused on a burned-out light bulb. During the troubleshooting, no pilot had been assigned the task of flying the aircraft and, although an altitude discrepancy was noticed by air traffic control, the flight gently descended without the crew noticing the critical controlled flight into terrain (CFIT) problem. [Cortés, et al, 2017, pp. 128]

In 1978, a Douglas DC-8 operating as United Airlines Flight 173 crashed near Portland, Oregon, after running out of fuel, killing 10 occupants. The accident resulted from the captain focusing too heavily on preparing the cabin for an emergency landing due to a gear malfunction, while neglecting both the fuel state and the increasing concerns of the other flight crewmembers who were rightfully worried about running out of gas. [Cortés, et al, 2017, pp. 128]

Note: Links to the case studies are provided in the references section of this book.

The National Aeronautics and Space Administration hosted a series of conferences in 1979 out of which Cockpit Resource Management was born.

NASA and Cockpit Resource Management

A 1979 NASA study placed 18 airline crews in a Boeing 747 simulator to experience multiple emergencies. The study showed a remarkable amount of variability in the effectiveness with which crews handled the situation. Some crews managed the problems very well, while others committed a large number of operationally serious errors. The primary conclusion drawn from the study was that most problems and errors were introduced by breakdowns in crew coordination rather than by deficits in technical knowledge or skills. The findings were clear crews who communicated more overall tended to perform better and, in particular, those who exchanged more information about flight status committed fewer errors in the handling of engines and hydraulic and fuel systems and the reading and setting of instruments. [Kanki, et al, 2010, §1.4.4]

The first generation of CRM placed its focus on changing behaviors, primarily of the captain, to emphasize that input from other flight deck crewmembers should be considered when making decisions. It was a revolutionary idea.

Part Three
The Crew

12: First Officer
May 2006

A view of a GV, how Dr. Jones checks the landing lights (Eddie photo)

Donald Robert Jones, Doctor Jones to me, had been Mr. Viceroy's airplane mechanic for over thirty years, back when that meant something with a propeller on each wing. Even though I was now in charge, I had no idea how much Don was paid, only that it had to be too much.

"Did you do a post flight, Don?" I asked. The hangar doors were closed and I could see the lights were turned out. A quick look at my watch and the flight log verified that we had been on the ground less than 30 minutes.

"Of course, I did," he said. "See you tomorrow." The door slammed behind him and through the window I detected a little anger in the way his truck kicked up a few rocks in the direction of my truck. Chip never wanted to talk about Don and warned me to tread lightly about my complaints about our maintenance. Now that Chip was gone, shortcomings in our aircraft's maintenance were my responsibility. Don's office was a mess – something to tackle sometime in the future – but I managed to find the Gulfstream maintenance manual and made a copy of the steps needed to do a proper post flight inspection. I left it on Jones' desk.

The next day I started out at the local Fixed Based Operator to prearrange our large fuel order, two sets of newspapers, and three bags of ice. I had already talked to Nigel who was preflighting the airplane and helping the flight attendant with the large catering order.

"Hey stranger," I heard from behind me. I turned to see Sid Justice wearing a Gulfstream jacket. "Where are you headed today?"

"Tel Aviv," I said. "And you?"

"Paris," he said. "I don't think we can do Israel in just one hop in the Four."

"How would you like to fly the Five?" I asked. "I'm hiring."

"As tempting as that would be, I think I'll stick with this job," he said. "The company is great, the passengers are great, and there is a rumor we're going to eventually trade our GIV in for something newer."

Sid said he wasn't permitted to talk about his company, as they were very private. But he guaranteed there was no one better to work for at Bedford. "Maybe anywhere," he added.

"No complaints then," I said.

"Only one," he said. He looked over his shoulder and whispered. "The management company."

"I have the same complaint," I said. "And a few others." Sid's airplane was managed by a small company based out of a small New York airport. He said his GIV was the only aircraft they had that wasn't at their home airport and they tended to be hands off. I related my problems with IFE, the uncurtailed center of gravity, and the poorly written manuals.

"At least you've got a company manual," he said. "The only good thing we have is a great dispatcher, she says she knows you."

"Linda Hodges," I said. "I would trade all of our dispatchers for her."

"You can't have her," he said, laughing. We talked sports, motorcycles, and food as we walked the ramp towards our airplanes. His GIV had certainly seen better days. It was easily fifteen years old and seemed to have its original coat of paint. As we got to his airplane, Sid shook my hand and I continued on to the prettiest bird on the ramp, our GV. I got to the steps just as Nigel was stowing the landing gear pins into a compartment in the stairs.

Flight Lessons 5: People

"Good bird?" I asked.

"Good bird," he said. "Your leg going east?" he asked.

"It's up to you, Nigel," I said.

"I think the PIC should always fly the first leg," he said. "It sets the tone for the trip."

"Okay," I said, "let's give that a try."

The passengers were on time and the flight attendant kept them happy and out of the cockpit as we settled in at 43,000 feet, safely above the airline traffic competing for the best winds going east. Nigel's oceanic plotting procedures were vastly improved but he still struggled with the post-position plot, a necessary plotting of the aircraft's position about ten minutes after passing a navigation waypoint. The rule said it had to be done "about ten minutes" after waypoint passage, but anything in the ballpark would serve its purpose. He wrote down our FMS's position exactly: 51°05.143 North, 48°25.003 West and carefully interpolated the position on the chart. The blue lines of the chart were drawn every 1° in longitude and latitude, so he had to estimate where exactly to place his dot. The dot was just a few millimeters off our plotted course.

"Best I can tell," he said, "we are on course."

"Good," I said. "There is an easier way to do this that not many people know about. The book says plot our position about ten minutes after the waypoint. When we are going east to west or west to east in these mid-latitudes, that happens about two degrees of longitude. So if you wait until an even two degrees of longitude, you cut the number of interpolations in half."

"That makes sense," he said. "But what if we get checked after landing and they discover we didn't do it at exactly ten minutes?"

"I'll dig up the regulation," I said. "It says 'approximately' and doing it at two degrees improves accuracy."

By the time we got to our next waypoint, I found the reference in our manual. Nigel waited until the airplane was at exactly 38° West longitude and noted that it had been nine minutes and a few seconds since waypoint passage. "Close enough," he said. Since his plotting now only required that he interpolate the latitude, he was able to draw his dot more quickly and accurately. "That's pretty neat," he said after showing me the plotting chart.

"That's the way Chip does it too," I said. "I can't believe he never showed you this."

"He never showed me anything," Nigel said. "The first time I asked him anything he made it perfectly clear that wasn't allowed."

"Really?" I said. "How did he do that?"

"It was on our first flight crossing the pond," Nigel said. "He told me we had to maintain our speed plus or minus point oh two Mach. I asked him where that comes from. He pulled out the big Jepp binder and said . . ."

"It's in here!" I said. "Yeah, he gave me that routine once."

"Well I vowed to never ask him another question," Nigel said. "And I never did."

"The irony of it is that he was wrong," I said.

"Wrong about the speed?" Nigel asked.

"Yeah," I said. "There used to be a Mach tolerance about ten years ago, but they did away with it. Now you have to be right on speed. No tolerance."

"That's what I thought!" Nigel said.

"I wish he told me that," I said. "I could have gotten another quarter."

Nigel laughed. He knew I was collecting them and ended up with nine on the chair rail. "You could have had an even ten," he said.

"Don't be afraid to ask me anything, Nigel," I said. "If I don't know something I'll say so. There is a lot not to know."

"Okay," he said. "How's this for a question: how do we find another pilot to take Chip's place?"

"How would you like to do that?" I asked.

"Not in my job description," he said.

Flight Lessons 5: People

"Okay," I said. "I'll get with IFE and see what we can do."

The next morning, I placed the call. "Chip Dawson," he said.

"So you've graduated from chief cook and bottle washer?" I asked.

"Oh, those were the days," he said. "This job sucks."

"You can have your old job if you want it," I said.

"This job sucks but I like to eat," he said. "What can I do you for?"

"I need another pilot, no thanks to you," I said. "I was wondering what IFE had to offer."

"Let me punch a few numbers on this phone thing," he said, "and a lovely lady in HR will help you right out."

The next thing I heard was the lovely lady's voice; Chip was gone. The lovely lady was helpful and promised to fax five resumes within the hour.

True to her word I had four resumes of pilots that appeared to be nearing social security retirement age and one who appeared to be too young to shave. None had any Gulfstream experience. Calls to local sources came up empty too. The supply of qualified Gulfstream pilots had dried up. Everyone good had a job, everyone who didn't have a job seemed to have a reason they were not employed. I placed the five IFE resumes plus three more from the local area on Nigel's desk and decided the best action for the day was inaction.

I showed up for our next flight to find Nigel doing the aircraft preflight and the resume of the youngest candidate on my desk. Nigel had written, "I know his uncle, gave him a call. He recommends him."

I wasn't sure that was the most unbiased recommendation possible, but it was a start. "He's single and doesn't mind moving," Nigel said after returning from the hangar. "He sailed through Challenger training and his current boss says he's the best. He thinks moving up to Gulfstreams is just the thing for him."

"He doesn't have a lot of experience with high density, New York to Boston traffic," I said. "He doesn't have any oceanic experience other than Hawaii." As soon as I said that I knew I would hit a nerve. "But I guess that's a start.

He doesn't have enough hours for captain, he'll have to be a first officer for a few years."

"We could use a genuine FO around here; we can mold him and bring him up right," Nigel said. "Besides, who else do we have to choose from?"

One phone call and three days later, Mick Riverton appeared at our hangar door. He was short, slender, and tanned. From his resume, based on his college graduation date, I guessed he was in his early thirties. He looked ten years younger. He greeted me with a firm handshake and a toothy grin. He answered our questions without hesitation and always with that high beam smile.

"How'd you get your start flying jets?" I asked.

"I got lucky, whenever someone needed someone for the next step up the ladder, someone I flew with recommended me."

"Did you ever have to tell your captain he was making a mistake?"

"Almost never, but I had to say something about not having enough gas once or twice."

"What's your favorite thing to do on the road?"

"History, mostly. That can be anything from a museum to a battlefield."

The next day, Mr. Viceroy's questions were aimed more at figuring out just how old Mick really was and if he really understood just how miserable weather in the Boston area was compared to the San Francisco bay area.

"Do you know this boy is only thirty-three?" Gail asked.

"No," I said, "I am not allowed to ask. But that was about my guess."

"Mister Viceroy just flat out asked," she said. "But he said that if Mick is okay with you, go ahead and hire him."

Mick loaded up his Nissan sedan and drove from Oakland to Savannah in three days, half the time it would have taken me, and started the next step in his career of getting lucky.

A month later I got a call.

Flight Lessons 5: People

"Your boy failed his check," Gary Storm said from his perch at IFE headquarters. "They say he didn't study as hard as he should have but with another day of class and a recheck he should be okay. But you're going to have to pay for two more days."

"It's a sunk cost," I said. "I can pay for another two days or consider the previous three weeks a total loss. Let's put him up for another two days and if that doesn't work we'll send him home."

"You don't need to check with the bean counters first?" he asked.

"No," I said. "I'll risk their wrath. I think this was a big jump for Mick. Let's give him the benefit of the doubt."

"Good call, Eddie," he said. "I wish more of our base managers had the balls to do that."

"We'll see," I said. "You might be looking for two more pilots if this doesn't work out."

"That's the risk you take when you step up to the big chair," he said, I suppose relating his fall from grace at Q-Tron to my possible demise at Gil Viceroy LTD. "You and I were both colonels in the military and we both saw some combat. But in the civilian world most guys don't have the stones to take command."

"I suppose that's true," I said, ignoring the fact that in both worlds it was optimal to get people to do things because they saw it in their best interest. Even in the military the "because I gave you a direct order" was the last resort of getting your point across.

"As long as we are being so agreeable, I got a question for you," he said.

"Shoot," I said.

"What in the hell is the problem with Chip Dawson?" he asked. "He's creeping out half the staff here. One moment he's laughing and yucking it up, the next moment he looks like a regular Norman Bates."

"He has his moments," I admitted. "I'm not sure what to do about it. He made half our flight attendants uncomfortable with that vacant stare of his. I talked to him about it, but he thinks it's a big joke. Maybe you can have more influence as his boss."

"The only influence I'm going to have is to fire his ass if he doesn't knock it off," Gary said. "Nice chatting with you, Eddie."

It was the most words Gary and I had ever exchanged without him yelling. It didn't make any sense. I didn't mention Mick's troubles to anyone except *The Lovely Mrs. Haskel* who was completely sympathetic.

"It's like you always say, on any given day the best pilot can bust a check ride and the worst can pass. Maybe it just wasn't his day."

Mick passed on his second try and showed up with his ever-present smile. IFE rules dictated that he do all his flying from the right seat so Nigel and I had to dust off true first officer protocols dealing with exchange of aircraft control during takeoff and landing. "We did this at the mainline all the time," Nigel said. "I'll train our pup to do this right."

"Then you can fly his first three and three," I said. I would have preferred to do it, but perhaps this was a way to get Nigel motivated to instruct.

"You don't pay me enough to instruct," Nigel said. That settled, I found a few days off in the schedule and devoted a day to crawling around the airplane and talking about procedures with Mick, followed by a day for his first three takeoffs and landings, making him qualified to fly with passengers on board.

I instructed from the left seat as Mick flew from the right, showing very good stick and rudder skills. "Remarkable," I said. "This is the largest airplane you've ever flown by a factor of two and you seem very comfortable. We have a domestic trip next week to Seattle, that can be you and me."

I gave Mick some homework to "chair fly" the checklist, meaning to practice it at home so as to become more comfortable. He promised that he would, and it appeared he had done so the next week. But there were other problems.

"We can do that," he said to Salt Lake Center when instructed to proceed

Flight Lessons 5: People

direct Billings. "Sure thing," when our next clearance was to Yakima.

"Mick, I prefer by-the-book radio phraseology," I said. "The pilot-controller glossary allows you to say 'wilco' in these situations. But I prefer to repeat the instruction exactly as given. That increases the odds we understood the instruction correctly and gives him a chance to verify that."

"Okay," he said. "I'm just not used to such a formal approach to flying."

"Well that's what it takes to fly at this level," I said. He did better and besides having to talk him out of saying "tally ho" and "bogey" when spotting traffic, I had no further phraseology complaints. His actual flying skills were very good, but he didn't have a complete grasp on how to program the avionics. But that was pretty normal for anyone new to the GV.

The winds were howling in Seattle and the autopilot struggled to center the needles during our ILS approach. With only 1,500 feet to go, I disconnected the autopilot and centered the localizer needle. After we landed and put the airplane to bed, I debriefed the flight from takeoff to landing. "I waited too long to get us back on course," I said. "So, shame on me. My question for you, Mick, is why didn't you say anything?"

"You were only a dot and a half off when you took over," he said. "That's not too bad."

"Next time speak up at half a dot," I said. "I'll do the same for you."

Two days later we were eastbound with Mick flying from the right seat and me doing the non-flying pilot duties from the left. I made sure to verbalize any procedures and techniques he didn't seem to have down fully, and he dutifully acknowledged each new morsel of information. As long as he was flying the airplane, he did well. He was going to work out.

"The new FO is not going to work out," Nigel said after his first trip with Mick. "He doesn't know any of the callouts, he misses checklist steps, and I don't think he knows the first thing about the FMS."

"That's why we are here, Nigel," I said. "The schoolhouse does a lousy job of all that and it is up to us to bring him up to speed."

"Training on a passenger carrying flight should never be allowed," he said. "If you don't know everything you need to know when you finish school, you need to go back to school."

"Did you know everything you needed to know?" I asked.

"I knew more than he does," Nigel said.

"Well let's work on him," I said. "It's you and me to Brazil next week. I got Mick into an international procedures initial at IFE headquarters starting Monday. I also enrolled him in a CRM course on Thursday. The following week I'll take him to Italy. The week after that its Los Angeles. You can take that if you want it."

"Good," Nigel said. "I'll get to beat up on him coast-to-coast."

"No beatings," I said. "It isn't good for morale."

Nigel always seemed to be on his best behavior when we flew overseas. While IFE blessed him as a captain before I took over, they would need my approval to elevate him to an international captain. It always seemed to grate on him that he was a "mainline" international pilot and he had yet to be the captain on an international trip. I enjoyed these trips with Nigel more and more because he was actually a pretty good pilot and could be receptive to instruction if he thought it was something he would need in the near future.

"Ask for a backup frequency," I said as we checked in with Amazonica Center, just crossing into Brazil.

"Why?" Nigel asked.

"Their infrastructure is pretty weak," I said. "Their controllers are known for stepping outside for several minutes with no warning. Brazil is a big country. Losing communications here is no fun."

Nigel did not comment the first time we had to go to the backup frequency, about fifteen minutes after entering Brazilian airspace. The second time he acknowledged the wisdom. "Good thing we had another frequency!"

That night at the bar Nigel was pretty pleased with himself and announced he was ready to upgrade. "I've done Europe, Africa, the Pacific, and now I've seen my fair share of South America. That should just about cover it, don't you think?"

"I suppose," I said. "The thing is you can never say you've seen it all, there is just so much out there. There is an important skill that has nothing to do with geography."

"Preparation," he said.

"Yes," I agreed. "But there is more to it than that. Even if you've been someplace a hundred times it is important to realize things change. And after you have done all the necessary research it is important to be skeptical that you know enough. There are just so many pieces to flying internationally you have to expect a few pieces to fall through your grasp. The skill is being able to pick up the pieces before they cause too much damage."

"Lots of pilots get thrown into the briar patch and learn as they go," Nigel said. "They seem to do okay."

"We don't hear about a lot of screw ups," I said. "Unless they end up killing someone. We don't want to rely on luck. But you are right. There is only so much preparation we can do, at some point we do get kicked out of the nest."

"So when do I get kicked out of the nest?" he asked.

"I've already signed you off," I said. "I turned the paperwork in yesterday. I'll take Mick to Italy next week and provided he gets signed off, it will be you and him the week after that to Paris."

Nigel bought me a beer – a rare thing – and the rest of the Brazil trip went smoothly. On our return I found a certificate of completion on my desk, telling me that Mick passed his international procedures course and was ready for his first trip across the pond.

A pilot's first trip beyond gliding distance from land can be a rite of passage for some. In the Air Force it happened early and was just another step of many. I suppose that could be said for any young pilot hired into a large airline with international routes. But among corporate pilots, it seemed to be a very big deal.

"How many crossings have you made, Eddie?" Mick asked as Newfoundland disappeared under our nose, replaced only by the blue of the Atlantic.

"I don't know," I said. "You will see that it isn't so hard as long as you stick to good procedures and keep up with the changes."

Mick listened carefully and did a fair job during his first High Frequency radio transmissions. The HF can be filled with static on one day and just like talking to someone on the phone the next. "What did he say?" Mick asked.

"He asked for the next waypoint," I said. "Tell him five nine north, zero three zero west." I had written a script for him but he forgot to add that last waypoint. On the next position report, he jumbled the order.

"Mick, try to remember the radio operator is sitting at a computer display wanting to fill in specific items on his screen," I said. "If you give him the information in the correct order, he types, tabs, and types some more. If you jump around, he has to. Let's make it easier on him. That gets the position report done quickly and frees the frequency for the next guy."

Mick listened to instruction and generally performed well at first. But he tended to forget his lessons and he became lazy after several successful attempts. I spent many of our off-duty hours in Rome rehashing procedures, which may have perturbed him. He wanted to focus on the historic sights while I kept up with the training regimen.

Our return flight did not start on a good note, with Mick giving up early trying to understand the Italian controllers. "What's on the ATIS?" I asked. It was his duty during the preflight to listen to the Automated Terminal Information Service on the radio, typically a recording of the weather and any pertinent airport information made by a tower controller. The total transmission was rarely longer than a minute.

"I couldn't understand him," Mick said. "His English isn't so good."

"You couldn't get anything at all?" I asked.

"No," he said. I selected the radio on my interphone panel and listened. The controller's accent was quite heavy, but I managed to get everything after three tries.

"Here," I said, handing my written transcription to Mick. He happily entered the information into our FMS and reported that the FMS was programmed. I knew the next challenge would be getting our en route clearance. In most U.S. airports this can be done prior to engine start. In many foreign destinations, like Ciampino Airport in Rome, this was done while the aircraft was taxiing. "Let's practice listening to clearances," I said.

"Okay," he said.

As soon as the controller said anything in English, I asked Mick, "what did he say?"

"I don't know," Mick said each time.

"You need to get good at this," I said. "Listen more carefully."

"If I didn't get it the first time," he said, "how is listening over and over again going to help?"

"Keep trying," I said. After a while he was starting to understand at about a fifty-percent level. "You know the structure of the clearance. You know you are going to get a departure procedure, an altitude, and a transition to the en route structure. You can study the departure procedure pages to get familiar with the names."

"All that just to get a clearance?" he asked.

"I never said it was easy," I said. "But if you want to be an international pilot, you need to get this down to a science."

Mick was nowhere near any level of science, but he managed to catch about half of the clearance. Once we were off the ground he did better and his second trip across the pond was better than the first. He was happy to have the rite of passage behind him but seemed less enthusiastic about his homework assignment.

"I'd like you to come in sometime between now and your trip to Paris," I said. "I would like you to memorize the names of every arrival and departure procedure into and out of Le Bourget."

"Really?" he asked.

"Yes," I said. "It may seem silly, but if you don't speak French, at least knowing the names will tune your ear. This is really important."

I called Nigel that night. "You need to be patient," I said. "Remember this will only be Mick's third flight over the North Atlantic. He's going to get this, but it will take time. Don't treat him the way Chip treated you."

"Okay," Nigel said. "I won't be a jerk."

"That's the spirit!" I said. "The key to surviving an oceanic trip with a new guy is to be prepared to do everything yourself, offloading only what the student . . ." I caught myself, ". . . the other pilot can handle as he is ready for it."

"I'm not being paid to do the work of two pilots," Nigel said.

"Neither am I," I said. "But that's the way it goes."

13: Captain
March 2007

The success of every flight rests on the captain's shoulders (Photo: Steven Foltz)

"The boys are in Paris," I announced to *The Lovely Mrs. Haskel*, in part to let her know that I wasn't working that day and in part to let her know my effort to get Nigel and Mick to get along without killing each other was progressing.

"This is Nigel's first time as the big cheese on an overseas trip, isn't it?" she asked.

"It is," I agreed.

"A rite of passage," she said. "I hope this straightens him out."

A rite of passage. The thought came to me often. My first solo in the Cessna T-37 Tweet was the first that has stuck with me over the years. Being strapped to an ejection seat, flying aerobatics without an instructor to save me, and then flying an overheard traffic pattern that began with a 2-G turn and ended with a descending final turn at 1,500 feet per minute without supervision was a rite of passage. I can add to that my first time in command of a crew, in a Boeing 707. On and on.

My first time in command of an international trip was also a big deal for me and it was, very much so, a rite of passage. That was also in the Boeing 707 and I still remember mechanically going through the crew briefing, thinking the crew of thirteen was wondering who the imposter at the head of the table was. But within a trip or two, the rite of passage was history and I had to wonder why it was so important after it had become routine.

I knew Nigel would be going through the same emotions, even with a crew of three. He started as a flight instructor and then had three jobs as a commuter airline first officer when he got picked up by his precious mainline. His only experience as a captain was with Chip and me in the other seat, both of us with considerably more experience. The day Nigel flew with Mick strapped into the right seat would have been his first time with a genuine first officer. It was a rite of passage I failed to notice; it completely got by me. In fact, I never thought of it until assigning the crew for the next trip to Paris.

The trip sheet to Paris Le Bourget placed Captain Nigel May's name on top, in the Pilot in Command block. Below him, on the sheet and in the eyes of all aviation authorities, was First Officer Michael "Mick" Riverton, the Second in Command. This was a big deal for Nigel.

Newly minted Certified Flight Instructors often worry that their newly approved students will fail to live up to expectations once kicked out of the nest. My instructor pilot experience began in the Air Force where we lived by a syllabus and the criteria for each phase of instruction was clearly laid out. When it came time to leave the nest, your students either flew or didn't. We didn't waste a lot of time thinking about it.

But, seeing their names on the trip sheet, I had to think about it. Nigel was the "captain" on several international trips with me as his first officer and he had done fine. Mick was competent. My rationale for signing Nigel off when I did was to take advantage of the simple Paris and back trip. It was easy enough I thought Nigel could do it solo. I already flew Mick's first crossing. This would force Nigel to realize the success of the trip rested on his shoulders and it would be in his best interest to get along with his first officer. His first officer. I noticed he would often refer to Mick as "my first officer." Sending the two out as a pair was a risk, but a necessary risk.

Back at Q-Tron, a large flight department, I was charged with upgrading all pilots each step of the way. Some of the newly minted captains would call during their first trips with questions but I made it a rule never to call them. They were captains and I wasn't going to deflate the experience by checking up on them. Back in our Bravo Zulu days I would get progress reports from our dispatchers, but not so with IFE. I made sure my cell phone was charged, just in case. There were usually no calls until they returned.

"Just checking in," Nigel said. "The airplane is in good shape, the passengers were happy, and everything went according to Hoyle." According to Hoyle, a Nigel-ism.

"How was the new hotel?" I asked, delaying the inevitable question while playing into one of his pre-trip suggestions.

"Good location, good rooms," he said. "Not quite up to your standard but it was cheap as chips." Another British idiom, I presumed.

"Is Mick getting a handle on dealing with foreign controllers?" I asked.

"Not really," he said. "You got to spoon feed that boy sometimes. I am starting to realize why some of our mainline captains seemed so grumpy all the time."

"Your efforts will pay off," I said. "Some of the best captains I've ever flown with got their starts as worthless and weak first officers. The light comes on later for some than others."

"All part of being a captain," he said. I smiled at the thought.

Over the next year we rotated with two pilots on, one pilot off. I adjusted the schedule now and then when Nigel's daughter had a recital or his son had a football game. It was actually soccer, but that was a subject one dare not bring up with Nigel. I also feigned the need for time off to making the timing work on our most demanding trips. While Nigel seemed to be up to speed on crossing the North Atlantic and most of Western Europe, I had never seen him operate in Eastern Europe, Africa, or Asia with the complete authority of a captain. I also wanted to have Nigel with me for some of those trips where playing the dual role of captain and instructor pilot would have taxed me to my limits.

Despite these scheduling concerns, my job had taken on the sense of being on autopilot. Paying bills meant verifying the charges were valid and putting those on Gail's desk once a week. Scheduling meant arguing with the dispatchers until they gave in. The trips were, for the most part, routine. The job was becoming fun again.

I had also resigned myself to the fact that International Flight Enterprises, our management company, was a lost cause. I dutifully asked each passenger for their weights, but nobody seemed to care. While I knew it was safer to fly a type of instrument approach that used a smooth, continuous descent rather than the more abrupt option, I could not do so on charters because IFE didn't have the necessary authorizations. So I had to use the "dive and drive" (some called it the "dive and die") option, with a steep descent followed by a quick level off. It was not as safe, it was uncomfortable for the passengers, and it was easily solved if not for IFE.

"You leave them alone, they leave you alone," I was told by a long time IFE pilot and former Air Force pilot. "It's better that way, you get to do what you want without some standards pilot looking over your shoulder all the time."

Of course, that standards pilot could have been me, back in the good old days with Bravo Zulu. I enjoyed giving check rides as a means of instructing and enjoyed all the writing projects. It was a part of my former life, both as a military and a civilian pilot, that I missed. I especially missed the sense of always needing to do something when spending several days in a location with nothing else to do.

Puerto Vallarta. Sure, lots of American tourists spend a lot of money to visit and spend several days here. But a week was too long for me. Even Mick was showing signs of boredom. We both resigned ourselves to a particular spot on the pool lanai, close enough to the bar so as to keep the beer cool on the way back to our reclining chairs. I brought two books, finished both, and still had two days to go.

"How's life?" I asked, giving in to the need to have some kind of conversation.

"Good," Mick said.

"Any complaints?" I asked.

Flight Lessons 5: People

"Not a one," he said.

"Nigel treating you okay?" I asked.

"Sure," he said. "I'd rather be flying with you, but Nigel's not too bad."

It was a non-answer, answer. But he was unwilling to go any further. Any further questioning would only taint the results of any forced answers. "Never bother your boss with your problems," the old saying went, "he has his own problems."

I got essentially the same line from Nigel and came to the same conclusion. But it was unusual for Nigel, who had been too easily prompted into complaining. At the height of his anti-Mick fervor, I accused Nigel of turning into Chip. "You once told me Chip treated you like an idiot when you asked him a question and you vowed to never ask another. And now you are doing the same thing to Mick." That must have stung because Nigel stopped complaining about Mick, robbing me of needed intel about the morale of my troops. It was, regrettably, a self-inflicted wound.

"We don't have the slightest idea where Captain May is," the dispatcher said. "First Officer Riverton is in his hotel room and says he hasn't seen him since they arrived on Monday."

I double checked the date and time on my watch, it was Wednesday. It would be about dinnertime in Casablanca, Morocco. "What's the urgency?" I asked.

"Their Friday departure moved up to Thursday," the dispatcher said. "I have to get his acknowledgement by midnight their time to make the trip legal."

"Let me look into it and call you back," I said.

Mick answered his cellphone on the first ring. "Last I heard from him was 'see you on Thursday,'" he said.

"You don't meet daily?" I asked.

"Nope," he said. "Nigel likes to do his own thing."

"Go to his door and knock on it," I said. "If that doesn't work, get the hotel to open it, tell them you are his colleague and are concerned for his health. If the room looks lived in, leave the room but leave him a note on the door to call me. By the way, you guys are leaving a day early. There should be a fax for you both at the front desk."

My cellphone range. "What's up?" It was Nigel. I looked at my watch again. It would be 10 p.m. in Morocco.

"You know your departure got moved up to tomorrow morning?" I asked.

"Of course," he said.

"Dispatch has been looking for you," I said.

"Yeah, I know," he said.

"Is it true you told Mick on Monday not to bother you until Thursday?" I asked.

"Yeah," he said again. "I don't really like his company, so I would just as soon not spend more time with him than I have to."

"How do you think that makes him feel?" I asked. "And what about crew integrity?"

"What I do on my time off is none of your business," he said.

"When you are on a trip your time belongs to me," I said. "You are responsible for the conduct of the trip as well as the assets, which include your aircraft and your crew. What if something happened to Mick on Tuesday or the airplane on Wednesday?"

Silence. I was expecting, "that's not the way it was at the mainline" but I didn't get that.

14: Instructor
October 2007

Mick's Elephant photo

It would be our first trip to Cape Town, South Africa as an IFE flight department and the first time we would need one of their contract pilots for a crew swap. Commercial rules allowed a two-pilot crew a 10-hour flight, a three-pilot crew a 12-hour flight, and a four-pilot crew a 14-hour flight. The Gulfstream GV has a 14-hour range, so anything longer required a fuel stop and crew change. Our charter passengers were departing from White Plains, New York, adding another hour to the 16-hour trip to Cape Town. Our last stop after eight days in Africa would be Cairo, Egypt, from where we would fly back to White Plains in just under 11 hours, requiring three pilots but no fuel stop.

"I'd like you to fly the first leg to Senegal, Nigel," I said over the phone. "It will be with an IFE contract pilot whom I've never heard of. Don't let him touch anything, don't let him break anything. Watch him like a hawk. From there you can airline home until we need you in Cairo."

"Do I get first class on the airline?" he asked.

"It's that or business class," I said. "I think even IFE does that on international travel before a trip."

"Okay, then," he said.

"I haven't flown a long trip with Mick in a while," I said. "What do I need to look out for?"

"Everything," he said.

"No, really," I said.

Nigel spoke for five minutes about all of Mick's faults, his efforts to fix them, and Mick's failure to improve. "It is almost like he is trying to get it wrong."

"I wonder if he's nervous," I said. "Maybe he is trying too hard to please the captain. Think back to your first trip on the mainline. Or better yet, think about someone with less experience than you on their first trip with even the nicest captain."

"I never thought about it that way," he said. "I suppose it can be intimidating."

"I think so," I said. "I've seen pilots do a lot better, but I've seen them do worse. I'll keep an eye on him, thanks."

"That was easy," I said to *The Lovely Mrs. Haskel*, after hanging up. "I was expecting him to want the part of the trip to South Africa and beyond."

"He does love the airlines," she said.

"Especially in first class," I said. It was starting to make sense.

I left my truck at the hangar and a suitcase on the airplane, Mick did the same. A limousine picked us up and drove us to Logan International, Boston's main airport. From there it was to New York's J.F.K. airport. Sarah Thomason, our flight attendant would meet us there. The airline flight to Senegal was nine hours long, a bit longer than what our GV would do the next day. But we were fortunate to be flying on the day of the week the only nonstop flight was scheduled. Nigel's return flight would be via London, nearly doubling the length of the trip after factoring the layover.

Nigel's crew was a pilot and flight attendant from the IFE roster, neither of which I had ever heard of. Nigel asked for his favorite, Claudia Lincoln, but I said no.

"Why not?" he asked.

Flight Lessons 5: People

"I don't think she is up to it," I said. "Besides, IFE already assigned someone else."

Nigel and crew arrived on time; the airplane was in good shape. "Bog standard," he said, lapsing into his Brit-speak. "That pilot is a few sandwiches short of a picnic," he said. "He doesn't know the first thing about plotting. Let's not use him again."

"Good to know," I said.

"I'm looking forward to a quick nap before good old B. A.," he said. British Airways, I guessed.

"I hope you enjoy it," I said. "See you in Cairo."

The next week was a blur, our passengers never spending more than one day in each location and adding a day to the trip for a night in Paris. Even with three days advance notice, the IFE dispatchers were at a loss.

"Operations says he has to go," the dispatcher said after my second call. "Something about flight and duty time limits on your crew."

"That was when we were going Cairo to White Plains direct," I said, again. "That flight would have been more than 10 hours. Now we are going to Paris one day and White Plains the next. Each day's flight is less than 10 hours."

"Operations has already ruled on this," the dispatcher said. "Nothing I can do about it. Besides, Captain May's airline tickets are non-refundable. He might as well go."

"We don't need him the way the schedule is now," I said. "I would like to give him the time off and I don't want our passengers billed for a third pilot if the charge is unnecessary."

"Operations has spoken, captain," the dispatcher said.

"Let me talk to Operations," I said.

"What?" the dispatcher said. "You can't do that."

I hung up and selected the director of operations from the directory. Gary answered immediately. "You got your orders, colonel." He hung up.

Mick was getting the hang of operating in Africa and learning to make the correct "broadcast in the blind" calls. The principle was air traffic control, what there was of it, didn't allow you to take off until it looked like you would have your route of flight free of conflicting traffic, provided everyone else flew their assigned routes. There wasn't a continent-wide radar system and you would be on your own most of the time. Once you were airborne, you transmitted your position, altitude, and route on published frequencies, and then kept a listening watch for others doing the same. Mick had learned to make the calls correctly, but there was a problem.

"I need you to not only monitor the frequency, but listen to what is being transmitted," I said.

"I don't understand their English," he said, reluctantly turning the volume up. "What good will it do?"

"If you hear a transmission from an airplane at our altitude, you will know there could be a threat," I said. "You know what airway we are on as well as our altitude. Scan ahead for intersecting airways and keep a listening watch for any airplanes on those airways at our altitude."

"What a screwed-up system," he said. "Why do they have to be so backwards?"

"Nothing we can do about that," I said. "There have been midair collisions here recently. Our goal is to get out of here without a scratch."

The ground controllers in Cairo were in rare form, sending us the long way to our parking stand and throwing in a few things not on our charts. "IFE 205," they called at one point. "Where are you going? I told you to turn left on alpha." I remembered the instruction, but it was given to us while we were moving at the tail end of a long list of turns. Mick sat in the right seat busy with his checklist, oblivious to the instructions, my mistake, or the correction. They gave us two lefts and a right to correct my error and with that, the worst part of the trip was completed. I reminded myself to critique my performance in front of Mick, to illustrate that the flight isn't done until you are in the chocks and that it takes two pilots to do that, but I forgot. Another mistake.

I've never had a trip to Cairo where I had enough time to visit a pyramid. In fact, the closest I've ever been to one was flying just a few hundred feet from one back in the days flying a U.S. diplomat who got the permission to do that. I was looking forward to an actual tour this trip, but our added Paris destination shortened our stay in Egypt to just long enough to grab dinner and a night's sleep. Nigel showed up a day earlier and had great photos of all the hot tourist spots as well as one of him on a camel.

Nigel was a good photographer and had one of those cameras with a lot of buttons, dials, and switches that only produced results if you knew what you were doing. Mick was also an avid photographer but Nigel didn't know that, since they had yet to do any touring together. After Nigel showed us his pyramid shots at dinner at the hotel restaurant, Mick excused himself and ran upstairs to get his camera. Mick was able to top Nigel's effort, not in quality but in sheer quantity after a week in four African countries. His best photos came from our day safari in Krueger, South Africa.

"How close did you get?" he asked about a particular elephant photo.

"About a hundred feet," Mick said. "The zoom lens did most of the walking."

After dinner we adjourned to the bar so the two shutterbugs could continue their talk of all things photography. It slowly dawned on me that I had never seen Nigel more relaxed and conversational.

I put Nigel in the right seat while I flew us to Paris, hoping a view from the jump seat would give Mick a perspective of a crew working well together. Once I started taxiing the ground controller revised our instructions with a path that was longer and more complicated. Nigel wrote the instructions on our flight plan and read the instructions back to the controller.

"Eddie, slow down," he said as I neared an intersection. "Stop, Eddie, stop." I stopped.

"Confirm left on Charlie for IFE 205," he asked the ground controller.

"Yes," the controller said. "That is what I told you to do."

"Thanks," I said to Nigel.

During our climb I was unsure of an altitude clearance about five minutes after we got it. "Are you sure it was flight level four zero zero?"

"It was," Nigel said, "but now I'm not so sure. Let me ask."

"Affirmative," the air traffic center controller said.

"Thanks for asking," I said after Nigel acknowledged the clearance we already had.

After a week on the road I was too tired to do the tourist routine in Paris and was happy to hear the rest of the crew felt the same way. In fact, the flight attendant excused herself from dinner, wanting the extra few hours of sleep. So we three pilots adjourned to the bar for more talk about photography. Or so I thought.

"That was pretty neat today," Mick said over his first beer after two glasses of wine at dinner. "It was impressive how you saved the day on our taxi out this morning. I had the same opportunity yesterday but blew it."

"We both blew it," I said.

"Yeah," he agreed. "But I missed my opportunity to be the hero."

"I can imagine that happened a lot at the mainline," I said to Nigel. "You guys flew a lot and to lots of busy airports."

Nigel took the bait and the rest of our bar time was a "there I was" soliloquy by former first officer and now captain, Nigel May. "Why don't you fly us home tomorrow, Nigel? I'll do the jump seat."

The next morning Mick managed to get the automated weather on his third try, notable because he didn't give up or ask Nigel to get it. As we waited for the passengers Nigel reviewed the challenges to come.

"You are going to have to ask for engine start here but they won't give us clearance until we have been cleared to taxi," he began. "We know what run-

Flight Lessons 5: People

way they are using for departures and we know what our entry fix into the high altitude sector will be, so we can narrow down what to expect."

He and Mick paged through the possibilities on their tablet computers and agreed on one of three standard instrument departures. "Let's practice. Pretend I am the snottiest French controller." Mick took out a pad of paper. "IFE 205, ready to copy your clearance," he said in a nasally tone that may have been more Russian than French.

Mick laughed but managed a reply, "Affirmative, ready to copy."

Nigel did a good job of butchering the Queen's English and I struggled to pick out a few words. Mick read back the clearance save one detail. "Say again departure procedure, slowly please." Nigel did so and Mick got it.

"Good job," he said, a second before I was going to say the same thing. When it came time to get our real clearance, Mick got it on the first try. "Bob's your uncle," Nigel said. From the jump seat, I detected a grin of satisfaction from both pilots.

The hop over the pond was routine and I struggled to keep awake in the jump seat while the two pilots did everything as well as I could have. Between position reports Mick talked about how much fun each of our African stops were and a few of the challenges at the airports not accustomed to handling a Gulfstream.

"Maybe I can be the PIC on our next African trip?" Nigel asked.

"Maybe," I said. "There are a few things you haven't seen yet, but I can say the same thing for me. We'll see what the schedule brings."

When we finally got home it was 8 p.m. and the office answering machine had a message recorded an hour before. "Call me tonight," Chip Dawson said. "I'm in my office."

"Yeah, thanks for calling," he said. "Remember Mr. Stefano Wayland?"

"Mr. Wayland," I said. "You mean the hospital guy?"

"No," Chip said. "He's the hospital guy who now owns IFE guy. He was in here this week yelling at everyone and their brother. Gary was sweating bullets. Do you know which IFE airplane has produced more charter revenue than any other so far this year?"

"Us?" I guessed.

"Yup," he said. "We got two more Africa trips and one to China all in the next two months. Mr. Viceroy has a personal trip in the middle of all that. Can you talk him into using one of our smaller jets while you do the big trips? He's done it before."

"I'll see what I can do," I said.

"We owe you one Eddie," he said.

I sat back in my chair. Of course, I knew about Stefano Wayland, the guy who took Bravo Zulu to court and lost. The guy everyone suspected was behind Bravo Zulu's demise. He was bad news for IFE. But that was their problem. In my part of the world things were going well. Nigel and Mick were working well together. IFE seemed to appreciate the revenue we generated. Things were starting to become sane again.

15: Manager
February 2008

The Forbidden City, Beijing, China (Eddie photo)

"Sanity check," I said to Nigel as he presented the trip plan. The times all worked out and he had done a good job with everything except one detail.

"Has she ever flown with seven passengers before?" I asked.

"Of course," he said. "It was you and me to Geneva, don't you remember?"

"Oh yeah," I said. "Something about that trip went wrong but I don't remember what."

"Well it couldn't have been too bad if you don't remember," he said. "Besides, I am the PIC and you told me I could call the shots. She is my choice."

"Okay," I said. I signed the proposed trip sheet and handed it to him. Nigel was a different person with all of our flight attendants but Claudia Lincoln somehow turned him into a schoolboy. I turned down every trip we had with her since the Geneva fiasco, but he had a point. If I couldn't remember what the fiasco was, how much of a fiasco could it have been?

A week later I was en route from Wilmington, Delaware to Dakar, Senegal. I had a contract pilot in the right seat and Sarah Thomason in back tending to seven passengers. It would soon be dinnertime. In Senegal we would refuel and hand the airplane over to Nigel, Mick, and Claudia. Claudia would have it easy, only having to tuck the passengers into bed and prepare breakfast before landing in Cape Town, South Africa. From there it was three more hops and back to the United States. It was the trip Nigel had been lobbying for all this time.

We landed just after nightfall in Senegal and Nigel and crew appeared well rested. "All set?" I asked.

"All set," he said. "Thank you for trusting me."

"You earned it," I said.

Two hours later I was in bed, twelve hours later I was boarding a British Airways Boeing 747 bound for New York City, and ten hours after that I was waiting for another flight headed to Boston when my phone rang.

"Fired," Gail said. "They fired the flight attendant. Can they do that?"

"Yes," I said. "But this is the first time I've heard of it ever happening."

"They tell me her only instructions were to wake them an hour before landing and serve breakfast," Gail said. "She didn't wake them until 45 minutes out, breakfast was rushed and not very good, and most of the passengers had no breakfast at all."

"That will do it," I said.

"They are charging us for the airline tickets to bring the bad flight attendant back home and a new flight attendant down to South Africa," she said. "This is going to cost us nearly thirty thousand dollars! Mr. Viceroy is furious."

I timed my next call to account for the time zones and Nigel's normal wake-up time. "This isn't a 'you are in trouble' phone call," I began, "I just need to hear what happened from someone at the front lines."

"I don't know what the big deal is," Nigel said. "She served us breakfast, it was delicious. She woke them up when they asked, served them breakfast, and they got rushed. It wasn't Claudia's fault that they didn't leave themselves enough time to eat. I'm going to call IFE and put in a good word for her. Claudia's reputation shouldn't take a hit because of her spoiled brat passengers."

Flight Lessons 5: People

"Okay," I said. "But keep in mind those spoiled brat passengers are paying the bills."

I wanted to call Mick, for a second source, but resisted the temptation. A week later he and I were on a trip to Omaha and I managed to sneak it into the conversation.

"It was pretty funny," Mick said. "Or maybe it wasn't. She spends a lot of time in the cockpit but since the passengers were asleep I guess that was okay. She brought us a big breakfast and ate hers from the jump seat. I was looking at the time and realized it was time to start getting ready for our descent and she was still there. I asked her if she needed to wake up the passengers and she said, 'Do I really have to?' You know, a joke."

"How much time before landing?" I asked.

"Thirty minutes," he said. "Tops."

I called the director of operations the next day. "I recommend you fire her."

"Already done," Gary Storm said. "Colonel you need to get control of that flight department of yours. It isn't so easy once you are in command, is it? Do it."

"You can't be serious," I said to the dispatcher, staring at the proposed trip sheet in my hand.

"That's the way it is," he said. "We got your email and kicked it upstairs to the head of personnel. He says you are just going to have to deal with it."

"Let me talk to him," I said.

"What? You want to talk to Mister McHenry?" he asked.

"Immediately," I said. The phone clicked a few times and I could hear the synthetic ring on the other end.

"Walter McHenry," he said.

"This is Eddie Haskel," I said, "with the Bedford GV."

"I know who you are," he said. "Do you know who I am?"

"I hear you are the head of personnel," I said.

"You don't remember me?" he said.

"Your name rings a bell," I said.

"I was with Air Force One while you were at Andrews," he said. "You flew back up for me a few times."

"Oh, yeah," I said. "I do remember that."

"So what do you have a problem about this time?" he asked.

"I have a problem with having you staff my Beijing trip with two contract pilots neither of which has ever flown a GV and the one who is going to China with me has never flown internationally," I said. "Meanwhile I have a fully qualified international pilot stuck on the domestic portion of the trip while a fully qualified first officer sits on his hands back home."

"The charter insists on at least a thousand hours in type," he said. "What do you want me to do?"

"Apply for a waiver," I said. "I did that just two trips ago. I tried to do that this time but they refused to talk to me."

"You haven't changed a bit, Colonel Haskel," he said.

"What?" I said.

"You think you are smarter than the rest of us and don't give us an ounce of credit for knowing what we are doing," he said. "It is our judgment that the two pilots we assigned you are better suited to the trip than your two, and that's that."

The phone went dead. I stared at it for a few seconds. I didn't remember clashing personally with Walter McHenry while in the Air Force, but as an Air Force One pilot he had rock star status and as a backup pilot I was just a member of the help. This particular trip was being paid by the U.S. sponsor of the 2008 Olympics in China and they had reserved every ultra-long-range

Flight Lessons 5: People

business jet on a certificate in the U.S. The rate was about fifty-percent higher than our usual rate and I could imagine IFE and Mr. Viceroy were salivating at the opportunity.

I reread the resumes. The customer insisted that every captain have 1,000 hours time in type and 5,000 hours as PIC. Additionally, the captain on any international leg had to have at least ten years international flight experience as a captain. I met all three requirements, Nigel only the first. So they scheduled our flight from White Plains, New York to Anchorage, Alaska with Nigel and an IFE Gulfstream G450 pilot. Then I would take the Alaska to China leg with another G450 pilot. The Gulfstream G450 is a smaller version of the GV with a nicer cockpit but smaller wings and engines. It technically shares the same design type, but it is a different airplane. Neither G450 pilot had ever flown a GV.

"Smarter than the rest of us." The accusation stung. I was sitting in my home office surrounded by notebooks from thirty years of flight experience, probably thirty of them. Most of them were filled with technical things with the aim of better understanding the machines and the precise processes needed to make it all safe. I had scribbled in some of those notebooks a few things about human factors, dealing with people. But there wasn't much. Nigel would be upset until he realized he would get two first class airline tickets from Anchorage back home while we were in China. So he would be okay with this. Mick would be upset until he realized he would be getting a week and a half off. I would be going to the Olympics, something I had never done before. Going along would make IFE and Mr. Viceroy happy after nearly a year of making both entities unhappy.

I signed the proposed trip sheet and fed it to the fax machine.

I stared at the message, willing it to go away. Our Quick Reference Handbook said what I already knew; it still didn't make any sense. A temperature bulb connected to the aft bulkhead of our left fuel tank was either less than -37°C or greater than +54°C. We were at 43,000 feet halfway between Alaska and Japan and had been airborne for nearly four hours. I could hear the ten passengers in back chatting comfortably with Chopin playing gently in the background. The sky was clear and blissfully calm. The outside air temperature was -57°C and the temperature of the fuel in the suspect tank was at -10°C.

"You ever see this before?" I asked Simon, the contract pilot assigned to us by IFE.

"Never," he said. "We don't have this message in the G450."

I was pretty sure he did, but I was also pretty sure Simon knew less about his airplane than I did.

"Smarter than the rest of us."

I squelched the thought. The fuel could not have been above +54°C unless there was a fire in the wing. I looked back out the window and laughed at myself. That couldn't be and even if it was, what were the odds I could see it from my vantage point. "Let me take a walk," I said to Simon. "You have the controls."

I strolled back to the galley and tried to nonchalantly look out the wing. "What is that, captain?" one of the passengers asked, pointing out the window.

I knelt down to look. The wing was perfectly normal. "That is the Kamchatka Peninsula," I said. The passenger smiled as I snuck a quick look at the opposite wing. Also normal. I returned to the cockpit, strapped in, and scanned the cockpit. The message was gone.

"When did the message go away?" I asked.

"What," Simon said. "Oh, I guess it went away. I hadn't noticed."

I looked at my watch and did some math. It would be about dinner time in Massachusetts. I picked up the satellite phone and dialed from memory.

"Eddie?" he guessed.

"Don," I said. "I had a red fuel tank temp message with normal fuel temperature and no other indications of cold or warm conditions in the wing. We

Flight Lessons 5: People

have been airborne for four hours."

"Did you say had?" he asked.

"Yes," I said. "It went out after ten minutes."

"So what's the problem?" he asked.

"Don, it's a red message," I said.

"I never heard of this before," he said. "Why don't you call Gulfstream."

"You call them," I said. "Then call me back."

"Yeah," he said. "Okay."

About thirty minutes later we got a text message from him. "GULFSTREAM NEVER HEARD OF THIS EITHER. IF MESSAGE OUT DON'T WORRY ABOUT IT. DRJONES."

"Who is Doctor Jones," Simon asked.

"Long story," I said. I would have normally entertained Simon with the Doctor Jones back story but I was all talked out. Simon had never flown outside of the United States, never used a High Frequency radio, never made a position report, and never plotted a position outside of his first international procedures course which he had taken the week prior. I normally enjoyed instructing but the fact I was doing so on this particular trip was galling.

"Let's talk about metric altimetry," I said after watching him fumble yet another position report. "This stuff is important." He was attentive as I covered the ins and outs of how getting meters confused with feet can end a flying career. I gave him play-by-play of watching Chip Dawson and Nigel May confuse 600 meters with feet.

"Unbelievable," Simon said.

Five hours later, descending into a strangely smogless day in Beijing we were cleared to 600 meters. Simon dialed in 600 in the altitude select knob.

"Really?" I asked.

"What?" he said.

"Meters," I said.

"Oops," he said.

We landed and parked in front of an elaborate terminal where our passengers were whisked away from us. An American from the sponsor company greeted us and explained she would accompany us as we repositioned the airplane to a new ramp built just to park all of us Gulfstreams. As we pulled into the ramp I saw a sea of T-tails.

"Wow," I said. "How many?"

"You guys are number 312," she said. "And there are more coming. There will be two billion dollars' worth of Gulfstreams here before the day is over."

"About that," I said. I explained that I would need some maintenance support regarding our fuel tank temperature issue. I parked the airplane, shut down, and inspected the airplane from nose-to-tail. All was as it should be. Simon and the flight attendant slept in the cabin, wondering why their captain was making a long day longer. Finally the Gulfstream mechanic showed up and after listening to my complaint, took a cursory look at our fuel tanks from the wheel wells.

"I don't know what to tell you," he said. "Must have been a queertron."

"A what?" I asked.

"A queer electron," he said. "Fly it home, if it does it again, give us a call."

The Olympics were fun but Beijing was not as I remembered it. The city was clean, desolate, and smog free. The Chinese had banned automobile travel for the prior month and shipped out most of the local residents. Simon was a good tourist and I was happy to have him with us. But he was of zero help in the cockpit.

"There she is again," he said, about three hours after takeoff. The Fuel Tank Temperature message was back. Ten minutes later it was gone.

"I don't know what to tell you, Eddie," Don Jones said. "I never heard of this before. Maybe you should take the airplane to Savannah."

Seven hours later we were on the ground in Anchorage, where Nigel and the

Flight Lessons 5: People

domestic version of Simon waited. "Good airplane?" he asked.

I gave him the play-by-play of our fuel tank message. "I'll see if I can get us a slot into maintenance in Savannah. If I can, I'd like you to fly it there after you drop the pax in White Plains. I'll airline there instead of Boston and bring her home with you."

Two days later I was in Savannah signing the work order for our repaired airplane. "Your GV does this every three years," the mechanic said. "If you would follow the normal maintenance schedule you could avoid this."

"We do follow the maintenance schedule," I said. "Don't we?"

The lead technician lowered his voice and showed me the work order. "Listen captain, I don't want to speak ill of another mechanic," he said. "You see how we charged you ten hours to do this. Between the temperature bulb and your cockpit there are three cannon plugs, one of which is under the cabin floor. It takes five hours to rip the cabin floor out and clean that cannon plug. Your mechanic can do this, but he doesn't want to. You guys seem to change chief pilots every few years so nobody remembers. But Don Jones knows how to do this. He just doesn't want to."

I flew the airplane home, compiled the paperwork from the previous two weeks, and drove over to Mr. Viceroy's office. It was late, but Gail was at her desk.

"You see this Africa trip they have for you?" She asked.

"Not the particulars," I said. "Any good?"

"Twenty days," she said. "That's a big pay day for us. We want you to do it, but we want you to personally fly it from start to finish. We don't want any screw ups this time."

"Sure," I said. "And I want Don Jones fired and replaced before I get back."

"That's not going to happen," she said. We talked for an hour but she wouldn't budge. "You are just going to have to deal with it, Eddie. That's why you are 'he who be in charge.'"

"What?" I said.

"Oh, sorry," she said. "That's what Mr. Viceroy calls you. That's what he calls pilots like you who enjoy making decisions. Some pilots will do anything to avoid making decisions, others seem to enjoy it. Pilots like you."

16: "He Who Be In Charge"

June 2008

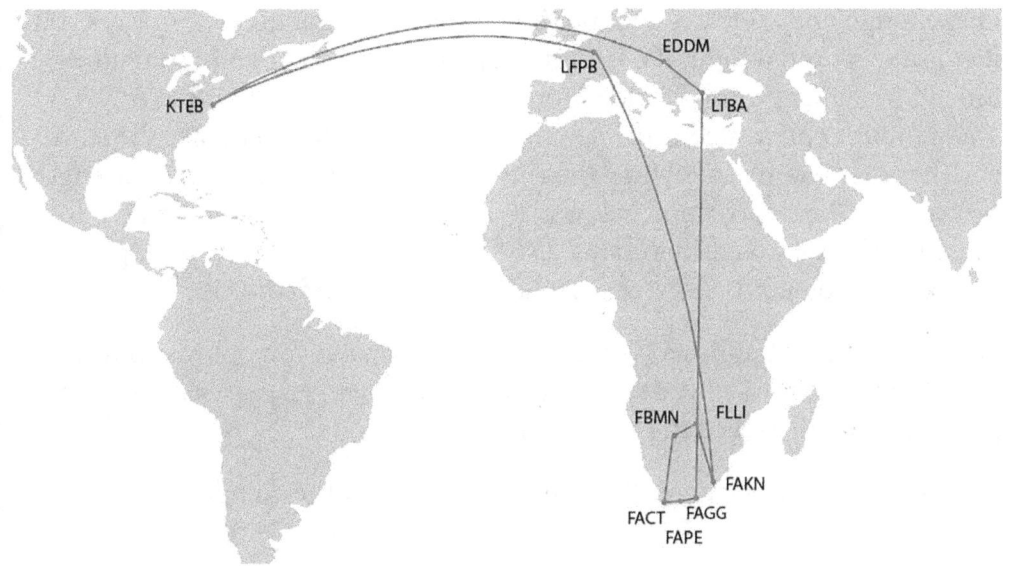

A thirty-day trip to remember

It was a long trip with lots of ground time in several countries I had never set foot on, but there was a problem. I looked at the itinerary and checked off the airports I had already been to and knew had adequate runways, approaches, and other facilities. The trip departed and returned to Teterboro Airport, New Jersey. Good old KTEB, easy. The next two legs were also familiar: EDDM, Munich International Airport, Germany and LTBA, Atatürk International Airport, Istanbul, Turkey. I had been to both many times and recently. At the end was LFPB, Paris Le Bourget, also familiar. And in the middle was FACT, Cape Town, South Africa and FAKN, Kruger Mpumalanga International, also in South Africa. Just a year ago I had never been to either, but since then had become a frequent visitor to both. All well and good. But then there were the four strangers in the list.

Of the four, I had only heard of FLLI, Livingstone, Zambia. Livingstone of "Doctor Livingstone, I presume" fame. It was the closest airport to Victoria Falls, a location truly in my childhood dreams and destined to be the highlight of the trip. FAPE was Port Elizabeth and FAGG was George, both in South Africa. Finally, there was FBMN, Maun Airport, Botswana. That's were the problem was.

The total flight time was just over 40 hours and two of the legs were over 10 and would require a third pilot. Each airport had the necessary infrastructure to support a Gulfstream GV but Maun had a marginal runway. It was long enough and wide enough, but it wasn't strong enough. A runway's ability to support the weight of a landing airplane was measured in something called a Pavement Classification Number and at Maun it was 18/F/B/X/T. The number represented the strength of the pavement, the higher the sturdier. The letters represented how the runway was constructed and its strength measured. I knew anything below a 26 required further investigation because the GV's ACN, its Aircraft Classification Number, never got higher than a 26. A quick check in the airplane's manual confirmed it.

"We can't do it as published," I told the dispatcher. "If you put Maun in the middle we can, but I can't depart Maun for Paris with enough gas. The airplane's ACN will exceed the airport's PCN."

"What are you talking about," the dispatcher said. "The computer says you can do it."

"The computer is wrong," I said. "Let me talk to the chief pilot, he knows about this kind of thing."

"Hold on," he said.

"Haskel, what are you crying about now?" It was Gary Storm.

"I asked to speak with Chip," I said. "He flew GVs and knows about this."

"Chip was fired last week," Gary said. "We packed his stuff in a cardboard box, confiscated his badge, and barred him from entering company premises."

"What?" I said.

"Sexual harassment," Gary said. "He couldn't keep his eyes off the women. Just kept staring at them with that freakish face of his."

"Well you know about PCN and ACN, right?" I said.

"All I know is our flight planning computer says it's a good trip, so it's a good trip," he said. "I don't want to hear anything from you but 'sir, yes sir, three bags full, sir.' So get to work and fly the trip. As scheduled."

Flight Lessons 5: People

"I can't do that," I said.

"We'll see about that," he said. I made note of the time and then rechecked my work. My phone rang about two hours later.

"Why can't you do the trip, Eddie?" Gail asked.

"They want to fly from a small airport to Paris," I explained. "The runway isn't strong enough to support the weight of the plane with the amount of fuel we will have on board. They can switch the order to put that leg of the trip anywhere before that. We can depart any of the other African locations for Paris, no problem."

"And you explained that?" she asked.

"I tried to," I said.

"This charter is going to net us a quarter of a million dollars," she said.

"That won't pay for the damage to the airplane if we sink through the pavement," I said.

"I see," she said.

Two days later I had a new proposed itinerary.

Date	From	To	Distance	Time
May 5	KTEB	EDDM	3,511 nm	7:48
May 7	EDDM	LTBA	850 nm	1:53
May 9	LTBA	FAPE	4,485 nm	10:18
May 9	FAPE	FAGG	161 nm	0:21
May 10	FAGG	FACT	188 nm	0:25
May 16	FACT	FBMN	876 nm	1:57
May 20	FBMN	FLLI	187 nm	0:25
May 21	FLLI	FAKN	540 nm	1:12
May 23	FAKN	LFPB	4,705 nm	10:27
May 25	LFPB	KTEB	3,158 nm	7:01

I signed the form and started to think about diplomatic clearances, antimalarial drugs, and mosquito repellent.

Having been asked to keep Nigel off the major part of the trip was actually easy. He had lost his taste for Africa after this last trip and for being the "He Who Be in Charge" after the flak of having his favorite flight attendant fired. The fact he would be getting four first class airline tickets out of the deal was the icing on Nigel's cake. The passengers requested a male flight attendant by name and he was someone I had flown with in the Air Force. Wesley Donaldson was a favorite of mine as an Air Force pilot and I knew I would have no worries from the cabin. The fact Nigel had no complaints about Mick for several months now told me the crew part of the trip wasn't going to be a problem. Even the primary passenger's name evoked a smile. Stanley Biggs.

"You're kidding," Mick said.

"No, that's his name," I said. We often joked about flying "Mister Big" in back, and now we were doing just that.

The flight from Teterboro to Munich was routine and as Mr. Biggs departed he handed me an envelope and said, "It was a pleasure, I hope to see you again."

"I'll see you in two days," I said. "We are with you the entire month."

"Really?" he said. "That's great. IFE usually swaps crews and airplanes around. This will be great. Let me have that envelope back, I'll have something for you when we get back to Teterboro."

The crew voted for just a short walking tour of Munich followed by a quiet meal, forgoing the usual drunken bier fest the city was so famous for. The trip was starting off very well.

Nigel was waiting for us in Istanbul, well rested after a day off and a trip on Turkish Airlines from the United States. All four of us were also frequent

Flight Lessons 5: People

visitors to Istanbul, but Wesley wanted to buy a carpet so we spent the day at the Grand Bazaar shopping. He made his purchase and had the carpet shipped home. Everything was going smoothly.

"Forty-five minutes on the ground seems a bit much if you don't need fuel," Nigel said from the jump seat.

"That's true," I said. "But that is the minimum allowed ground time on the schedule by IFE. If we can beat it, we should. It just depends on how long it takes the terminal to get our passenger to us."

I studied the trip sheet with renewed interest. We were stopping in Port Elizabeth, South Africa to pick up two more passengers, both acquaintances of Mr. Biggs, who would be accompanying us through Paris. Our next leg to George, South Africa, was barely half an hour en route.

As we neared the airport, Mick called the terminal using the frequency given on the trip sheet. "They say to expect parking spot alpha three and that our passenger hasn't shown up yet."

"So much for beating the forty-five minutes," Nigel said. I looked at the clock and did some math. With three pilots we didn't have any duty limits to worry about but the George Airport was scheduled to close early that evening for construction.

After we landed ground control cleared us to spot alpha three but there was nobody to greet us. I punched in the numbers for our local contact printed on the IFE trip sheet. "We are here, captain," the voice said in broken English. "But we don't see any American airplane and we don't have any passengers."

I hailed the nearest person in a yellow vest and was given little more than a shrug of the shoulders. Walking around unescorted on an airport ramp with airline service is never a good idea, especially in a foreign country. But at least they spoke a form of English I could understand. With the clock ticking, I found the terminal manager who said they had no idea we were coming until the flight plan arrived and they didn't know about our passengers.

I returned to the airplane. "We have to be off the ground by 1740 or we aren't going to be able to land at George," Nigel said. I looked at my watch. It was 1700. I called the IFE dispatcher.

213

"I don't know anything about it," the strange voice said. "Another dispatcher set it up. Do you know what time it is here?"

"I don't care what time it is there," I said. "If I don't get some answers we are either going to have to leave two passengers behind or spend an unscheduled night at an airport without hotel arrangements. I need some answers."

"Just deal with it captain," he said. "Sheesh, all we get out of you is problems. We don't get this from our other charter captains."

I hung up on the unhelpful dispatcher and selected another from my phone's address book.

"Eddie?" she said.

"Hi, this is Eddie, your former pilot," I said.

"This is Linda, always your dispatcher," she said. I explained the problem and she listened carefully. "Give me your contact's phone number, I'll see if I can make sense out of this."

I relayed the number. "I'll call you right back," she said.

Mr. Biggs approached, not a good sign. "Eddie," he said, pointing across the ramp to the other side of a chain link fence. "Henré and Frieda are right over there." I looked and two nicely dressed people waved. They were flanked by two suitcases.

"Thank you, sir," I said. "I'll get them."

"How are you going to do that," Mick asked as I walked off.

"I don't know," I said. My phone rang, it was Linda.

"Didn't you say you are, right now, in Port Elizabeth? South Africa?"

"Yes," I said.

"That number you just gave me has a Namibia country code," she said. "I called it and the handler is in Windhoek. They are on the tarmac, right now, waiting for you."

"Typical!" I said.

Flight Lessons 5: People

"Oh how I miss Bravo Zulu," she said. "Be careful out there."

I pulled out my wallet and found three twenty-dollar bills. I found the nearest gate with an attendant wearing a yellow vest. I approached and flashed my crew badge with the sixty dollars underneath. I pointed to the couple. "My passengers need to come over to my airplane, can you help?"

The attendant examined my badge, taking the cash. He waved to the passengers. Fifteen minutes later we were in the air.

We had a relaxing day in George, mostly spent walking the beach and enjoying the local wines. We flew to Cape Town the next day and spent the first day walking around as Nigel and Mick tried to outdo each other's photographer bona fides.

On day two in Cape Town Nigel left us, bound for the U.S. until he would return in twelve days. Mick, Wesley, and I became fully engrossed in the tourist economy. Mick would bring up apartheid now and then to a local and was never answered with anything but a diplomatic and polite answer.

"Ugly times," our cab driver answered. "We are a better nation now, for sure. But we still have a ways to go."

"We should go out and visit the real South Africa," Mick said at dinner that night. "Get to know the real people. We still have three days here."

Wesley looked at me, knowing the answer. "Mick it is admirable that you are seeking deeper knowledge and wanting to go beyond the beaten path. That is fine. But as crew we have two more burdens that a tourist doesn't. The first is to the aircraft owner. That's an expensive asset they have parked on the ramp and if something happens to you, their asset is stranded. Second, to our passengers. They paid for the trip and we can't have you endangering yourself if that could impact their schedule."

"Six days in any location can get stale," Wesley added. "But the food here is great. We should take advantage of it."

Mick behaved himself for the rest of our time in Cape Town. I greeted Mr. Biggs at the airplane for our flight to Botswana and he asked about our plans.

"We have a hotel room in Maun and I guess we'll see what kinds of tours are available," I said.

"Really?" he said. "That's it?"

"Pretty much," I said.

"Cancel the hotel," he said. "I'll have something better."

We flew on to Maun where we were the largest airplane on the ramp. After our passengers left I wondered about the "something better" but busied myself with getting the airplane put away for five days. Out of the corner of my eye, I spotted a young man wearing short pants and a white shirt with four epaulettes. I guessed he was a local pilot who wanted to see the cockpit of a real jet, so I approached him.

"Hallo," he said in a Dutch accent. "I am Gunter, your pilot for your trip to Camp Okavango." He pointed to a high wing Cessna, reminiscent of my first flight lesson, back in 1976. "It will be my pleasure to stow your baggage at this time."

"Gate One" at the Okavango Airport (Eddie photo)

Wesley and I sat in back as Mick sat in the copilot's seat for our thirty-minute flight to Okavango. It became apparent to me that we were landing on a grass strip but that didn't bother me. What bothered me was the stall warning horn about a hundred feet above the grass just seconds before landing.

Flight Lessons 5: People

"That's normal," Mick explained. "How long has it been since you've flown a prop?"

"Yeah, old man," Wesley said. He winked at me and whispered, "I was scared too."

The camp was quite nice and we each had our own cabins. We couldn't walk about without an armed guard. "Don't let the lions, tigers, and bears get you," Wesley said. "If you see a bear, let me know," Mick said.

The entire camp was designed to make us tourists happy. Each day we took a boat to another island where we got up close and personal with all manner of wildlife, a nice box lunch, and ended each evening with a gourmet meal. The day before departure our pilot for the next day joined us for dinner. He explained that he was one of twenty Dutch pilots trying to build time and experience for the airlines. "Good luck with that," I said, trying to be less sarcastic than my words.

Mr. Biggs and party showed up, tanned and somewhat the worse for wear. He explained they had a very nice safari but were exhausted. "All we want now is a few days off," he said. The weather for our flight to Livingstone was excellent and we spotted the falls from nearly thirty miles out.

Aerial view of Victoria Falls, (Photo: Benard Gagnon)

The falls were just as spectacular up close and personal. Mrs. Biggs handed us three tickets and pointed to a gentleman waiting at the airport. "That gentleman will take you." And he did.

"Bucket list!" Wesley and Mick both said when we first walked up the Victoria Falls close enough to get drenched by the mist, which appeared to be defying gravity. "The falls are 108 meters in height," our guide said, "the water hits the bottom with such force that the mist travels upward to heights over 400 meters."

I had never heard of the "Bucket List" movie that had apparently come out the previous year, but the upward "falling" water exceeding the downward water's drop definitely interested me. I spent the night thinking about it and came to the conclusion nature's wonders exceeded my ability to understand it.

The next morning we greeted our passengers who seemed to be in much better spirits than the day before. "Good time in Livingstone?" Mr. Biggs asked.

"It was fantastic," I said. "I've wanted to see Victoria Falls all my life, and thanks to you now I've done that. Didn't you think that was the most spectacular piece of nature you've ever seen?"

He looked a bit embarrassed. "To be honest, Eddie, we missed it," he said. "We all agreed we were too tired and all we wanted was a quiet night at the bar. But now our batteries are recharged! On to Kruger!"

Before we landed at the Kruger Mpumalanga International Airport, Mr. Biggs came to the cockpit with his usual question, "what have you got planned?" After my answer failed to impress him, he handed me a card. "Call this number, they are expecting you. We have a safari planned that will knock your socks off!"

And it did. Three days later Nigel joined us; two days after that we were in Paris; and two days after that we were back in New Jersey. As the last bit of luggage left the airplane, each passenger made sure to shake hands and thank each of us. Mr. Biggs handed me an envelope. "I've heard that you give all your tip money to the flight attendant," he said.

"I am paid too much as it is," I said. "Sarah does a great job and deserves everything she gets plus more."

Flight Lessons 5: People

"She is marvelous," he agreed. "But I already gave Sarah her own envelope. This is for you. If I hear you gave it to anyone, I am going to be upset. Go buy the lovely Mrs. something nice. Promise me that."

"I will," I promised, smiling at his usage of "the lovely Mrs."

The trip wasn't complete, of course, until all the paperwork was done. One of the IFE forms was called "Post Trip Report" and gave the captain about two inches to comment about anything good, bad, or indifferent. I attached about twelve pages of typed text. That would give them something to chew on. The next phone call had nothing to do with the trip.

"We have your 299 scheduled for next week," the dispatcher said. "The director of operations is looking for a suitable inspector right now, but you can set aside Wednesday for it. Just you two captains, as you know."

"We will be ready," I said. That call was on Wednesday, the week prior. Things started to turn ugly on Thursday.

"Who the hell do you think you are?" Gary was in full Gary mode. "It's bad enough you listed every single person in the company you don't like, but the fact you sent it to the president of the company is a step too far. Did you ever think for a moment what this is going to do to the morale at headquarters?"

"I did, actually," I said. Gary must have been done with me because he hung up. The next call was from the FAA.

"I'm inspector Rasmussen," he said in a voice quiet enough I had to check the volume setting on my phone. "I'll be flying in Wednesday morning and would like you to pick me up. You should plan one leg out and one leg back, with you flying one leg and Captain May flying the other. Plan on a two-hour oral before we fly."

"I will do that, inspector," I said. "This is a 299, is it not?"

"Yes it is," he said. "You seem surprised, you do this once a year, don't you?"

"I do," I said. "I've just never heard of a two-hour oral prior to a 299."

"Just do your best," he said. "I hardly ever pull anyone's ticket."

I hung up the phone and had to wonder. The 299 check is so-called because it can be found in the Code of Federal Regulations, Part 135, Section 299. It is more commonly called a "line check" and need only examine three things: a flight over a route segment, a takeoff, and a landing. I had flown many where that's all we did. Others were more involved, but not much more. The oral exam, the part where the inspector asks you enough questions to insure you know what you are doing, are usually reserved for other checks. Our previous 299 under IFE was very brief, very easy, and did not include an oral.

I showed up at Boston's Logan International Airport and Inspector Rasmussen appeared on schedule. He shook my hand and buckled into the right seat of my truck. "Can we stop by a Burger King?" he asked. "My blood sugar is low."

He was on the fat side of pudgy, about five-foot-six, and wore thick glasses of the type you would see on Japanese caricatures of the late sixties, in the pre-politically correct days of late-night television. I tried to ignore the trough-like noises as he devoured his double Whopper with cheese. He wadded everything up into the bag and left that on his seat after we arrived at our hangar's parking lot. I introduced him to Nigel and we all sat down in my office.

Inspector Rasmussen pulled out a black wallet and presented us his FAA Form 110A, his credentials as an inspector of the Federal Aviation Administration. "Okay," he said, "let's get started. If things go smoothly we should be done in about an hour and thirty minutes. I'll ask you each a question, alternating between the two of you. You may not help the other person unless that person first acknowledges that he doesn't know the answer. Do I make myself clear?"

We nodded and Nigel got the first question. "Landing environment," he said. The inspector looked to me. "Once inbound and on course," I said.

Inspector Rasmussen was picking these questions from a spiral notebook of laminated pages. Looking at the book after thirty minutes, I guess we were more than halfway through. Nigel was surprising me with his depth of knowledge and, between us, we had correctly answered at least 50 questions.

Flight Lessons 5: People

The inspector got to the last page and started to say something, then paused. "This is pointless, let's go fly."

I purposely filed a flight plan from Bedford to Nashua, New Hampshire in hopes of flying the Non-Directional Beacon approach into Runway 14. The approach normally required pilots to configure for landing 1600 feet above the terrain, then dive down to 640 feet above the tree tops until in a position to land. Commercial operators with special authorization, called an Operations Specification, were allowed to do this much more safely, with a gradual, continuous descent. We had the authorization at Bravo Zulu Aviation, but not at International Flight Enterprises. I flew the approach as published and landed. On the ground I swapped seats with Nigel and he flew us back to Bedford. It all went well.

"I must admit I am a bit surprised," Inspector Rasmussen said. "I was told you guys didn't know what you are doing but it appears to me you are among the best I've ever seen. Here is your paperwork, congratulations." Nigel was all smiles and the inspector stood. "Captain Haskel can I impose upon you for a ride back to Logan?"

"Sure," I said. As we drove back he sat silently. "I've given a fair number of check rides over the years," I said, breaking the silence. "Certainly not as many as you. But I always ended them asking the pilots if they had any comments for me. That allowed me to see what kind of job I was doing and to get any feedback for the company."

"That isn't my job here," he said. "But, okay, do you have any comments for me?"

"I was wondering if you noticed we didn't curtail our center of gravity," I said.

"No, not at all," he said. "IFE doesn't have Operations Specification A097 so you can't do that."

"Doesn't it strike you as odd that an airplane the size of ours doesn't have A097?" I asked. "Can you imagine me asking for the weight of every passenger who boards?"

"I just assumed you did that," he said.

"I do," I said. "I might be the only pilot in the entire company who does."

"Oh," he said.

"Also, did you notice my 'dive and drive' approach into Nashua?" I asked.

"Well, yes," he said. "But that is the nature of a non-precision approach, isn't it?"

"Not if you have C073," I said. "That approach allows it, our airplane has the capability. But IFE refuses to adopt C073, making us all less safe."

"That's between you and the company," he said.

"Are you the principle inspector for IFE?" I asked.

"Yes," he said.

"Well doesn't that makes it your business?" I asked.

The pudgy inspector's pudgy cheeks were drained of color. I imagined I had just ruined his day, forcing him to pick between doing his job and keeping the foxes in his particular hen house happy. We got to the airport and he left, without saying goodbye.

I knew this was drastic action on my part and I knew retribution would be violent and swift. But I failed to predict the intensity and the speed. My phone rang the next day. I was expecting Gail, but it was Mr. Viceroy.

"I like you a lot, Eddie, really I do," he said. I predicted his next words with absolute certainty. "But IFE says they will no longer use you on charters and I need the airplane to fly charters. I am afraid you are going to have to find another job."

"He who be in charge is now he who be unemployed," I said.

"What," he said, "Oh, yes, I guess that's right. Nice to know you still have your sense of humor."

The next call was from Nigel. "I heard you and Mick got huge tips from Mr. Biggs," he said. "Nice of you to think of me."

"You know I give my tips to the flight attendant," I said.

"I never agreed with that," he said. "Well Mick was bragging to me about the thousand bucks he got. That's the straw that broke the camel's back. I cannot fly with him anymore. It is bad enough I have to do his job for him, but if I find out he's making more money than me, I, I don't know what I'm going to do!"

If things are going to fall apart, I thought, they might as well all fall apart all at once. In a flight department of only four, the troops were at war with each other despite the best efforts of their boss. Ex-boss.

The Lovely Mrs. Haskel took it in stride. "Things were trending that way," she said. "I see you write furiously in those computerized notes of yours. It's like you were getting ready to defend yourself in court. If you were that worried about the company's safety practices, you shouldn't have been flying for them. Don't worry about it, something will turn up for you. It always does."

Flight Lessons: The Crew (Second Generation CRM)

By 1982 many believed Cockpit Resource Management was a game changer and captains who learned to tolerate second opinions in the cockpit would drastically reduce the number of pilot error accidents that could have been prevented had somebody spoken up. All of that changed on January 13, 1982.

The negative lessons of Air Florida Flight 90

On January 13, 1982 an Air Florida Boeing 737 departed the gate at Washington-National Airport, DC with a crew of 5 and 74 passengers, bound for Tampa International Airport, Florida. The crew made several mistakes prior to takeoff, during the takeoff roll, and shortly after takeoff. All but one of the crew and four of the passengers were killed. The lessons learned:

1. If you are still in conditions conducive to ice, snow, or frost accumulation, you need to check the aircraft prior to takeoff. Getting de-iced and anti-iced does not relieve you of this responsibility. (The aircraft was de-iced about 50 minutes prior to its eventual takeoff.)

2. Do not use reverse thrust for push back with snow or ice on the ramp. (The crew did so, despite a warning from the ground crew that this was against company policy.)

3. Use engine anti-ice according to your flight manual procedures. (The crew did not.)

4. Increase your distance behind other aircraft when taxiing over contaminated surfaces. (The captain elected to closely trail the aircraft in front in an attempt to blow the snow off his aircraft.)

5. Monitor engine performance. (The thrust was set too low because one of the engine's probes used to measure engine pressure was blocked by snow.)

6. Whenever you think you need additional performance, push the throttles forward. (If at any point they simply pushed the throttles forward they would have survived.)

7. If the other pilot voices a concern, listen and consider. (The copilot said during the takeoff roll "that's not right," but the captain said "yes it is." Still below V1 the first copilot said, "I don't know.")

The positive lessons of United Airlines Flight 232

On July 19, 1989, a United Airlines McDonnell Douglas DC-10 departed Denver Stapleton International Airport, Colorado for Chicago-O'Hare International Airport, Illinois, with a crew of 11 and 285 passengers. Just over an hour after takeoff their tail-mounted engine failed and took out all three hydraulic systems. The cockpit crew, with the help of a dead-heading United training check airman, were able to control the airplane in pitch and roll using the two operating engines. Their superb crew coordination allowed them to make an approach to the Sioux Gateway Airport, Sioux City, Iowa. 10 of the crew and 175 of the passengers survived the crash landing.

The performance of the crew of United Airlines Flight 232 has become a textbook example of how Crew Resource Management should work, and rightfully so. United had thrown itself "all in" with CRM programs for a decade prior to this mishap and it shows.

Note: Links to the case studies are provided at the end of the book.

Consider the captain

1) **Accomplishes tasks.** Besides routine flying duties, the captain's tasks include directing the activities of members of the crew, establishing priorities, "thinking ahead of the airplane" (anticipating what is yet to come), mentoring the rest of the crew, assuming responsibilities for the crew, and monitoring crew performance.

2) **Communicates.** The captain is in many ways the focal point of information in a crew and must regulate the flow of that information to ensure the crew has what it needs and can provide the rest of the crew (including the captain) with what they need. This can be formalized as required call outs. It should also include more informal means, such as asking for opinions and feedback.

3) **Establishes and maintains a positive environment.** A good captain creates the proper climate to encourage good crewmember relations and participation. This climate must maintain positive relations, resolve and prevent conflict, and encourage critique and feedback. A positive environment encourages good situational awareness and avoids "tunnel vision" or "target fixation."

4) **Makes decisions.** The captain's decision-making process must begin with gathering and evaluating information and end with assuming responsibility for those decisions. Along the way the captain must encourage a monitoring – feedback – adjustment loop, as time permits.

5) **Avoids Potential pitfalls.** The captain may be tempted to retreat into the familiar – flying the airplane – at the expense of taking command of the unfamiliar. Captains may convince themselves that flying the airplane is the most important task and that relieves them of the burden of confronting the unknowns in a situation. Captains may convince they are crew resource management gurus because they never receive (or listen to) any evidence to the contrary. This only worsens negative CRM behavior.

Consider the crew

1) **Accomplishes tasks.** Each crewmember has specific tasks to accomplish that often require coordination with other members of the crew. Their tasks may also include additional duties assigned by others which should be accepted, if possible. If not possible, the issue needs to be elevated as necessary so the task is not neglected.

2) **Communicates.** Each member of the crew is responsible for the two-way flow of crew communications; they must not only receive but also transmit. An important facet of this exchange of information is that the message must not only be sent or received, it must be understood. Members of the crew are responsible for providing opinions and feedback.

3) **Establishes and maintains a positive environment.** Every member of the crew shares the captain's responsibility to create the proper

climate to encourage good crewmember relations and participation. Interpersonal grudges and other "baggage" must be compartmentalized and removed from the flight environment.

4) **Makes decisions.** While all crewmembers have individual decision-making responsibilities, they must recognize the captain's decision-making process is the most consequential and requires active monitoring and feedback. Disagreements are to be expected and should be handled by an inquiry / advocacy / assertion process (discussed below).

5) **Avoids potential pitfalls.** Falling prey to complacency is a risk for every crewmember but the captain has the added responsibility of managing the crew's performance. Presumably, the captain's additional experience allows a deeper understanding of the pitfalls of succumbing to complacency. (And so is better able to recognize and manage it.) Other members of the crew are at increased risk because they have less to "worry about" and may feel they have mastered the job before the hard experience of realizing the job can never be mastered.

More about the decision-making process

Many books on the subject will talk about a process, from start to finish, when making decisions. In aviation, where time is a factor, it may be helpful to think of decision-making in the form of a cycle. The following steps are repeated as necessary and as time permits.

1. Identify the issue that requires action.
2. Collect information.
3. Solicit input from within and outside the crew.
4. Identify and evaluate possible solutions, including those provided by other crewmembers.
5. Implement the decision.
6. Review the consequences, adjust as necessary.

7. Repeat the process, as necessary.

Inquiry/Advocacy/Assertion

Inquiry.

In a healthy CRM environment, questions are encouraged and answered openly and nondefensively.

[CRM Leadership & Followership 2.0, Antonio Cortés] Show Respect for Fellow Crewmembers. Showing respect to the other members of the crew, naturally including the captain, is not just a matter of courtesy, it is fundamental to fostering a sense of shared purpose that is the building block for teamwork. One of the most important ways of showing respect is by listening to others. This means actively listening for content in what another crewmember is saying, not just "hearing" what is being said.

Advocacy.

In a healthy CRM environment, crewmembers are encouraged to speak up and state opinions with appropriate persistence until there is a clear resolution. This can be encouraged by captains who ask the right questions. "Do you have anything to add?" prompts a yes/no answer and a "no" can appear to the timid crewmember to be a threat to the captain's authority. On the other hand, "what am I forgetting?" will be seen as a request for help and encourages input.

Assertion.

In a healthy CRM environment, crewmembers are allowed to question the actions and decisions of others and to seek help from others when necessary. Of course, the final arbiter is the captain, who must weigh all concerns before deciding. An important point is that the captain must err on the side of safety. A crewmember's concern, which may or may not be valid in the captain's view, may carry the day if the action lowers potential risk.

[CRM Leadership & Followership 2.0, Antonio Cortés] Regardless of what tone has been set by the captain, crewmembers have an obligation to be assertive and to voice concerns and opinions on matters of importance to the safety of the flight.

Crewmembers must understand that there are few things more corrosive to a crew's integrity than to have a crewmember disagree with the captain in front of the rest of the crew or passengers. A good way to show respect for good crew resource management is to disagree with other crewmembers (including the captain) in private, if time permits.

If the captain is not listening or doesn't grasp the gravity of a situation, the following techniques may prove useful:

1. Get the captain's attention (use name or crew position/opposite typical): "Jim, I have a concern I want to discuss with you."

2. State the concern: "I am not comfortable with this heading that we are on."

3. State the problem and consequences: "If we continue on this heading, we will be too close to the buildup."

4. Give solutions: "I think we should turn 20 degrees further west."

5. Solicit feedback and seek agreement: "What do you think?" or "Don't you think so?"

Note: See the References at the end of the book for much more about these CRM techniques.

Part Four

Management

17: Top Draft Pick
January 2009

Tom Brady, the 199th pick of the 2000 National Football Team Draft (Photo: Keith Allison)

"You are getting pretty good at these post mortems," *The Lovely Mrs. Haskel* said at last, after her second cup of coffee in silence. "Though I think you are being hard on yourself."

"Maybe," I said. "But there is an approved solution at IFE that starts with keeping your mouth shut and doing the job the best you can."

"Cooperate and graduate?" she asked.

"No," I said. "It is more like ignore and accomplish. If you just paid as little attention as possible to management, they would pay as little attention to you, and things got done."

"Like arranging for a handler in the wrong country," she said. "Or refusing to get the right authorizations for you to fly safely, or . . ."

"Okay," I said. "Your point is well made." More silence. "I guess it could be worse," I added. "I could have just soundly beaten the Buffalo Bills thirteen zip and still be denied a playoff position for the first time since 2002."

"Not funny," she said.

To say *The Lovely Mrs. Haskel* was a diehard New England Patriots fan would be an understatement. After nearly a decade in New England, our year was no longer based on January to December, but from February to January, from Superbowl to Superbowl. If they won the Superbowl, it was the start of a dynasty. If they lost, they were robbed. If they didn't make it to the final game, she would proclaim, "the season is over!" This year, the season ended in December.

"I guess you are unhappy because you pushed too hard with the FAA inspector," she finally said. "You could have survived had you stopped just short of doing that. But your motive was to effect change of a system that was inherently unsafe. That is hardly a sin."

"And now I am unemployed," I said.

"We have savings," she said. "I have a job and you have a reputation that will cause the phone to ring."

The phone rang.

"Eddie, it's Sid," he said. "Sidney Justice from your Q-Tron days."

"I know your voice," I said. "You are flying Gulfstreams for that medical company, right?"

"Exactly," he said. "I hear you are looking for a job."

"News travels fast," I said. I had yet to make a single phone call so the news must have come from IFE or someone in the old flight department.

"Our CEO asked me to keep my eye out for Gulfstream talent with good leadership skills," he said. "I told her about you but that you already had a job. She told me if you suddenly became available, we would suddenly interview you."

"Wow," I said. "Okay, tell me about the job."

"Very secret," he said. "Too secret for a phone line. How about lunch?"

We met at a hole in the wall café in Concord, Massachusetts. I remembered that Sidney hated chain restaurants and favored places where he could get food he had never heard of before. The sandwiches were familiar as was his easy-going nature. "The meal is on me," he said. "I don't want to bite into your food stamps."

"Funny," I said. Sidney explained that he worked for A Priori Biomedical. "From the earlier," I said.

"What?" he said.

"A Priori," I said. "I think the Latin means 'from the earlier' or about being based on previous knowledge."

"If you say so," he said. "It is a good job. The GIV is old and tired, but the pay is good and we don't fly too much. Two pilots and one mechanic. We've been looking for a third for quite some time. We use a lot of contract pilot help. The CEO keeps turning down candidates."

"Is it run 'in house' or do you have a management company?" I asked.

"It's a small company you never heard of," he said. "Scontro Aviation. They are based in upstate New York and we are the only airplane they have outside their little airport."

"Scontro?" I asked, thinking of words I knew in Italian.

"Yeah," he said. "It is a partnership between Richard Sconyers and William Troy. They both owned Queen Airs, decided to go in together on a larger turboprop and have been buying airplanes ever since. They have a bunch of Learjets and Citations. We are their only Gulfstream."

"That doesn't sound too good," I said.

"No it's perfect," he said. "They leave us alone and we pretty much do as we please."

I thought back to IFE and my war of wills with management. "I guess that is okay if the guy running your flight department knows what he's doing."

"He's okay," Sidney said. "Ollie McShay is a product of Boston; he is as easy going a chief pilot as you are ever going to find. Nothing rattles him and his goal in life is to 'maintain an even strain.' He says that all the time."

"The only place I've ever heard that was in the movie 'The Right Stuff,' or maybe it was the book," I said.

"He's not military," Sidney said. "But he's easy to like."

After lunch I followed Sidney to his hangar and met Ollie. He was a bit taller than me, quite a bit heavier, a bit older, and had a smile a bit wider than mine. He was a bit more of everything.

"I have heard so much about you," he said with a vigorous shake of my hand. "Boy oh boy, could we use you around here!"

Ollie showed me the airplane, an old Gulfsteam GIV in need of a paint job on the outside and reupholstery on the inside. The avionics were fairly standard for a GIV, which is to say dated. Both pilots' seats had tears on their backs and the sunscreen shield on the pilot's side of the cockpit was also torn. The cabin was neat, but it appeared they were doing the best they could without spending any money on a refurbishment.

"How's the budget?" I asked.

"We don't talk about that," Ollie said.

"Fair enough," I said. "How are your trips?"

"Pretty good," he said. Ollie explained that most of their trips were domestic with just a hop to Europe every other month. "All of it business, no personal stuff."

"Sign me up," I said.

The A Priori Biomedical website was unlike any I had ever seen before. There was no "about" page with tedious biographies of the top company officers. There were no product demonstration pages or testimonials. In fact, it was hard to discern exactly what it was they were selling. As an economics professor of mine in school said, if you can't explain what a company does in a short paragraph written so someone with a sixth-grade education could understand it, walk away. But that was in the days before computer-controlled pacemakers, medicated heart stents, and all those other marvels of science that didn't exist when I took that course. A simple Internet search of the two company officers I was scheduled to meet only revealed both were graduates of the nearby Massachusetts Institute of Technology, one with several degrees in math and electrical engineering, the other in architecture and design.

The company headquarters was hidden away in the forest tucked away inside the infamous "Route 128 Technology Corridor," a 55-mile stretch of highway that was mostly Interstate 95 but also a state road that the locals refused to give up. You could tell a local from someone with less than a few decades pedigree by their choice of pavement nomenclature. They shared a campus with a few other high-tech firms, but only A Priori refused to hang a sign of any kind. Ollie McShay drew a crude map that ended with a three-story building with glass walls and no signs.

I checked in at the front desk and told the receptionist I had an appointment to see Laurence Fitzsimmons, the company president. "Larry," the receptionist said, "yes, I did see him walk in a few minutes ago. Up the stairs, third floor, right turn, snake through the cubicles, last office before you get to the ten-foot-tall dinosaur."

With twenty years as an Air Force officer and now ten as a civilian pilot, both experiences filled with flying people with big, important titles, I wasn't ready for a receptionist referring to the company president as Larry. No matter, I needed to focus on her directions. It wouldn't do for a pilot candidate to get lost in the company headquarters. I didn't need to worry; the dinosaur was easy to spot. The cubicles, however, almost threw me off. They were not the boxy cubicles one would expect at a "normal" office. There were no square spaces anywhere to be seen. It all looked rather random. I found Mr. Fitzsimmons' office, a small affair shaped like a pie wedge with the outer circumference bordered by a glass wall and a door. Inside a man of slight build, my height and weight, and hair starting to gray sat at a desk, typing away at a computer. There was no sign of any kind on his office. I looked around for a receptionist, secretary, anyone.

"Excuse me," I heard from the glass office, "do you need help finding someone or something?"

It was him. "Sir, I'm Eddie Haskel," I said. "I believe we are meeting soon."

"Eddie!" he said. "Yes, of course. I see you admiring the floor plan. I read that you are an engineer. What does your technical eye say about all this?"

"I was just wondering if there was any pattern," I said. "It seems everyone has a view of a window, which is very nice." Even on the third floor, most of the view was of trees.

"Good, good," he said. "More?"

"It also appears the clusters, if I can call them that," I continued, "are meant to keep groups together. I suppose each team member has a direct view of others on their team."

"Very good," he said. "Hardly anyone gets that right off the bat. Let's sit and talk."

Larry – I was forbidden from calling him Mister Fitzsimmons – spoke easily about how A Priori was designed to allow each person do whatever it was they wanted to do to further the company's mission, with just gentle guidance along the way. "Let's say you build widgets. We engineers love those widgets, don't we?" I nodded. Of course, the widget is the standard output of any engineer's hypothetical. "In a typical company, you have them build the widget to certain specs and once that's done, you move on. But what if you, the designer, aren't satisfied? If the 95 percent design sells, why waste any time getting that extra 5 percent?" I didn't answer, often the best choice in an interview setting. "Because it is going to gnaw on the designer if he, or she, is a perfectionist. And that is the kind of person we hire here. So we allow them to keep at it until they are satisfied. We get a better widget, they get more job satisfaction."

"What about your return on investment?" I asked.

"That is something we never mention around here," he said. "We take care of the widget; the ROI takes care of itself. How does being an engineer help with being a pilot?"

I spoke, briefly I thought, about the challenges of prioritizing one's attention in a cockpit flying in a world of distractions and how that has been made better, and worse, in our high technology cockpits. Larry asked probing questions, indicating an understanding of modern jet aircraft and an interest in all things high tech.

Flight Lessons 5: People

"Does being an engineer help you when leading people?" he asked.

"They say a good engineering degree will erase the strongest personalities and in my mostly male class at Purdue they said it was the purest form of birth control," I said, chancing the joke. Larry laughed. "I think a good engineer has a logical mind and can sort through minutiae to identify the important bits of any problem. If you have more equations than variables, you have a solution."

"Only if you know how to build the equation," he said.

"Exactly," I said. "And that is the biggest challenge, isn't it?"

I spoke, briefly I thought again, about the differences between leading a military squadron of 150 officers and enlisted personnel and that of leading a flight department of four or five. Both had their own unique challenges, but in both cases a logical mind helped in the drive towards solutions. A young woman appeared at his door.

"I really enjoyed this, Eddie," he said. "I think Elizabeth is ready to see you. I look forward to more discussions just like this." He offered his hand, which I shook. As I left his office I was surprised to see it was dark outside. I looked at my watch. I was with Larry for two hours. I followed the young lady, thinking about a restroom break only to be deposited in another small, pie shaped office with a glass wall, door, and no signs. The room was identical in size to Larry's no longer than 12 feet on its longest side. We stood outside as Ms. Scaling stood inside talking to a group of three young women. She was striking, in a "Miss Manners" sort of way. She stood about five-foot-six in a handsome suit you could easily picture on a man, except for the light blue color. While Larry was obviously ten years my junior, Ms. Scaling appeared to be my age or slightly older. She made eye contact and smiled.

The three younger women filed out and she gestured me in and pointed to a chair. "I trust you had a good talk with Larry," she said.

"Yes," I said. "We talked about a wide range of subjects and I have to admit the time just flew by. He is an interesting man."

"That he is," she said. "But so are you. I don't normally look at resumes but yours is quite a doozy."

"Really," I said. "I think it is rather subdued."

"Exactly!" she said. "That is the perfect word for it. Every line opens the door to huge stories. Tell me about your parents."

My parents?

"My dad was an officer on a Navy ship stationed in Yokosuka, Japan," I began. "It was a three-year assignment during which he met my mom who lived with her parents who owned and operated a futon factory."

That begat a series of questions about my ethnic background, a topic the company's legal team would have an aneurism over. But no matter, the conversation flowed easily. "Who do you take on after, your mom or your dad?"

This went on and on and I had hardly thought of the time until she did. "Oh my goodness," she said. "It's midnight. You need to go home or your family will think we are monsters here."

There are two main training vendors for the Gulfstream GIV and those of us who trained with the primary vendor often referred to the lesser version as "Brand X." I hadn't trained with SimuSafety since 1992 and always considered that a blessing. The fact A Priori used Brand X was a disappointment, but something I would deal with. I walked into their New Jersey training center and was pleased to see that I knew the center manager, Mister John Katzenberg, formerly known as Colonel Katzenberg or, more commonly, *The Katz*. I signed in at the front desk, collected my badge and a manila envelope, and made my way to the classroom with a small detour. I found his office, a large affair with a blank whiteboard on one wall. The office was open but there was no Katz. I found a red marker and drew a math formula:

$$GIV\ Type = \frac{GIII + GV}{2}$$
$$\therefore \text{ No training needed}$$

Flight Lessons 5: People

The first morning of class managed to be tedious and aggravating at the same time. "Don't worry about the check ride," the instructor said. "We will teach you what you need to know and half the sim rides are check profile flights. Nobody fails." She handed us our books and a photocopied sheet of things to concentrate on. "No memorization!" she said. "I know pilots like to memorize numbers but don't do that. Don't make it hard on yourself when it should be easy."

After our first break a parade of center personnel stopped by, starting with *The Katz*, who walked into the class, spotted me, and said, "Eddie your math is still wrong after all these years, so you better pay attention in class!"

The entirety of ground school was mind numbing, each system finished with the instructor saying, "And that is all you need to know about . . ." followed by me saying "What about . . ." and them cutting me off saying "Don't make something hard when it can be easy."

Our simulator instructor was a short woman of four-eleven with arms covered in tattoos and a large piece of metal stuck in her tongue that would make a clanking noise when she wanted to fill the silence. My simulator partner took to calling her "The Stud" behind her back, which I thought was funny but started to worry I might let that slip within earshot. She confirmed that every other lesson was a carbon copy of the check ride to come because, yes, don't make something hard when it can be easy.

By the sixth simulator I was comfortable with the airplane, even while uncomfortable with my knowledge level, and had already memorized the check ride profile that our instructor was following exactly. My simulator partner was doing well, but he was a timid youngster who wanted only to walk away with his GIV type rating and never failed to answer any question exactly as SimuSafety wanted the answer given. I was too busy making friends and influencing people to bother with convention. I was first up for the night and the first takeoff and approach were right out of the check ride profile. For the next takeoff, the right engine failed just as predicted; I got the airplane airborne and cleaned up when it really began.

"Drift up, Eddie," said *The Stud*.

"What?" It wasn't my most articulate response, but when confronted with lunacy I guess I am tempted to respond in kind.

"Once you've retracted the flaps after an engine failure," she said from the jump seat, "you need to fly drift up speed."

"I am flying VSE," I responded while pointing to the display controller, "just like the book says."

"Yes I know," she said, "but after VSE you fly drift up."

"Show me."

```
        S.E. FIXED ALT CRZ 1/1
        S.E. CRZ        DRIFT UP
       FL279            SPD   198
        RANGE<-RES  FUEL->ETE
       520                   01+50
        RANGE<-ZERO FUEL>ETE
       939                   03+26
       ◀CRUISE    S.E. CRZ CLIMB▶
```

GIV Drift up page (Photo: Kevin Knecht)

With a few button presses on the FMS she brought up the aircraft's single engine performance page, something we didn't have in the GV. It clearly said, "DRIFT UP SPD" and had a number which was quite a bit higher than VSE. So I pushed the nose down and accelerated, wondering what part of aerodynamics I had slept through in college. Fortunately, this was Friday and I had until Sunday before my next simulator. I spent all day Saturday looking for something, anything, about drift up. Even the GIV manuals were silent on the subject.

For the Sunday simulator, while in the right seat, I snuck a peak at the offending page, it said DRIFT DN SPD while we were at high altitudes getting ready for our rapid depressurization, a part of the check ride profile. The speed agreed with the book value for drift down and it showed the correct drift down altitude as S.E. CRZ.

Flight Lessons 5: People

GIV Drift down page (Photo: Kevin Knecht)

As we descended, I kept sneaking a look at the page and realized that as the airplane flew below drift down altitude, the DRIFT DN turned to DRIFT UP. I've spent a fair amount of time over the years programming computers and can recognize a mistake from a programmer that doesn't know the first thing about flying. That's what this had to be. The programmer thought you shouldn't drift down to an altitude that is above you, so DN became UP.

After we swapped seats, I waited eagerly for my next engine failure. I dutifully cleaned up the aircraft and zeroed in on VSE.

"Eddie," the instructor said as if on cue, "don't forget drift up speed."

"I don't believe in it," I said, "and telling anyone to fly that speed jeopardizes the safety of the airplane, violates the flight manual, and I am not going to do it."

She said nothing. Not even during the debrief. My sim partner kept silent as well, perhaps feeling his type rating was in as much jeopardy as mine.

The next morning, I was greeted by *The Katz* and the senior GIV instructor, a distinguished gentleman I knew only as Adam. *The Katz* and I were longtime friends and he usually treated my academic acts of terrorism with caution, lest they be right. The senior GIV instructor I knew only by reputation, and he had a good one. Adam had been flying the GIV since day one and knew it better than just about anyone.

"Eddie," *The Katz* said, almost embarrassed, "I know you know the airplane backwards and forwards already but so do our instructors. You have to learn to fly it our way if you expect to pass the type check. Adam here tells me if you don't fly drift up speed, he can't pass you on the ride."

I looked at Adam, who kept silent. "Tell you what," I said, "you find even one place in any Gulfstream manual that mentions the phrase 'drift up' and I will fly your speed and I'll buy you a case of wine. But if you can't, you stop teaching it and you buy me a case of wine."

"You got it!" Adam said immediately. "I'll see you after your sim."

After the sim Adam was nowhere to be found. The morning of our check ride began with an oral exam taken right out of the SimuSafety playbook. "When does the 'wing hot' message come on," the examiner asked.

"At 180 degrees Fahrenheit," I answered.

"No," he said. "Try again."

The number was identical in the GV and GIII and I was certain of it. I knew some of the overheat numbers in the GIII were given also in Celsius, but this wasn't one of them. I did some math.

"At 180 degrees Fahrenheit, or 82 degrees Celsius," I said. The examiner looked truly peeved.

"I am only going to ask you one more time," he said. "When does the wing hot message illuminate?" He emphasized the key words.

"When it is hot?" I guessed.

"There!" he said. "Was that so hard?"

The check ride itself went exactly as our practice profile had. My sim partner flew a perfect drift up speed and I did not. We both passed.

Coming onboard with A Priori was simply a matter of signing a contract and nondisclosure agreement, picking up a laptop computer and cellphone, and

Flight Lessons 5: People

bypassing the rest of the company's indoctrination procedure.

"Most of the company doesn't even know we exist," Ollie explained. "And we like it that way. If anyone asks who you work for, say 'a private company' and leave it at that. And that website of yours, well that's a problem."

"You know about my website?" I asked.

"Yeah," he said. "At my last recurrent the instructor used it to explain minimum control speeds. I got to tell you, it is a great resource. But you can't have anything with your personal name on it out there on the Internet. You need to take it down."

I knew the switches in the HTML code were not bulletproof. Those switches, known as robots, simply told all search engines to pass the website by. But if someone knew the exact address, they would have access to it. Ollie was right about my name on the website. I logged onto the server controlling www.knownprocedures.com, hit Command-A to select all of it, and hit the delete key. The server kindly asked me if I was sure. I pushed the button that said "yes."

Of course, I had a copy on my laptop's hard drive. That meant I could no longer give friends a copy of my notes without risking the notes themselves. I would have to ponder.

It was fitting that my first flight with A Priori would be to Teterboro Airport. Ollie McShay warned me that over half his logbook entries since taking the flight department over were to Teterboro. I showed up at the appointed time but Ollie was nowhere to be found. I opened the airplane and did the external preflight, checklist in hand. While inside the aft equipment bay I heard his familiar Boston twang from eight feet below. "Good morning Mister Haskel! What you doing up there?"

"The external preflight inspection," I yelled from above. As I descended the ladder I lowered my voice, "in accordance with the flight manual."

"Oh we never do that," he said. "Sully does a good preflight and we trust him."

"Trust has nothing to do with it," I said. "If the book says do it, I do it."

"Suit yourself," Ollie said. He ambled off, coffee in hand, no sign of displeasure with me, his newest subordinate. Our passengers were on time and Ollie did a competent job from the left seat, though I was disappointed by his landing. As soon as we cleared the last obstacle coming into Runway 19 he pushed the nose over and headed for the first inch of usable pavement and then skimmed the next 3,000 feet before gently touching down. Despite this, he never touched the reversers. "No pressure, Eddie," he crowed. "It's gonna be tough to beat that one!"

"I have never seen wheel brakes get so hot after a single landing," I said as Ollie brought the airplane down to normal taxi speed. The airplane was light, the braking was a bit heavy, but certainly not worth the temperatures on the indicators. Ollie looked at the indicators.

"Nah that's perfectly normal," he said. "This airplane is like that."

"I get concerned at 100 degrees C," I said. "At 200 degrees I start to think about problems. At 300 degrees I start to wonder about fire coverage."

"This is nothing!" he laughed. "Don't worry so much."

After a few hours on the ground in Teterboro we came home. It was just below freezing and the brakes reflected the outside air temperature once we extended the gear, plus a little for the friction of the air. I made note of the four "0° C" readings, one for each main gear wheel.

I landed normally, perhaps a little firm in any other pilot's judgment but what I call a good landing. We were on speed in the touchdown zone at Bedford's longest runway. I used the thrust reversers as soon as they became available and I kept them for as long as permitted. By the time we had 1,000 feet of runway left, we were doing 50 knots and I had yet to touch the brakes. I looked down and saw all four numbers above 100° C. "That ain't right," I said.

"What?" Ollie said.

"Nothing," I said. By the time we were back at our hangar, after minimal use, three of the four indicators topped 180° C and the fourth wasn't far behind. As soon as the passengers were gone I approached each brake cluster carefully. No doubt, the brakes were hot.

"What are you doing down there, pilot?" Sully said. Richard Francis Sullivan

Flight Lessons 5: People

was destined to be called "Sully" from day one and though he answered the phone "Richard," he insisted on being called Sully. He was just a few inches taller than five feet even, but he was probably wider. His face portrayed an age probably a decade older than did his birth certificate, and the rasp in his voice betrayed a lifetime of smoking unfiltered cigarettes.

"I barely touched these things and now they are almost hot enough to call the fire department," I said. "They still have another 30 minutes of temperature rise. We may want to hold off on towing the airplane into the hangar."

"Har, har, har," he laughed from the gut. "Welcome to the gee four. All my fours were just like this. You ain't in your fancy five anymore!"

"I flew threes as well," I said. "This isn't right."

"Hey leave him alone," Ollie said. "Let him do his job so we can do ours."

I came in the next day to study the airplane manual, since I didn't have a copy of my own. While replacing the books onto the airplane I spotted Sully spraying something from a can onto the brakes. "What's that?" I asked.

"M.E.K.," Sully said. "You never heard of this, Mister Air Force?"

"Sure," I said. "Methyl Ethyl Ketone."

"I don't know what it stands for," he said. "I just know there's nothing better for keeping a set of brakes shiny and clean."

"I'm not telling you how to do your job," I said.

"So don't," he said. "Har, har, har!"

"I've never heard of anything but compressed air or water used to clean carbon-carbon brakes," I said. "I think those two are the only things allowed. And if you use water, you need to give them a day to dry out."

"Well it's a good thing I'm the mechanic and you're the pilot," he said. "Har, har, har!"

I retreated to the hangar office, telling myself more research was needed. Our office had a large window overlooking the hangar floor and I noticed Sully reading the back of his MEK can with the magnifying glass he kept in his back pocket. A few moments later I saw him lugging a water hose underneath the airplane. He doused each brake assembly for five or six minutes each. There was water everywhere.

I was the captain on the next trip with Sidney as the first officer. "Scontro says I need a thousand hours in type before I can be the pilot in command," he explained.

"I've got three point four hours in the GIV," I said. "I guess nobody is in command today."

"Well they make things up as they go," he said. "You'll get used to that."

"I was going to ask you about that," I said. "How does a newly hired pilot get a company manual around here?"

"We don't have one," he said.

"Well I know that isn't true," I said. "The FAA isn't going to let them operate without one."

"Well good luck finding one," he said. "I'll do the exterior preflight. Ollie says we are checking the aft equipment bay now."

"Good," I said. Sidney left and I busied myself with the flight plan. As I walked out Sidney was just buttoning up the aft equipment bay.

"Hey buddy," Sully said to him, "don't forget to check the thrust reverser accumulators."

"The what?" Sidney asked.

"Don't you know nothing?" Sully asked.

"Don't expect anything from me," Sidney said, "I trained at SimuSafety!"

Sully opened a compartment and revealed two accumulator gauges. They both laughed. "No problem Sidney," Sully said with his booming laugh. "We are all learning!"

I pulled Sully aside and said, quietly, "Sully, I don't have a lot of time in this airplane, but I am pretty sure it doesn't have thrust reverser accumulators. Those gauges are connected to the thrust reverser lines all right, but that's because that gives them direct access to the combined and flight hydraulic systems."

"No that ain't right," he said. "Let me call my buddy Georgie. Don't you worry, I'll get to the bottom of this."

I flew us to Teterboro and noted with satisfaction the brake temperatures never exceeded 100°C, but that also included a touchdown in the proper zone with full thrust reversers. The real test would be Sidney's landing back at Bedford.

During our ground time a familiar face from Q-Tron tapped me on the shoulder. "How you doing, stranger?" Jeff Lombard asked. We caught up for a while until he changed the subject. "You remember those notes you lent me a while back?"

"Yeah," I said. "I never did find them."

"That's because I still have them," he said. "They were stuck under one of my couch cushions. I'll mail them back to you. But you've got to put 'known procedures' back up. I tell people about it all the time and now it's gone. We need it back."

My cellphone rang, it was Larry. "We are leaving the meeting, see you in forty-five minutes."

"I have to go, Jeff," I said after finishing the call. "I'll come up with something."

Sidney flew a textbook perfect approach to Bedford's shorter runway, which meant he had to get on the brakes. I was hoping he would be able to do as well as my 100°C braking. The temperatures were even lower. After he pulled us back into our hangar I placed a set of chocks on one of the main gear as Sully got the other. I put my hands on the brakes. "Nice and cool, the brakes did nicely today."

I thought he took offense because he didn't acknowledge; it seemed he noticed Sidney closing the baggage door. "Hey Sidney," he yelled. "I got to correct what I told you this morning. I told you these gauges were thrust reverser accumulators," he said pointing to the closed panel. "Eddie told me that wasn't right so I called my buddy Georgie who told me I was right and Eddie was wrong. But I thought why would Eddie think that wasn't right? So I called someone at Gulfstream. As it turns out, they are not thrust reverser accumulators at all! They are hydraulic system accumulators. So I just want you to have the straight story!" He gave us both a wide grin. "Har, har, har!"

"Nicely done," I said to Sully.

"I gotta tell ya," he said. "Ten years I've been saying those were for the TR's. Ten years!"

I thought about a new website, one that I would take care to keep free of my name or other things that could trace it back to me. I needed a name. The purpose of the website would be to educate pilots so they could avoid having an inflight emergency as well as how to handle just such an emergency. There is a transponder code that alerts the world to an airplane in distress. It was settled. I checked and the name was available. Ten dollars later I was the owner of the www.code7700.com domain.

"Where's the plotting chart?" I asked. I was in the left seat and had waited as long as I could before reminding Ollie about what he should be doing. We were headed to Europe with the CEO and President of the company onboard. The faxed copy of our flight plan was acceptable for oceanic operations but just barely.

"Why do we need one of those?" he asked. I reached into my brief case and pulled out a blank plotting chart and a plotter. I drew our route, measured the course and distance of each leg, and compared the results to our flight plan and FMS. Ollie was fascinated by it all, as if he had never seen such a thing before. "I remember doing that in school," he said. "I've never done it in Gulfstreams."

Ollie was an attentive student. As I was explaining how to manually plot an equal time point I heard a female voice just over my shoulder. "Are we lost?" Elizabeth said.

"Oh no, ma'am," Ollie said, violating Elizabeth's dislike of the m-word. "We just got to do this to keep the lawyers happy." She looked unconvinced and

Flight Lessons 5: People

then turned to me.

"Elizabeth, the airplane does a fine job of navigating," I said. "We have three independent computer systems as well as GPS. If you look at the screens here, you will see we are right on course. But that isn't good enough. Flying over domestic airspace we have air traffic control's radar keeping an eye on us, backing all of this up. Flying this far away from land we don't have that. So it is up to us pilots to independently back up all those high tech gizmos with good old fashioned pencil and paper navigation charts. It's extra work for us and we'll probably never need it. But if we do, we'll have it."

She smiled and pointed to the plotting chart. Larry was standing right behind her. "They are doing everything manually to ensure the computers are doing their jobs. It's a backup."

"Smart," Larry said. "It's good to know they are doing that."

As the top two officers of our company returned to the cabin I wondered how badly Ollie would react to being upstaged, at best, or thrown under the bus, at worst.

"That was pretty neat!" he said. "I've never heard it explained like that." Ollie wasn't easily upset.

We had barely two days on the ground in Paris, which may have been one more day than I could take. Ollie was pleasant enough but didn't care for museums and his taste in French food went as far as pomme frites, but not much further.

Returning to Bedford, we spotted the airport from twenty miles east and somehow got cleared straight in and cleared to land with five miles still to go. "I'll set you up on the ILS," I said.

"Nah, don't bother," Ollie said. "I can see the airport just fine."

I knew a lot of pilots relished the chance to fly visually without any electronic aids at all, but prudent pilots tend to stack the odds in their favor. I set up the Instrument Landing System because I wanted it, and Ollie would have it on his side of the cockpit whether he wanted it or not. "You are a dot low," I said, as our glide path drifted a degree below where it should have been.

"I'm okay," he said.

"Below Vee Ref," I said.

"Okay," he said.

V-REF, more properly called 'reference speed,' is the slowest we are allowed to get on final approach. Our target speed, however, was ten knots faster. Getting too slow was removing our stall and maneuverability margins. At 100 feet above the runway, Ollie slapped the throttles to idle and we sunk like a rock. He flared a bit early but milked the last several inches until the airplane gently alit onto the runway.

After we parked we both set out to help unload passenger baggage. As I made the last trip to Elizabeth's vehicle she stopped and faced me. "Well, what do you think?"

"It's all good," I said. "We have room for improvement, but the fundamentals are all here."

"How do we compare with other flight departments?" she asked.

I measured my words carefully and tried to paint a picture that didn't so much as falsify but, let's say, sugar coat my observations. If she had asked me if this was a poorly run flight department I would have given her an honest answer. But she didn't ask. She had obviously "heard between the lines."

"Can you fix it?" she asked.

"I can certainly help," I said. "I'll give Ollie all the help he needs."

18: Coaching
February 2010

Bill Belichick, Coach of the New England Patriots (Photo: Keith Allison)

"I need you to drive me someplace," Elizabeth said while standing behind the cockpit. "Can you get us a car?"

"Sure," I said. "I'll just call in to the FBO and ask."

"If Sidney stays with the airplane can we leave right away?" she asked.

"Yes," I said. "That will work."

We were headed for Appleton, Wisconsin but our trip sheet didn't reveal where Elizabeth was going. I knew Gulfstream had a service center at Appleton, but we were going to the FBO, on the other side of the airport. Our trips were usually scheduled by someone at A Priori through a phone call to Scontro Aviation. I had no idea where we were going.

"She talks to you differently," Sidney said after she returned to the cabin. "Sully thinks something is going on."

"What does that mean?" I asked.

"I don't know," he said. "But everyone notices. With the rest of us we get a polite hello and every now and then a 'how are you doing?' But with you, there are these long conversations."

"I don't know about that," I said. "I am comfortable speaking with her and Larry. Maybe they sense that comfort as an invitation to talk."

The FBO provided a nice, clean, midsize sedan, removing one of my concerns. "Where are we going?" I asked.

"To Gulfstream," she said. "They should have someone meeting us at the main gate."

It was no more than a five-minute drive and from the gate we were taken to a large hangar. There were ten new Gulfstreams, most of which were green. "Why are they green?" she asked.

"It is a corrosion inhibitor," our guide said. "We don't paint them until the very end."

"When will that be?" she asked.

"December," he said.

At last we stopped at a green Gulfstream G450. It was the newest aircraft in the Gulfstream stable, the one with the high-tech cockpit most Gulfstream pilots dreamt about. "What do you think?" Elizabeth asked.

"I like it," I said. "Can I have one?"

"This one is yours," she said.

Elizabeth explained that A Priori bought the airplane about a year ago but kept it a secret. The company knew the GIV was getting old and would soon have trouble meeting newly evolving worldwide navigation and environmental standards. But Elizabeth and Larry were uncomfortable with Scontro Aviation in general and Ollie in particular.

"We want you to take over," she said. "We told Ollie when we hired him that he was the chief pilot temporarily. We would like him to stay on as a pilot, but not the chief pilot. I would be surprised if he didn't see this coming."

"I got to be honest with you, Eddie," Ollie said the next day, "I never saw this coming!" I stared at him, speechless. "No, I'm joking," he said. "The minute I first met you I realized you were taking my place."

Flight Lessons 5: People

"I am relieved to hear you say that," I said. "I am going to be counting on you to help me through this. What is it that you do, as the chief pilot here?"

"Nothing," Ollie said. "This is the easiest job I've ever had. Scontro does all the scheduling, gets all the legal authorizations, and pays all the bills. They deal with A Priori for us. I don't do nothing at all!"

"You will be doing all of it," Elizabeth said the next day. "We want you to get rid of the old airplane as soon as we get the new one, and once you've done that we want you to fire Scontro. And don't bother coming to us for permission for this or that. Just do what you have to and get it done. Have you picked up how we organize our staff?"

"I noticed you don't have managers," I said. "And it looks like most departments are called teams. So that means you must have coaches."

"Exactly," she said.

As much as I hated leaving the Gulfstream GV's ultra-long range and modern systems for the antiquated GIV, I was looking forward to stepping into the next generation of business jets. I momentarily entertained immersing myself into aircraft manuals and all things related to the G450. But in the end, I knew standing up a flight department from scratch was going to take all of my time for the next few years. Two of the challenges I anticipated were not challenges at all.

"This has been a huge load off my shoulders," Ollie would tell anyone who would listen. "You know me, all I want to do is maintain an even strain. With Eddie in charge, that's exactly what I am going to do!"

Every time I heard him mention his even strain, I reminded myself that we would one day need to have a talk about my philosophy about easy going pilots: they don't belong in professional aviation. But that would have to wait.

Richard Sconyers, as it turned out, had passed away a few years ago and was only still present in the company's name. The president and CEO of Scontro Aviation was William Troy, he could have been an Ollie McShay clone, and seemed to be operating on autopilot.

"Okay," he said. "If you need anything give the girls a call." That was his standard answer. The girls, his staff of dispatchers and schedulers, would handle it all. I had just told him that his highest paying client was leaving within the year and the airplane that generated their largest take in maintenance and fuel was going up for sale. "Okay," he said again. "If you need anything, well, you know."

"Everything happens for a reason," *The Lovely Mrs. Haskel* was fond of saying. It appears all the flight operations manuals I had written over the years were a prime example. I took the most recent one, the version I wrote for Bravo Zulu Aviation, and did a whole-document find and replace. We now had our very first A Priori Flight Operations Manual. I printed four copies.

"What?" Ollie said at our first ever flight department team meeting. "We got rules now?" His wink betrayed the joke.

"Har, har, har!" Sully added.

"Not quite yet," I said. "But I want it in place by the time the new airplane shows up. I want us all to go through this manual, word by word. We are going to end up rewriting this a few times before then. But let's not put this off."

Ollie, Sidney, and Sully each lifted their binders, as if in an effort to weigh the task before them. After many years of dispensing unpleasant news, I could tell each was starting to realize their lives maintaining an even strain were coming to an end.

That Sunday I sat at home reading the manual while paying just enough attention to the game to convince *The Lovely Mrs. Haskel* we were having some quality time together as a couple. The Patriots sneaked by the Bills for the season opener, winning it in the last two minutes. They had a few chances to repeat the last minute save against the Jets in the second game, but sloppy play denied them. They were one and one, and game three would set the tone for the rest of the season. By the end of the first quarter, it was 3 to 3. For the first time in my short career of watching football from the sofa, I noticed the choreography between the many coaches and players. Everyone had a job to do and, even playing a game, everyone had some kind of book, manual, or card that required reference. I was suddenly interested in the game.

As an Air Force squadron commander, I realized early on that if you could motivate the troops to do something, you were ahead of the game. You could not only bypass the "I order you to . . ." step of the process, but the troops were apt to do a better job. Coach Belichick had obviously done his job. The Patriots took the lead in the second quarter and never looked back.

"Tell me the pros and cons of training together," I asked Ollie and Sidney.

"We can be sure we aren't paired with some loser," Sidney said.

"Don't you hate it when you have to carry the other pilot?" Ollie said.

The two went on and on, making it clear they wanted to attend initial training as a team. The G450 shares the GV type rating and I had already done the short course needed to transition from the GV to the G450, so I didn't have to go at all. "I'll think about it," I said.

I had actually already made up my mind and arranged for a month of contract pilot help on our GIV while they would be gone. I knew the problems of being paired with a "loser" but I was also afraid Ollie's "even strain" could turn him into that loser. If he had Sidney with him, he might be more motivated not to look stupid. Besides, I wanted them looking forward to the new airplane.

The season ended early; the Patriots lost the divisional playoffs to the Baltimore Ravens, trailing 24 to 0 in the first quarter. Sully finished his G450 maintenance course with flying colors, graduating top in his class. I heard Sidney did quite well and that Ollie did "well enough." We took delivery of the new airplane in March, started flying trips with it in May, and sold the old airplane in August. I realized in September that I couldn't survive without sleep.

Our company rules for when a coach needed help was to drop the CEO a cryptic email with a blank subject line and only three words in the body of the text: need to talk. You would then get a meeting location and time.

"What's up?" she asked.

"I need a dispatcher," I said, "stat."

"Only hire the best," she said.

"I already know the best," I said. In the months since we became our own flight department, that is to say, without a management company, she wasn't interested in any of our operating procedures or expenses, so long as everything went smoothly. I was hoping I could have the dispatcher question settled with an equal level of *laissez faire*.

"I want to meet him," she said.

"Her," I said.

"Even better," she said.

I knew Linda Hughes would never leave any job unless forced to; but I also knew she got hired by Scontro after Bravo Zulu folded. But that job only lasted a year before Scontro downsized and foolishly decided their most junior dispatcher had to go. Linda was scooped up immediately by an industry starved for talent.

"This is Linda," she said on the phone, "your soon-to-be unemployed dispatcher."

"This is Eddie," I said, "your former and hopefully future pilot."

"Funny thing," she said, "I was just thinking about you. I knew you left Scontro and I was hoping your new company was hiring. My fly-by-night operation just flew the coop."

"How soon can you be ready for an interview?" I asked.

"It depends on traffic," she said.

Elizabeth didn't have a schedule, per se, but getting on her list of things to do within a week was very hard to do. Predictably, she pushed back. "I'm just too busy," she said. "Maybe next week."

"We can't afford to lose her," I said. "She will be off the market tomorrow if we don't act today."

"What's so good about her?" she asked. I had a catalog of Linda stories but the one that came to mind seemed the most appropriate.

Flight Lessons 5: People

"I was in South Africa a few years ago, getting ready for a morning flight across the continent," I began. "She called me out of the blue to warn me about a war that broke out along our route of flight and to suggest a different airway that would take a little more fuel but was safer. I asked her what time it was in Massachusetts and she said it was 2 a.m. I asked her if she ever slept and she said not when her pilots were on the road."

"Tomorrow then," Elizabeth said. "It will have to be late, but have her come by around 9 p.m."

The next evening, I got the call. "It was love at first sight," she said.

"You can't have her," I said, "unless we can still use her as a dispatcher."

"Very funny," she said. "Larry said she is fantastic but I was in another meeting so we asked her to hang out on the bottom floor. I got a look at her from the balcony and knew, instantly! She has that look. And then I met her, and I was convinced. She is very smart. I don't know a thing about her job, but I can tell she knows all there is to know about it."

"That is definitely true," I said. "Our timing was perfect. We are lucky we got her because she will be off the market within a week, no matter what we do."

"Find out what her top salary was and add five thousand," Elizabeth said. "Do not lose her."

Linda was the highest paid dispatcher in Bravo Zulu's office of eighteen. I knew she took a pay cut going to Scontro and again after that. Our offer was the highest I had ever heard for an airplane dispatcher. Linda accepted immediately. I spent the next week fielding calls from one Bravo Zulu veteran after another, wondering how I managed to pull off the magic of getting the dispatcher everyone else wanted.

After a year we had a dispatcher, two fully trained pilots, and a competent mechanic. Everyone was settling into the routine of flying a high-tech airplane with barely a year of mileage on it and a brand-new operation with a brand-new manual. There was still room for improvement.

"The hydraulic system isn't behaving the way it should," I said to Sully after a flight home from the west coast. "The quantity on the left system dropped point five pints right after takeoff and then slowly climbed back over the next four hours."

"They do that," Sully said. "The fluid gets hot after takeoff and takes a while to cool off."

"That is true," I said. "But the gauge is temperature compensated. Besides, it didn't behave that way until last month. What has happened in the last month?"

"Nothing," he said. "I'm telling you, Eddie. There is nothing wrong with that hydraulic system. Maybe you need new glasses. Har, har, har!"

"Service it," I said.

"Already did," he said.

"Do it again," I said.

The next flight the left hydraulic system showed half a pint low right after takeoff. "That isn't right," I said, pointing to the synoptic display.

"Sully's pretty pissed as it is," Ollie said. "He's usually a pretty easy-going guy about these things, but he was wondering where you got your A and P, ordering him to service the system when he already did."

That was a valid complaint, I thought. While some pilots also had one of the top mechanic ratings, the Airframe and Powerplant license, I did not. Moreover, Sully had the highest license of all, he had the so-called IA, the inspector authorization.

"I've been flying Gulfstreams since 1992," I said. "I've never seen a hydraulic system behave this way."

"I've been flying them almost as long," Ollie said. "But this is the first one with a synoptic page. Maybe it is the electronic stuff getting in the way."

"This system is identical to the GV," I said. "This isn't right."

"Well he's going to be pissed," Ollie said. "You never heard this from me, but he calls you 'mister make work' sometimes."

Flight Lessons 5: People

"Am I 'mister make work?'" I asked.

"You do what you have to," Ollie said. "You aren't going to hear those kinds of complaints from me."

"Good," I said. "Because I have some work for you. I want a Safety Management System in place within a year. You are our safety officer, I need you to get smart about it, and take us there."

"I don't know anything about SMS," Ollie said.

"Well it's your job," I said. "Time to step up to the plate." Ollie gave me his usual smile, but I could sense he was unhappy at the loss of his "even strain."

A week later I was in the hangar office when he returned from a flight with Sidney. "Good flight?" I asked.

"Good flight," he said. "I sure love that airplane!"

"What about the hydraulics?" I asked.

"Two point seven and rock steady," he said. "Sully said he serviced it and like magic it worked."

"Tell me about SMS," I said. Ollie's smile disappeared.

"About that," he said, "no can do. That is pretty involved stuff and, if you ask me, it is all unnecessary bullcrap. I've been flying airplanes since Christ was a corporal and I never needed an SMS to fly airplanes safely and I don't need one now."

"You've been flying airplanes longer than I have," I agreed. "But back then the sky wasn't filled with so many of them and they certainly were not flying as fast and as high. We need an SMS system and we need you to get us one. Find an SMS school and enroll. We'll take you off the flight schedule as best we can, but we need you to do this."

"Listen, Eddie," he said. "You are the boss and I'll do what I have to so I can keep flying airplanes. But my job is as a pilot, not a pencil pusher. I got to tell you, I am not happy about this."

"I'm sorry you are not happy about it," I said. "But if you want to be a pilot and only a pilot, I suggest you call the airlines."

Ollie shrugged his shoulders but turned when Sully entered with his usual, "Har, har, har!" Sully approached us and looked at me. "I got to tell you, Eddie, you were right. I was servicing the hydraulics with the gear doors open, because in the GIV, they didn't matter. But I thought maybe things were different in the G450. And son of a gun if they are different. The gear doors have to be closed! I did that, and bada bing, bada boom, that did it. I called Gulfstream up and they said leaving the doors open means you could have air in the system. I don't know how that is, but it is."

"Excellent," I said. "I didn't know about any of that. But now I do."

"It just goes to show you," Sully said. "You don't know what you don't know. Har, har, har!"

Over the next month I found a weeklong course designed to help corporate flight departments become SMS certified. Having an SMS program would soon be mandatory in certain parts of the world, but by then there would be countless programs that didn't accomplish anything other than make you look good. I wanted a real SMS program to help us anticipate things we didn't know. I enrolled Ollie for the next course and Linda made airline and hotel reservations for him.

"He is pretty upset," she said after confirming the arrangements. "You need to know that I think he was in Dallas last week."

I knew he asked for a week off but I didn't know why. But I soon found out. "I just got hired by American Airlines," he said. "My class date is next week. I know it doesn't show a lot of class to give less than two weeks' notice, but you left me no choice, Eddie."

"I suppose that may be true," I said. "Good luck with American, Ollie. I think you will do great there."

"I got to get back to the game," Ollie said. "No hard feelings?"

"None," I said.

I cradled the phone, returned to our living room, and plunked myself down on the sofa. *The Lovely Mrs. Haskel* was fully engrossed. New England was behind by three. They and the New York Giants were both looking for their fourth Super Bowl win. The Giants were lucky to be there, coming off a 9 and 7 season. The Pats had won 13 and lost only 3. On paper, from the perspective of a non-football fanatic, it should have been an easy game for the Patriots. They lost by 4 points.

19: Rebuilding Seasons
January 2013

The 2013 New England Patriots training camp (Photo: MD Faisalzman)

"Why is Brady in red?" I asked.

"This is a practice with our guys on defense and offense," *The Lovely Mrs. Haskel* said. "It tells everyone 'no contact' is allowed. It wouldn't do to injure your quarterback during practice."

"But it is okay to injure the other players?" I asked.

"Well no," she said. "But you have to take special care with the quarterback. It is like how everyone in the flight department is important, but without pilots the airplane doesn't fly."

It made sense, I concluded. They had two seasons since their last Super Bowl, and that was a loss. While they won their conference championship both times, that wasn't considered a victory for the franchise that had so many appearances at the big game.

Ollie's departure was a big setback and it took us more than a year to replace him. It took me an average of two months to find a candidate we thought would pass what we called the "A Priori Beauty Contest," only to have them shot down in flames after a two-hour interview. Based on our six failures, the candidates were either "not very smart" or didn't have enough "backbone to stand up to you or Sidney." We were fortunate to have a few contract pilots, but none of them would pass the beauty contest. The irony was that we were spending twice as much on per diem fees as a full-time pilot would cost.

"That isn't important," Elizabeth said. "What matters is finding the right person. Be patient."

Sidney took over Ollie's safety officer duties, attended the Safety Management System class, trained Sully, Linda, and me on our SMS duties, and got us through the first-year audit. He did all that without a single complaint and the only questions I ever got were about how to make a PowerPoint presentation. We both spent more time flying with contract pilots than each other, but things were getting done and A Priori rewarded everyone with the largest pay bonus I had ever seen. "Things are good," Sidney would say whenever I asked.

There was a rhythm to it all: two pilots, a mechanic, and a dispatcher getting it done. But it was obvious we couldn't survive much longer without a third pilot. Both my children were away in college and *The Lovely Mrs. Haskel* was fully engaged as a nurse in Boston, so the fact my bride and I hadn't had a vacation in two years escaped everyone's scrutiny. Our annual August heavy maintenance provided our only opportunity. I talked *The Lovely Mrs. Haskel* into two weeks in Savannah, one of which would be with me in G450 training and the second checking in on the airplane. Knowing every evening would be at another world-class restaurant, she agreed. That was a big advantage of the name brand training vendor over SimuSafety. We traded in New Jersey for my favorite food city in the country.

Of course, there were better times in the year than August to visit Savannah, but most of A Priori was on vacation in August so that was the best time to do our annual maintenance. It also meant we could fly our airplane down and avoid airline seats. *The Lovely Mrs. Haskel* sat in the jump seat for the flight, something she had done many times over the years.

"How did we do?" I asked that night at dinner.

"Excellent crew resource management," she said. "I can tell you two think

Flight Lessons 5: People

alike."

"Let's hope that is true," Sidney said. "We have a check ride to pass."

The simulator cockpit was identical to ours, the visual displays outside the windows were quite good, and the six-axis motion made everything about as realistic as it could be. The entire contraption sat on huge hydraulic arms lifting the cockpit twenty feet in the air. I sat in the left seat with Sidney in the right when our instructor, playing the role of the air traffic controller, cleared us for takeoff. I pushed both thrust levers forward and then engaged the autothrottles.

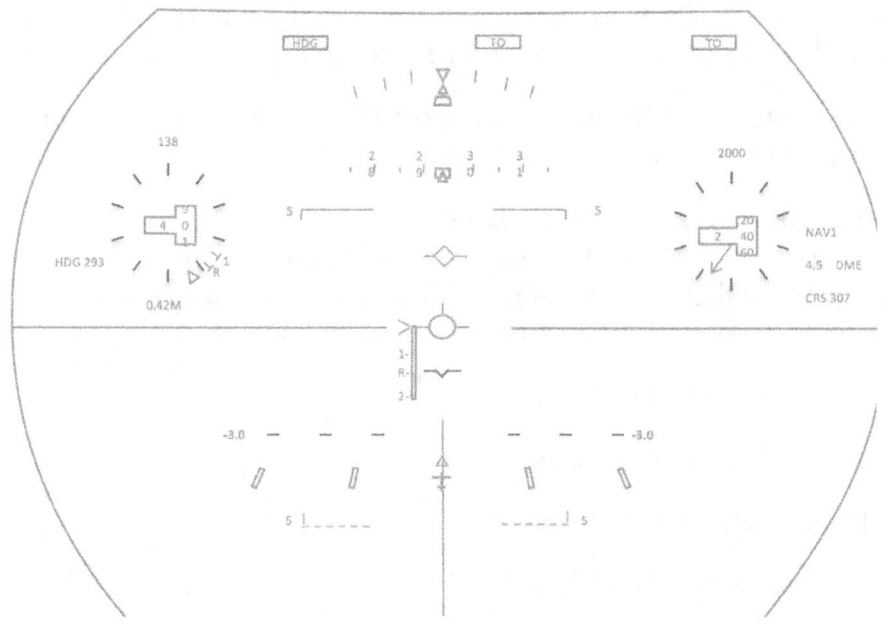

G450 Heads Up Display

"Sixty knots, power set," Sidney called.

"Roger," I said after a quick glance. I was looking straight ahead, keeping the airplane pointed down the center of the runway, watching the airplane's airspeed increase on a gauge on the HUD, the "heads up display," which projects much of our instrumentation onto a plate glass in my line of sight.

"Eighty knots," he said.

"Roger," I said. I verified the speed on a round dial on the left side of the

HUD. At this point our abort criteria changed and I would only reject the takeoff if we lost an engine, had a fire of any type, or if for some reason lost directional control. My primary focus would be on the middle of the HUD, where a small circle with two horizontal lines and one vertical line represented the airplane's path. The left horizontal line represented the left wing and off that was a compressing vertical line with letters and numbers. The speed tape showed our future speed and signified the events during the takeoff roll. The next events were "1", denoting V1 our decision speed, "R", denoting our rotation speed, and "2", denoting V2 our takeoff safety speed. If we lost an engine before V1, I was to abort. After V1, I was to continue the takeoff.

As the speed tape's "1" disappeared from view I took my hands off the throttles just as all hell broke loose. "Abort," Sidney called. "Too late," I said.

The world froze. "What are you supposed to do if you lose an engine before V1," the instructor said from behind us.

I turned in my seat. Gil Desjardaines, our instructor, was an ex-Army pilot with thousands of hours in helicopters and hundreds in an Army turboprop but no actual flight hours in any Gulfstream. He seemed very knowledgeable and had been a great instructor in the previous session.

"We were past V1," I said.

"Sidney didn't call it yet," he said.

"I didn't," Sidney said.

"I think you should have," I said.

"But that's not the point," Gil said. "The rule is you abort if he didn't call it."

"I don't think that is what the rule is," I said. "I think you will find the rule is above V1, you continue. We were above V1."

"Okay," he agreed. "That is the rule. But that's not very good Crew Resource Management, ignoring your copilot like that."

"It's a Catch-22," Sidney said. "I can't call it until we are there, and by the time I call it it's too late."

"I think you are supposed to call it earlier," I said. "I always time the call so

Flight Lessons 5: People

the pilot hears the call just as we get to V1."

"Okay, let's not get bogged down here," Gil said. "Let's continue and we can talk about this later."

After the session and a short break we sat down for our debrief. Gil had a slide up on a computer showing the takeoff roll call outs, as required by Gulfstream. "As you can see here," he said pointing to the V1 arrow on the slide, "the rule book really doesn't say. So I asked around the office and all the old heads agree with you, Eddie. The call out has to be made a little early."

"My bad," Sidney said. "I guess I learned something today."

"Not a bad thing," Gil said. "We are all here to learn."

I had to wonder about Sidney having missed what I considered such a fundamental procedure in flying large airplanes. Of course, my background in heavy Boeings meant the G450 was one of the smaller aircraft in my logbook whereas it was the largest airplane Sidney had ever flown. But, more importantly, after having flown with Sidney in three airplane types, why had I never noticed the late V1 calls? Gil's point about my breach of CRM was also valid. We all took away serious lessons from our simulator session.

"He's pretty sharp for an Army guy," Sidney said that night at dinner. "He taught you a thing or two."

"He did indeed," I said. "I like how he admitted he learned something too. Most of these instructors would rather lie than admit weakness."

"We should hire him," Sidney said with a wry smile.

"He doesn't have any real Gulfstream experience," I said. "He knows the airplane, but he's never really done what we do for a living."

"I didn't have any Gulfstream time when A Priori hired me," Sidney said. "Besides, aren't you the one who always says you hire the person first, the pilot second?"

Gil passed the A Priori beauty contest and eagerly left his simulator instructor position. He rented an apartment near the Bedford airport. "We want to get a feel for the area before we buy," he said. All of his children were either in college or moved out. He found another simulator instructor to rent his Savannah house. It appeared he was keeping his options open; probably a smart thing.

His taxi technique was sloppy, but that was to be expected from any pilot graduating into heavier iron. The nosewheel tiller and wheel brakes can seem overly sensitive at first, but he gradually improved. He continued to have a problem keeping his brain ahead of the airplane. That too was a skill learned with experience.

The G450 is an overpowered beast that likes to climb, likes to fly fast, but does not descend gracefully. Many airplanes will dutifully descend when you pull the throttles to idle and point the nose down. And in most Gulfstreams that works until you run into a speed limitation on the flaps, the landing gear, or the airplane itself. The pilot needs to carefully plan out the descent profile before getting to that point. Gil wasn't doing that. Repeatedly.

We were about 20 miles out at 10,000 feet, with Bedford's Runway 11 clearly in front of us. Our ideal altitude would have been 6,000 feet but Boston Approach Control often kept us high because of crossing traffic from Boston or Manchester, New Hampshire airports. This would be a repeat of his previous arrival from this direction. For the second time, he pressed the "Flight Level Change" button of the autopilot and began his descent at 250 knots, the maximum allowed below 10,000 feet.

"Is this going to work?" I asked, from the right seat.

"I'm doing the best I can," he said.

"Level off," I said.

"What?" he said.

"Idle now," I said. "Trust me." He pulled the nose up. "I'm going to get you as dirty as possible."

"That's not going to help," he said. That was a common mistake for pilots who didn't have a lot of real-world experience. Getting dirty simply meant

Flight Lessons 5: People

adding drag by extending the flaps and landing gear as a means of flying as slow as possible while still descending. There was magic to be had with the airplane's limitations.

"Here comes the gear," I said. "Flaps, next." Once the flaps were down, I said, "Descend at 175 knots." The limiting speed was 180 knots. By the time we were through 5,000 feet things were starting to look normal. By the time we got to 2,000 feet, they were.

"Well that is a technique nobody knows about," Gil said. "Where did you learn that?"

"Out in the real world," I said. "This works in the GII and every Gulfstream since."

"I gotta tell the guys at the training center," he said. I would leave that to him, knowing any Gulfstream pilot with more than a year of real-world experience would already know it. The problem of getting down is more than one of vertical dimensions, the longitudinal distance matters too. Slowing down meant you consumed longitudinal distance at a slower rate, giving you more time to take care of the vertical challenge.

Sidney had years ago, back in the Ollie days, come up with the "What's the DEAL?" check when debriefing each flight. The right seat pilot would look at the left seat pilot and say, "What's the deal?" Then it would be up to the left seat pilot to critique the flight, including the [D]eparture, [E]n Route, [A]rrival, and any [L]ogbook issues. It was our custom for the flying pilot to critique himself and the non-flying pilot only to offer supportive comments unless the flying pilot had a specific question.

"What's the deal?" I asked Gil as he finished the last piece of paperwork.

"It was a good departure," he began. "Nothing to report on the en route phase and the arrival was okay except for the way Boston dicked us over on the descent. Nothing to log on the airplane."

"'Why do you say Boston dicked us over?" I asked.

"Because nobody can handle a descent that steep," he said. "They had to have violated a bunch of rules setting us up like that."

"And yet we dealt with it," I said. "You are going to find that this happens a lot, especially in the northeast. You should try to run the math in your head all the way down. Just divide your altitude in thousands by three for an idea of where you need to be distance-wise. That will be a good heads up to realize if you are going to need a steeper descent."

Gil remained quiet. I was hoping he might ask a few follow up questions or at least take a few notes, but there was none of that. If anything, he behaved as if I had reprimanded him. I didn't push him further but reminded myself it was something I needed to figure out.

"Some people are beyond figuring out," *The Lovely Mrs. Haskel* said that evening. "But it isn't that hard. He's an ex-Army guy used to yelling at others or being yelled at. You yelled at him with your tone of voice."

"I am pretty sure I said, 'you should' as opposed to 'you must,'" I said.

"When the boss says, 'you should' it is the same thing as 'you must,'" she said. "You know that."

"Maybe a demo is in order," I said.

"A conspicuous demo," she said. And that was true. It was a concept she came up with many years ago when I came home frustrated by my efforts to get a squadron of very good pilots to adopt some very good habits that would have made them even better. I thought setting a good example was enough to drive home the message. I learned that setting the best example does no good if nobody notices.

Sidney and I had the next trip, which was due to return early in the morning, so we scheduled our monthly safety meeting to take advantage of having the rest of us already at the hangar. It was Gil's turn to host the meeting and he had an agenda ready to go. I may have been a little distracted, or perhaps I was getting lazy, but I landed about ten feet left of centerline. Sidney remained silent, perhaps seeing that I was in the process of correcting.

Sidney and I entered the small conference room in our hangar office to see Gil had his laptop hooked up to the projector. Linda and Sully were already seated. "No rush," Gil said. "We know you still have your debrief to go."

After Sidney and I put our gear away it came to me. "Let's have a public debrief," I said. "Maybe we can demonstrate how to do this to those who can't seem to get it."

"I have an idea where you are going with this," Sidney said. "I like it."

We returned to the conference room and took our seats. "Sidney and I still have to debrief, but it won't take long. Do you mind if we do that right here?"

"Not at all," Gil said.

"What's the deal?" Sidney said, on cue.

"The departure was good," I said. "I almost forgot the speed restriction. Who am I kidding, I did forget the speed restriction. But you reminded me, and I corrected immediately."

"Whoa, that's not good," Sully said. "You forgot something?"

"Happens all the time," I said. "This particular airport lies underneath a bigger airport's airspace, so I couldn't accelerate as quickly as usual. Sidney remembered so we were covered."

"Nice job, Sidney," Sully said. "Har, har, har!"

"Let's see," I continued. "En route was fine and so was the arrival. I landed left of centerline for the first time in a long time. I need to work on that."

"That might be my bad," Sidney said. "The tower gave the winds as calm but I noticed the speed readout showed the crosswind we really had. I should have said something."

"Maybe so," I said. "But I got eyes too! And finally, just one write up for a light bulb in the galley. We logged that in the forms, Sully."

"Har, har, har!"

As we spoke, I noticed Gil following along closely. But he didn't comment so we started the safety meeting and covered his agenda. In the weeks to come, he never admitted to a mistake but continued to critique Sidney or me as if he was still the instructor and we were still the students.

"First up," I said, "we need a cash machine." The Prague hotel was regal and our rooms, though small, were beautifully appointed. It was an unusual trip for us and Gil's first real trip outside our normal London and Paris routine. He had prepared himself well and other than some help with interpreting the broken English on the radio, he handled almost everything on his own. The hotel clerk described a bank down the street which was also near a good restaurant.

It was well past normal banking hours but there were two Automatic Teller Machines, one inside and the other outside. An older man dressed in a threadbare coat lingered nearby, but was careful not to crowd our access to the outside ATM or the door enclosing the indoor ATM. I looked at Gil who stopped and opened his right hand, pointing to the door. "After you," he said.

I walked into the enclosed room, inserted my card in the machine, and punched in a few numbers. After acknowledging that I would be charged a fee of 100 Kč, Czech Korunas, I withdrew 5,000 Korunas in four 1,000 Koruna bills and an assortment of smaller folding money, about 200 U.S. dollars. The 1,000 Kč notes had a distinguished looking gentleman in a purple hue, the 100 Kč notes were green with someone with a long beard and a threatening stare. I stuffed the bills into my shirt pocket, double checked my wallet in my front pants pocket, and left the glass room.

Gil was outside talking with a local. The two exchanged money and Gil turned to me. "Dinner time?" he asked.

"Right across the street," I said. "What was all that about?"

"Oh that man said he needed a large bill to pay his rent and wanted to exchange with me," Gil said.

"Really?" I said. "And you did that?"

"Sure," he said. "I want to be a good American."

"What did he need and what did you give him?" I asked.

Flight Lessons 5: People

"He asked if I had any one-thousand Koruna bills," Gil said. "He said he would give me 500 Koruna bills in exchange. So I gave him four one-thousand Koruna bills for eight of the five hundreds. No problem. Besides, smaller bills should be easier to spend."

I let the subject drop and we found the restaurant right where the hotel clerk said it would be. The food was very good and the check came to less than 2,000 Kč, around $80 US. Gil reached for his wallet and placed his four bills on the tray with the check. They were red.

"Can I see that?" I said. He handed one of the bills over. It had the "500" numerals on it. But where my bills said "Korun Českych" his said something in letters that were mostly non-existent in English. The waitress came by and I handed her one of Gil's notes. "Excuse me, could you tell me what this is please?" I asked.

She blushed, smiled, and returned the bill. "That is a Russian Ruble," she said. "I should say, was a Russian Ruble. They changed their currency last year."

"What is it worth today?" Gil asked.

"It has no worth," she said. "It is, I think you English say, it is rubbish."

"What a rotten country," Gil said after she left.

"It happens to the best of us," I said.

"Ever happen to you?" he asked.

"No," I said. "But I think I am naturally suspicious."

As we walked back to the hotel Gil wasn't in a mood to talk, which worked out because I was in a mood to reflect. Why had it never happened to me? My first overseas trip as a pilot was to London. I was 23 years old and every mistake was greeted by the old men on the crew laughing. No mistake was too little not to be pointed out; the sport of belittling a second lieutenant has a long tradition in the U.S. military. This caused you to grow a thicker skin, but it also trained you to laugh at yourself. Gil spent twenty or more years in the army as a warrant officer, which is to say more than an enlisted soldier but something less than what the army called a second lieutenant.

Our next leg was to Amsterdam where we limited our monetary exchanges to dealing with machines and not shadowy figures waiting on the street. I had a number of examples where I had been an idiot and learned from it; but offering any of these would be seen as pandering. I needed a way of demonstrating to Gil that our human frailties are to be expected; moreover, our frailties as pilots need to be acknowledged as a part of the learning process. I had worked with other pilots with fragile egos, but never one in such a small flight department. When one-third of the pilot force is dysfunctional, two-thirds of every crew has a problem. Our next day would be from Amsterdam to Paris, and then back to Bedford. The day would be long enough where we needed to have Sidney airline to Paris to provide a fresh pilot for the long flight home. Perhaps he could figure this out.

I flew the takeoff with Gil in the right seat, hoping to give him some practice with the various radio calls and the procedures for entering oceanic airspace. Despite the linguistic ability implied by his last name – Desjardaines – he had a particularly difficult time with the French controllers. Once we had coasted out, Elizabeth came forward with an offer of croissants.

"These are the most delicious croissants ever!" she said. "They are so flaky and they are filled with rose petals that have to be the tastiest thing you've ever had. But I don't want you eating them in the pilots' seats; you will get the crumbs all over the instruments." She pointed to Sidney, in the jump seat. "You can have yours now, then trade places with Eddie. And when Eddie is done, Gil," she paused, "No with your short fingers maybe you should wait until we land." Sidney and I laughed, Gil only smiled.

"The best thing ever!" Sidney said. From my seat I twisted hard to look. It was a huge croissant with a dusting of red flakes. Sidney showed us the insides, filled with more of the red goodness.

"Hurry up," I said.

"Not a chance," Sidney said. "This must be savored."

After an interminable delay, we swapped seats and Elizabeth returned with my croissant. "This is about the best thing I've ever eaten," I said. "It's the best thing that didn't come from a mammal." Elizabeth returned with one final croissant with instructions to swap seats again.

"I'm not eating that thing," Gil said.

Flight Lessons 5: People

"She was joking," I said.

"I don't care," he said. "I'm not eating it."

The next morning, in Elizabeth's office, I got approval for our plans to bring the airplane to Savannah for some maintenance. She was rarely interested in the why but keenly interested in the when. As usual, the conversation ended with, "How is everyone doing?"

Thoughts of Gil's hurt feelings flooded my frontal cortex but then retreated. It would do no good for Gil or Elizabeth to bring it up. "Everyone is doing well," I said. "Sidney is chugging along, doing great. I think Gil is making good progress. Sully is a work in progress. Linda is a godsend."

"A godsend?" she asked. "Do you believe in God?"

"I do," I said.

"What about evolution?" she asked.

"I do not," I said.

"How can you not believe in evolution?" she asked.

"I believe in entropy and the two ideas are incompatible," I said.

"Always the engineer," she said. "Are you bored yet?"

"Bored?" I said. "Why do you ask?"

"I asked Sidney why you quit your last couple of jobs," she said. "He said you get bored easily. I don't want you to get bored. I'm sorry we don't have more flying for you. What do you do to keep from getting bored?"

My mind raced. It seemed like the right time. "Well, I have a website." I explained my need to keep notes which morphed into a need to provide notes to the aviation community at large. I told her the precautions I had taken to protect my identity and that of the company. But I told her I was worried about her reaction to the fact the coach of our flight department was doing such a thing.

"It sounds admirable," she said. "Give the website address to our chief counsel and have him weigh in on it. I can't imagine it will be a problem. And if it keeps the boredom away, I am all for it."

"I told you as much," *The Lovely Mrs. Haskel* said that night. "You are giving back to aviation and making everyone safer. What's not to like about that?"

The next week the chief counsel called. "We think your website is great," he said. "This is right up A Priori's alley. The reason we exist as a company is to do good. You are doing good. Elizabeth is in full agreement."

"Nice approach and landing," I said from the right seat as Gil pulled off at the end of the runway. "I think you are getting the hang of the Boston slam dunk."

"Well it's a lot easier when the guy in the right seat isn't talking nonstop," he said. "I can't get Sidney to stop talking on final."

"That is unlike him," I said. "What is he talking about?"

"Oh, about I'm a little high," he said. "Or a little low, or left of course, right of course, too fast, too slow. Or it is time to add some flaps. That sort of thing."

"You know how long Sidney has been flying Gulfstreams?" I asked.

"I know," he said, "longer than me."

"No," I said. "He hasn't been flying them very long at all. I think he has four years now."

"So what does that matter?" he asked.

"You were an instructor pilot in the Army, right?" I asked.

"Yep," he said. "I instructed in the four models of the Huey and two versions of the C-12."

"We had this saying in the Air Force," I said. "It basically says you should never let the student exceed your limitations."

"I'm not a student," he said.

Flight Lessons 5: People

"I got news for you," I said. "We are all students. I've been flying Gulfstreams for over twenty years now and sometimes I get distracted, or sometimes I miss something. Sometimes I make mistakes. If you see me going a dot high, I would like you to tell me about it. That's what CRM is all about."

"You are forgetting that I was in charge of teaching CRM for over five years," he said. "I know all about that. CRM also means knowing when to shut up."

"Give him another chance," I said. "And please keep in mind it isn't personal. He is reminding you of our stable approach criteria because it makes his job easier. If the needles are centered he can concentrate on other things, like looking for the runway. If he is more talkative than me it is because he has less Gulfstream time than me. He needs to stay ahead of the airplane and that's taking more effort than he is used to. It isn't personal. Remember you are both on the same team and you should both be trying to make the other pilot's job easier."

"Okay," he said. I wasn't sure he was convinced or just resigned to the fact I wasn't going to agree with him.

A week later I flew with Gil and purposely deviated a dot right of course, feigning the crosswind pushed me to one side. "A dot right," he said. In my efforts, I dipped below glide path. "And a little low," he added.

"Thanks," I said. After the flight, he asked me, "What's the deal?" I mentioned my failures. "For the arrival I kind of lost focus right after glide slope intercept. I don't hand-fly a lot of approaches and today was a perfect opportunity. I guess the lesson is that even in great weather you need to treat an instrument approach seriously."

"Yes," he said. And after a slight pause, "that is exactly right."

A week later Gil was on vacation and I flew several trips with Sidney. After one of his "What's the deal?" admissions, he added news I was happy to hear. "For the first time ever, Gil admitted to making a mistake. He asked for the landing gear when we were too fast. I put my hand on the gear handle, thinking something wasn't right. I looked around the cockpit and spotted it the same time he did. So we didn't overspeed anything but we could have. During the debrief he mentioned it. Not only that, he thanked me for hesitating."

"It sounds like we've made a breakthrough," I said.

"And it only took two years!" Sidney said.

"Did you make a big deal of it?" I asked.

"No, not at all," Sidney said. "But there is more. I told him that this flight department has made me a better pilot because I no longer blow off my own mistakes and I've learned to always look for ways to improve."

"That is true about you," I said.

"He said that he has come to the same conclusion," Sidney said. "He said that even though he taught CRM for years, until he came here he never realized that CRM is useless unless the boss really believes in it and demonstrates it."

Neurons fired. I pulled out my laptop and brought up the CRM page. It was starting to make sense.

The Patriots won the Super Bowl but, if you believe the press, they did so only after deflating the footballs to Tom Brady's liking during the conference championship. I didn't watch the game but the morning radio shows were filled with commentators saying the Patriots shouldn't have made the Super Bowl after stealing the conference championship.

"Talk to me about 'deflategate,'" I asked *The Lovely Mrs. Haskel*.

"Everybody loves to hate my Patriots," she said. "They invent things to make it seem they are cheating, and this one is the silliest of them all. The balls were checked before the game in a warm locker, and confirmed to be between 12.5 and 13.5 psi. They were brought out to the field and used. During halftime five of the eleven balls were found to be at 11 psi."

"Wasn't it cold at that game?" I asked.

"Exactly!" she said. "The Ideal Gas Law says as temperature goes down, so does pressure."

Flight Lessons 5: People

"You know I can't concentrate whenever you talk science," I said.

"I am being serious," she said.

"Me too," I said. "So, I assume they reinflated the balls for the second half. How did that turn out?"

"The Pats led twenty to seven after the first half," she said. "They scored twenty-eight unanswered points in the second half."

"So, it is all about nothing," I said.

"You watch, they are going to make it a big deal," she said. "That's the way the world works."

Of course *The Lovely Mrs. Haskel* was right; they did make a big deal of it. By May, Brady was suspended without pay for four games for the upcoming season, the team was fined a million dollars and was forced to give up a first-round draft pick. *The Lovely Mrs. Haskel* was in a sour mood as I started salary negotiations of my own.

"How is everyone doing?" Elizabeth asked. A Priori did not do personnel evaluations and the only measure of a team member's performance and value was from their coach. In the five years I had been doing this, we never failed to get raises and the bonuses were equally generous. In each of those years I answered the first question with "everyone is doing well," and the next question with, "I think everyone deserves an above average raise." Then we argued about what above average meant and agreed that we were actually paid well above average, exceptional, in fact. It happened this way every year.

"Everyone is doing well," I said, playing my role in the Kabuki theater she was expecting. But then I took us off script. "Something has changed in our industry, but I'm not sure what. It may be related to that Gulfstream crash last year."

It was a topic she brought up often. A pair of very experienced Gulfstream pilots attempted to takeoff with their gust lock engaged, having failed to verbalize a single checklist. They crashed after failing to abort the takeoff and attempting to disengage the gust lock at a speed that made doing so impossible. While the investigation wasn't yet complete, it was becoming apparent that both pilots were intentionally disregarding all accepted procedures and flying recklessly. They died and took five innocent people with them.

"People are starting to realize you get what you pay for," Elizabeth said.

"I think so," I said. "The caliber of people calling me, looking for jobs, has fallen. I think all the good pilots are staying put because they are being paid what they are worth. The only pilots on the market are unemployed for a reason."

"Are you afraid our pilots might jump ship?" she asked.

"Maybe," I said. "I can't imagine Sidney leaving, but I can't rule it out. I'm not so sure about Gil."

"What do you want to do about it?" she asked.

"Ten percent raises," I said. It would be our largest since we started the flight department. "And we'll look at it again next year."

"Your call," she said. "But that sounds wise."

Everyone was happy with their raises but circumspect amongst themselves. I always cautioned them to avoid talking about salaries with others, knowing that it was an unspoken rule in business aviation and, besides, just good manners. That had never been a problem until now.

"I didn't bring it up," Sidney said, "just so you know. But Gil has been asking Sully and me about how big a raise we got. Sully told him it was none of his damned business and I told him I was uncomfortable talking about it and that he should talk about these things with you."

"I suppose I should have anticipated this," I said. "In the military everyone's pay is a matter of public record. In his simulator company I am betting there were so many of them it was probably a union shop and salaries were common knowledge. I guess I need to talk to him about etiquette."

"We were in Washington last week and he was yucking it up with a bunch of guys from another flight department," Sidney said.

"Which flight department?" I asked.

"That's the thing," he said. "He wouldn't introduce me. After they left I kind of looked at one of their badges. They were FBI."

Flight Lessons 5: People

"FBI as in spooks, FBI?" I asked.

"Yes," he said. "But not spooks, they had pilot badges. I found out they have a large flight department in D.C. with a couple of Gulfsteam G550s and a GV or two. Not that there is anything wrong with any of this, but I think he is shopping around. Do you have any experience with the FBI?"

"Only with the spooks," I said. "We dealt with them now and then in the Air Force and we had one as the chief of security back at Q-Tron, he was the person we answered to."

"And?" Sidney pressed.

"The first thing and last thing that guy ever said to me was a lie," I said. "And I am pretty sure most of everything in the middle was too. Years ago I had a few run ins with those types in the Air Force. The sampling of agents I dealt with all seemed to be little Napoleons who wouldn't last a day in the field. I think they gravitated towards their desk jobs because they didn't have the stomach for their real jobs and being shoe clerks allowed them to call themselves FBI agents without having to do anything of consequence."

"You got some pent-up anger, Eddie?" Sidney asked.

"I guess so," I said, laughing.

Gil never brought up his salary and only answered my usual "How are things?" with "Good, things are good."

I signed off his latest upgrade, to International Captain on a Tuesday and by Thursday it was on his social media pages: Gilbert "Gil" Desjardaines, Gulfstream G450 International Captain, A Priori Flight Department Director of Safety. I don't have a social media page but a friend emailed a screen shot with the subject line, "I thought you would like to know."

That was Thursday. On Friday Gil emailed to ask if I would be in the office on Monday, and if I could make time for him; he wanted to talk about something personal. I made the time.

On Monday he asked to speak in our conference room. He closed the door behind us. "Thank you for the raise," he began. "I am now making double what I was at the schoolhouse and more than just about all of my Army buddies who got out when I did."

"You deserve it," I said.

"I want to know what kind of job security we have with A Priori," he said. "I need to think about the future and my family."

I knew he had an Army pension and that all of his kids left the house and were self-sufficient. But he was also paying a huge mortgage for his Georgia home and had payments for a boat and two cars. I recognized the pattern of the conversation and resigned myself to play my part.

"The company is doing very well," I said. "They fully support the flight department and I've never heard even a hint about us going away."

"But can you guarantee that?" he asked.

"No, of course not," I said. "The biomedical field is very competitive and so is corporate aviation."

"Well that leaves me no choice then," he said. "I am going to have to resign my position here and take an offer from the FBI. They have a large flight department and the chances of them going away is zero."

"Okay," I said. "I wish you well." Gil left the conference room, leaving me with my thoughts. I was thinking that I didn't wish him well at all. He wasn't a *Friend*, to be sure, but he wasn't really a *Foe* either. He was just a mercenary.

My next call was to Linda. "Gil quit," I began.

"Oh, no," she said.

"We need to scarf up as many contract pilots as we can for the foreseeable future and put out the word we are hiring," I said. "I'll call Elizabeth next."

"I hate to add to your burdens," Linda said. "But I've been hearing rumors that IFE is looking to meet with Elizabeth. It sounds like they want our account."

"Terrific," I said. "I'll mention that too."

"I had a feeling about this," Elizabeth said. "He never seemed to really commit to us. He was my mistake."

Flight Lessons 5: People

"I hired him," I said.

"I should have detected the problem," she said. "I am usually pretty good about seeing through people, but he fooled me. Don't worry about him or some company trying to move in. What did you say their name is?"

"IFE," I said. "International Flight Enterprises."

"Well don't worry about it," she said. "Go find us a good pilot who won't stab you in the back."

I thought about that phrase over the next few months, as well as the fact Gil had fooled Elizabeth. I guess that meant he fooled me too.

"Did you get Gil's Christmas card?" Sully yelled into the phone. His Boston accent took on an edge when he was upset. His volume was always on ten, but when he was upset it seemed even louder. "It ain't right. It ain't right."

"I threw it away," I said. "I never opened it."

"Eddie, you got to read it," Sully said. "It had one of those two page letters from his wife bragging about the kids and telling the world about their year. You got to read it."

The next call was from Sidney and then from Linda. Everyone was upset. I found the unopened envelope in the trash, somewhat worse for the experience underneath a rotten tomato. Appropriate, I thought. The letter was protected by the card.

"Greetings from Virginia!" the card began. "We just moved here at last. Gil promised me we would only have to spend one winter in that awful cold that is New England. Well, it took three years but we finally made it to Virginia! Gil is now with the FBI! It is like old times in the Army. In fact, three of the pilots are from our last squadron!"

I stopped reading. Gil had played us. I had been warned that some simulator instructors would grab any offer to fly, just as a means of building flight time and experience before leaving to where they really wanted to be. I couldn't believe it. We trained Gil to deal with the real world and upgraded him to international captain. He had quite the resume when he was done. And now he was with the FBI. It was a match made in heaven. *Foe.*

Tom Brady's suspension was vacated in federal court and he suited up for the season opener. The ruling was that the National Football League failed to give Brady due process. They managed a winning season but failed to capture their league's championship. In March, Brady's suspension was reinstated. He would miss the first four games of the next season.

20: The Team
February 2016

The New England Patriots grand entrance (Photo: Saboteur)

The New England Patriots began the 2016 season without Tom Brady. The lifted suspension from the previous season was reinstated, despite a preponderance of evidence showing the commissioner of the National Football league had jumped to conclusions about the inflation of footballs two seasons earlier, and then refused to admit he was mistaken. The Patriots managed a 3 and 1 record with their backup quarterbacks. Brady took the Patriots 80 yards on their first possession of game five to the end zone. He was a man possessed.

Kidney stones took Sidney down for three months and I became a one-pilot show for the duration, using a cadre of three contract pilots. A Priori rules would not allow a non-company pilot in the left seat, so my proficiency was going up even as my patience was growing thin. Approaching my next recurrent training Elizabeth suggested I fly our airplane to Savannah. "We can't use it without you," she said. "You might as well take it."

News had traveled about our pilot shortage and there was no shortage of volunteers from the simulator company. Many looked promising but the thought of the knife in our back left by their former colleague ruled out any consideration. Our next pilot had to come from a more reliable source.

Sidney's condition forced me to cancel several speaking engagements, my newly acquired hobby of talking in front of crowds about all things aviation. Code7700.com was building a following and with that came speaking opportunities. One such invitation was from an Air National Guard unit in Portsmouth, New Hampshire. I told them I could do it, with the caveat of a last-minute cancellation if a trip came up. Fortunately, I was able to make the speech. My topic was about the normalization of deviance, the tendency for experienced crewmembers to give up standard operating procedures once they became highly experienced and complacent.

As these things usually transpire, I fielded a few questions from the stage and a lot more after we broke from the formal event. Most of the audience were military and many of them were in flight suits. A lieutenant colonel with pilot's wings and a patch proclaiming he flew the Lockheed C-5 Galaxy approached with a business card.

"Good afternoon, sir," he said. "I am Kyle Reasoner from the Westover Air Force Reserve Base. I have been following Code7700 for several years now, in fact I use it as a teaching resource." He explained that he recently left the active duty Air Force and chose the reserves over the airlines so as to be able to spend more time at home. "I have three in high school right now," he said. "I don't want to be an absentee dad. So, I am happy to be a reserve rat. I am the chief of training and was wondering if you could make it down to Westover one of these days and give us a speech. We'd love to show you around."

Kyle said their crews were having the very problems that I spoke about. "Unlike in the active duty," he explained, "some of our pilots have been in the squadron for almost twenty years. I think our average is over ten."

"That will do it," I said. "But knowing everyone is susceptible is the first step to beating it. Why don't you stop by Bedford? I'll show you something high-tech you might like."

"I'd like that," he said.

True to his word, Kyle called on Monday and on Tuesday he showed up before I did. Luckily, Sidney was there, having just received his medical clearance to return to flying. "I'll give him the nickel tour," Sidney said when he called to let me know. "You'll get here when you get here."

I had been called into A Priori headquarters to explain an unsolicited letter they had received from IFE. Larry was more confused than anything else. "We didn't contact them, this came out of the blue," he said. "Everyone is very happy with your team and we have no intentions of replacing anyone. They say they can get us two pilots right away and they can lower all of our costs. How can they do that?"

"They can't," I said. "First off, we need one more pilot, not two. Sidney is back."

"That's good news," Larry said. "Tell Sidney we are looking forward to seeing him again."

"They can get us pilots," I continued, "but no pilots that measure up to our standards. They can lower our costs, but only by cutting corners by using the worst vendors."

"That's what I thought," Larry said. "Now I can tell them no with a better idea of why I am saying no."

By the time I got to the hangar, Sidney had moved Kyle's tour to the airplane. I found them both in the cockpit. "What do you think, Kyle?" I asked.

"It's a part of aviation I only see in magazines," he said. "This is a beautiful airplane."

"With the wings off, we could probably fit it inside your airplane," I said. "Feeling claustrophobic?

"Not at all," he said. "The cockpit is smaller, but you do need that pointy nose to fly as fast as you do."

"Did you know Kyle was a squadron commander?" Sidney asked.

"No," I said. "Really?"

"Yes, sir," he said. "At Dover Air Force Base. That was my last active duty assignment."

We finished his tour and agreed on a reciprocal tour of his unit in Westover. After he left Sidney shot me a thumbs up. "You know what I am thinking?"

"I have an idea," I said. "But you tell me."

"Elizabeth once told me that we need to find another you," he said. "I told her they broke the mold. But it seems to me Kyle is pretty close."

"Maybe," I said. "But I think the reason he is running the training squadron in Westover is he wants to stay at home for his kids. I doubt he wants to resume a heavy flight schedule."

Sidney laughed. "We don't have a heavy flight schedule."

"That's a good point," I said.

With Sidney back in action, the schedule returned to normal. Actually, a little busier than normal. We came back from a two-day trip and spotted Sully bent over from the waist with both hands on the aircraft tug. When he heard our engines he stood upright and picked up his marshalling wands. As he crossed both wands in an "X," telling us to stop, I detected a slight dip in the arms. I pushed myself up in my seat. He recovered and picked up the red carpet and carried it to where our air stairs would open. After our passengers departed, I went straight to Sully.

"Are you okay?" asked.

"It's my hip, buddy," he said. "Just a sign of old age, I guess. Har, har, har!" The last "har" was feeble at best.

"You need to get that checked out, Sully," I said. "I got to get another two years out of you before you can retire."

"Har, har, har!"

Flight Lessons 5: People

The drive from Bedford Airport to Westover Air Reserve Base was just under two hours, but that included an hour on the Massachusetts Pike, a toll road prone to horrendous traffic. I thought about the possibility of hiring Kyle Reasoner and our requirement that all pilots live within a two-hour radius of the airport. The thought was premature, I knew.

Kyle met me in front of his wing's headquarters and led me through the building to his office. As we walked, I remembered how the Air Force Reserve was becoming the better equipped and dressed part of the Air Force when I retired, sixteen years ago. The "weekend warriors" were no longer flying the Air Force's used equipment. While many of the personnel appeared very young, many of the officers appeared to be closer to my age.

His office was just big enough for his desk, a credenza, and a large white board filled with training objectives and schedules. "I think our training manuals are about the same as the ones you had on active duty, maybe a little simpler," he said. "We have to schedule around our part timers, but everyone knows the routine and things get done."

"Do you have more part timers than full timers?" I asked.

"It's pretty much a fifty-fifty mix these days," he said. "We have a lot of guys on deployment. I am one of the lucky ones who don't deploy at all. I think the wing wants me to go part time or deploy. One or the other. It's a tough choice, I don't think I can make ends meet on a part timer's pay and I don't think my family can deal with the deployments."

"Can I suggest a third option?" I asked. I described our normal flight schedule and that he would likely only need to fly ten days a month with half of those overnighters. I told him A Priori was fully supportive of Reserve and Guard personnel and that he would be on a full salary. He seemed genuinely interested. "But before we get too serious," I said, "I need to know how far away from the airport you are. Where do you live?"

"Southbridge," he said. "I hope that's close enough."

"I am not familiar with Southbridge," I said.

"If you came down on the Mass Pike you passed right by it," he said. "It's about an hour and fifteen from Bedford."

"Perfect," I said.

Our hiring process had evolved over the years but had so far failed us with Gilbert Desjardaines. We reviewed the resume and had the candidate fill out a pilot history form required by our insurance broker. If all that looked good, A Priori would run a background check. The next step was a simulator check that Sidney would conduct. And if all that went well, we sent the contestant to A Priori for the beauty contest.

"He's a good pilot," Sidney said over the phone. "Very methodical and he doesn't get rattled. You are going to like him."

I had two topics for Elizabeth on her next "how are things going?" call. The calls usually came after dinner. "Am I interrupting dinner?" she would ask. "Dinner is a distant memory," I would say. "But it's only seven," she would say. "What time did you eat?" And I would say, "Five p.m. on the dot." And then she would say, "that's what old people do."

"Sully needs his hip replaced," I said. "He will be out of action for five months. We can get per diem help and he can do a lot of his paperwork from home. But I don't think he should put it off."

"Yes," she agreed. "That is very important."

"Sully has been asking about disability and who he needs to arrange that with," I said.

"I don't know about that," she said. "Did you ask Esther?" I knew what Esther's answer would be, most Human Resources people would have the same answer.

"I didn't ask," I said. "I would rather not put him on disability. He has a family to feed and keeping him on salary telegraphs a good message to the rest of the team."

"You are thinking like a true A Priori coach," she said. "You do what you think is right. Anything else?"

Flight Lessons 5: People

"I have a new pilot for you," I said. "I think he is very good. He is in the Air Force Reserve and will go part time with them to go full time with us. He was an Air Force squadron commander. He can take my place."

"Don't you say that," she said. "You aren't going anywhere. Okay, I'll meet him."

The view 90° after turning from the ILS and 90 before turning final at Teterboro

I failed to mention to Kyle one of the few minuses of our operation, that we spent about half our time at Teterboro, one of the more challenging airports in the country. Nestled underneath the heavily trafficked approach and departure paths of La Guardia, JFK, and Newark, Teterboro is one of the busiest in the country. It is also home to some of the gustiest winds. Even on a calm wind day, Teterboro was a challenge.

"Winds 360 at 25 gusting to 40, cleared the ILS 06," approach control said, "circle to runway 01."

I repeated the instructions and pointed to Giant Stadium. "You got the stadium?" I asked.

"In sight," Sidney said. "Looking for the towers. That's a big-time overshooting wind, isn't it?"

I didn't need to do the math; a 60 degree angle comes to about 90 percent of the component. "It is as good as a direct cross for your turn," I said, "but well within limits once you line up on final for zero one."

"Aiming outside the towers," he said.

"Good plan," I said. It was a common mistake at Teterboro. Many pilots didn't understand that clearance to circle wasn't the same as clearance to fly an instrument circling approach. There was no reason to keep the turn tight. I got some pushback on the website from pilots who refused to believe that, until the previous year when two Learjet pilots were killed attempting to keep the circle in tight. In fact, Sidney was in the keep it tight crowd until I showed him the regulations. "Safer is better," he said.

His circle worked out well and we made ourselves comfortable in the FBO's lounge while our passengers sped off to their Manhattan meeting. The top floor of the FBO had a nice view of the ramp and we both had our usual spots where we could plug in our laptops while keeping an eye on the world.

"Hey you're the Code7700 guy, aren't you," I heard from across the room. I rose and extended a hand.

"Eddie Haskel," I said.

"Todd Lindsey," he said. "I heard you speak in Vegas last year. I am a big, big fan." We spoke for a while until he had talked himself out. "One other thing," he said. "I hear you guys are coming to IFE."

"I think you heard wrong," I said.

"Well we fly the only G450 in the company and we had a meet and greet with the IFE owner," he said. "We have a hard time finding per diem help and that has been one of our complaints. Mr. Wayland said your G450 would soon be on our certificate."

"When was this?" I asked.

"Last week," he said. "I hope it's true for our sake, but I hope it isn't true for yours. IFE is one messed up company."

Flight Lessons 5: People

"How dare you do that to me," Elizabeth said. It wasn't the answer I was hoping for. I was speechless.

"Hello?" she said.

"Hello," I said. "I guess I am at a loss for words."

"I'm kidding!" she said. "I love, love, love him. He is so intelligent; he has done so many things. I can't imagine a better fit for you and Sidney. You must hire him as soon as you possibly can!"

That was the answer I was hoping for. Despite never having flown an airplane built after 1980, Kyle sailed through initial training. His first flights were very good indeed and I started to suspect he was quickly becoming Sidney's favorite travel companion. The two had a lot in common. They both owned a couple of antique cars, they both were avid skiers, and they both tried to never miss a Patriots game. By the end of the year, as defined by Super Bowls, Kyle was fully checked out, Sully had a new hip, and we presented ourselves for an inspection by the local Safety Management System auditor.

"I cannot tell you how impressed my team is by your team," the inspector began.

"Please give it a shot," I said. Laughter.

"I think the best way to describe it," he said with a smile, "is that this is a small flight department run like a big flight department. You guys do everything right."

I was starting to think spending my first Super Bowl in front of the television with *The Lovely Mrs. Haskel* was a bad idea. The Patriots were 14 and 2 and easily beat their rivals in the divisional and conference championships. It was their ninth Super Bowl appearance, having won four in the 15 previous years. The Atlanta Falcons had a relatively dismal year, with an 11 and 5 record. It was their first Super Bowl appearance. And yet, by the middle of the third quarter, the Patriots were behind 28 to 3.

"Twenty-five points is nothing," *The Lovely Mrs. Haskel* said. "Never count out number twelve."

I couldn't see how number 12, Tom Brady, could fix what was broken. But then came 25 unanswered points. When the Patriots won the coin toss for overtime, I knew what *The Lovely Mrs. Haskel* knew at the beginning of the game. It was a forgone conclusion.

21: Free Agent (At Last)
February 2018

A green Gulfstream GVII

"What do you know about that new Gulfstream?" Elizabeth asked. "The one they call the seven."

"Not a thing," I said.

"Really?" she asked.

"I assumed you wouldn't want to buy anything until it was tried and tested," I said. "I heard the Gee Seven is a clean-sheet design. They started over. That is unlike Gulfstream."

"So you do know something about it then," she said. "Get smart on it but keep it to yourself."

The team was doing well but I continued to worry about Sully. His new hip was treating him well but now his knees were bothering him. There is no age limit for mechanics and he didn't do a lot of heavy lifting. But still I worried. He was 64 with no plans to quit.

"There has to be more to life," I said, in a not so obvious hint.

"Yeah I know, Eddie," he acknowledged. "The cabin is paid for and the kids are doing good. But I got no reason to quit now. Besides, how are you going to survive without me. Har, har, har!"

Now that the traitorous Gil Desjardaines was two years in our rear-view mirror and Kyle Reasoner was fully checked out, the pilot situation was finally good. His command experience in the Air Force translated into getting along with everyone and accepting every assignment cheerfully. His time as the chief of training at his Air Force Reserve unit meant he was the perfect candidate for many of the things Sidney and I did in addition to our normal jobs. Sidney had completed several leadership courses and was enrolled in business aviation's largest Client Aviation Manager course. It was very obvious he wanted my job, but was willing to wait for my retirement.

Retirement. Both of my kids were out of the house and doing well. *The Lovely Mrs. Haskel* bristled every time I told her about Elizabeth's reaction when I brought the subject up. "I will pitch a tent in your front yard until you change your mind," she once said. "I have friends in the government and will have you put on the no-fly list," when she thought I was being tempted to move to Australia. "You will go insane with boredom," was her latest tact.

That last bit was a real threat. The website took some time but it was manageable. I averaged a speech every other month and could easily double that. An aviation magazine had taken to publishing me monthly so there wasn't a shortage of things to do. I could retire any day. A new airplane changed everything.

"It will take a year to deliver," I explained to *The Lovely Mrs. Haskel*. "Then a year to get everyone checked out and comfortable. I think we can retire in two years."

"That sounds optimistic," she said.

"You retire first," I said. "We'll see how that goes and then I'll think about it."

"Okay," she said, calling my bluff. "I'll put in my papers tomorrow." And she did. After raising two kids and two professional careers, *The Lovely Mrs. Haskel* hung up her medical scrubs and stethoscope for the last time. The ball was in my court.

Flight Lessons 5: People

The airline experience from Boston to Savannah used to be tortuous, involved a plane change or two and hours in very small, uncomfortable seats. You had to allot a full day for travel and multiple stops meant the chance of missing a flight were doubled or tripled. Finally a new upstart airline started offering once daily service and the experience was much improved. An extra fifty dollars gave you "even more leg room" and the day was shortened considerably.

I stretched my legs and realized buying a new Gulfstream would mean frequent flyer status with the new airline. That was not a good thing. The new airline offered free Internet access, which was a good thing, but the recently arrived email was not. Gordon Citolini, Esquire, representing International Flight Enterprises, notified me of a defamation suit against Code7700, Limited Liability Corporation, and that my presence was required for a deposition. I did a word search of the website and there were no hits on "International Flight Enterprises" at all. The acronym IFE also stands for Inflight Emergency – appropriate, I thought – and that appeared three times. I read each of those articles carefully. Not an issue.

I pulled out my invitation from Gulfstream, inviting me to tour the GVII plant and fly their non-motion simulator. The airplane wasn't yet certified and there were no motion simulators available. I reviewed my list of fifty-three concerns about a "clean sheet" airplane, particularly this one. Still something was nagging me.

I found the complete set of code for my previous, now offline, website and repeated my search for International Flight Enterprises and IFE. Same results. I had nothing to worry about.

To say Gulfstream is a major player at the Savannah airport would be an understatement. Each of their several complexes dwarf the main airline terminal. Pilots are not normally shown the red carpet when coming to the front door asking about a new airplane. But since they had me on record as the person who bought our G450, the red carpet treatment is exactly what I got. After a slide presentation extoling the virtues of their clean sheet design,

I was introduced to a senior test pilot who would walk me through the production plant and eventually to the simulator.

"Hi, I'm Parker Samuels," he said. "I was the lead on the cockpit design and I hope I can answer any questions you might have. The airplane has been great so far and we hope to have her certified early next year. I am a big fan of Code 7700. I hear you have some concerns about the new bird, maybe I can put those to rest."

He was in his late forties, slim, and in the five-foot-eight range. Gulfstream tended to favor Navy pilots for their experimental airplanes and Air Force pilots for their proven birds. Both services tend to favor shorter pilots for fighters, since a shorter distance between heart and brain increases g-tolerance. Air Force fighter pilots tended to be stockier and less articulate for some reason, so I guessed Parker was of the Naval pedigree.

I allowed him to go through what had to be a canned presentation by now. The airplane was fly-by-wire with absolutely no mechanical connection between the cockpit controls and the rudder, ailerons, or elevators. It was the first Gulfstream with a side-stick, the first without the conventional yoke. Most of the avionics were accessed through touch screens. They called it a clean sheet airplane, but the basic guts of the fuel, electrical, and pneumatic systems appeared to share much in common with the GV and GVI series.

The first time I had ever walked through a Gulfstream plant I was alarmed. Back in the nineties, the GIII plant reminded me of an auto repair shop, replete with airplanes parked haphazardly, tool and parts bins scattered at random, and loud noises from a potpourri of rivet guns, grinders, and even hammers. The GVII plant reminded me of a hospital operating room. There were neat lines of airplanes, workstations and tools. All of the workers were dressed in what looked like sterile surgical gowns. We started at the end where the fuselage was being built.

"Do you know how a stringer is normally built?" Parker asked.

"You take a piece of aluminum and rivet it to the inside of the fuselage," I said. "I guess it makes the fuselage stronger without the additional weight of a thicker skin, plus it ends up being stronger because it doesn't flex as much as a single piece of aluminum."

"Exactly," he said. "And each one of those rivets is a point of weakness. Rivets can leak cabin pressure and rivets can corrode. We reduced the number of rivets on some Gulfstreams by bonding some of the stringers."

"The airplane is glued together?" I asked.

"Essentially," he said. "But that was only on some of the stringers. In the GVII we bypassed that by etching some of the stringers. You familiar with that process?"

"I think so," I said. "Something like what you do on a circuit board."

"Exactly like that," he said. He explained that by starting with a thicker piece of metal you paint on a chemical resistant coating where you want the stringer and then bathe the piece in a chemical that eats away at the metal you don't want. "We still have rivets," he said. "But we have less than half of the number of rivets on your G450."

Everything about the production line was impressive. We stopped at the wing assembly area and I stared for a while at the wing. "Beautiful," I said.

"She is that," Parker agreed. I long ago assumed you could not build a prettier wing than what Gulfstream put on the GV. The GVII's wing was even prettier.

"Is this the highest wing sweep Gulfstream has ever built?" I asked.

"I think so," he said. "We needed the sweep to get the top end." The angle of the wing to the fuselage is known as its sweep. A straight wing tends to have about a 90° angle to the fuselage. The further back the wing is swept the faster the wing can go, but that tends to harm low speed handling. It was a tradeoff.

"What about the low end?" I asked.

"Not as slow as a GV on final approach," he said. "But slower than your G450."

"So it can use shorter runways then?" I asked.

"Yes," he said. "You will have an approach speed around ten knots slower," he said. "Plus, you will have automatic brakes. This airplane will stop on a dime."

"I know you are advertising point nine," I said. "Is that point nine for a short while or point nine all day long?"

"Right to point nine," he said. "Here to Paris at point nine. Not only that, but she'll do that using less gas than your G450 at point eight three."

That was news to me. The G450, indeed most Gulfstreams, cruise at Mach 0.80, that is at eight-tenths the speed of sound. It is called Mach number because Austrian physicist Ernst Mach was the first to quantify it. We could push that to Mach 0.83 by burning a little more fuel, but anything faster than that was fuel prohibitive. Mach 0.90 would be a game changer.

An hour later I was in the left seat of their simulator with Parker in the right. "You flown a stick before, Eddie?" he asked.

"Not since the Air Force," I said. "That was pulleys and cables in the T-37 and hydraulic lines in the T-38. And they were both sticks in the middle, between your legs."

"This one is easier," he said. "When we get to rotate speed, just ease her on back."

I pushed the thrust levers forward and engaged the auto-throttles with the same type of switch used on our G450. The airplane accelerated very quickly and in no time it was time to pull back on the stick. The airplane rotated easily. Once we got to altitude Parker asked me to pull the throttles to idle and pull the stick full aft.

"Stall it?" I asked.

"You can try," he said.

The nose came back easily at first but then required a definite pull. Once the airspeed fell below a yellow line on the airspeed indicator the nose fell smoothly of its own accord. "She won't let you stall," Parker said.

The instrument approach was easy and the landing was quite nice. "The benefit of a non-motion simulator," I said.

"The airplane is just like that," Parker said. "She makes the pilot look good."

We returned to the meeting room where the day began and Parker sat opposite me. "Questions?" he asked.

"Fifty-three of them," I said. One-by-one, Parker answered each and I was convinced. "I think you have a winner here."

I was home the next day and that evening Elizabeth called, "Am I interrupting dinner?" "Dinner is a distant memory." I gave her a complete report. "Go buy us one," she said.

"I can do that," I said. Left unsaid was yet another deposition, this one aimed at me.

The office was behind a huge glass wall that ran the length of the hallway from the elevator to the side of the building. The wall along the hallway was opaque, the wall at the end offered a view of Manhattan and Central Park, thirty-seven floors below. The first door on the right informed me I was at the correct law firm and there was a list of several attorneys, none of which were the ones I was scheduled to see. I pushed the door open. The receptionist took my name, offered a coffee and a seat. I declined the former and accepted the latter. Within minutes another door opened.

"Hello," she said, extending a hand. "I am Sally Harlan. You are right on time and we are ready for you. Please follow me." She opened another door to another glass-lined hallway. "Is this your first time?" she asked.

"First time for what?" I asked.

"First time giving a sworn court deposition," she said.

"No," I said. She didn't react. It was, in fact, my third time at bat. I knew she was trying to rattle me, to get me nervous. In fact, her question reminded me that what was to follow was a chance for everyone in question to put on an act. Actor. I was playing a role. The conference room was fairly plain, except for a beautiful long table. At the head of the table, farthest from the window, sat a young lady with a laptop computer and stenotype. I first got a look at one while in the Air Force, when I was called in to testify against my commanding officer at the time. On the far end four people came to rise, with Sally taking a fifth chair. On the near side was a solitary chair.

The lawyers introduced themselves, the stenographer swore me in, and we all sat. The attorney opposite me reminded me that I could have brought an attorney and gave me a chance to reconsider my decision to represent myself. I did not, remembering the old saying "he who goes to court as his own attorney will be represented by a fool."

The lead attorney explained that IFE was suing for defamation about things I had written and said about them. "I'd like to enter the following exhibit, five articles taken from the defendant's website, Code 7700, dot com."

"So entered and marked," another attorney said, pushing the bundle to me.

"Mr. Haskel, are these articles from your website and did you write the words on the pages shown," the first attorney said. I took the first of the stapled bundles and started to read. The first was an article I had written about sophistry, the art of stating a lie with such conviction that it seems true. The article was ten pages long. After a few minutes the attorney's patience was exhausted. "You don't have to read the entire article," he said. "You wrote it, after all."

"You asked me if I wrote the words," I said. "I just want to be sure." I continued to read. The five attorneys were abuzz with whispers. I continued reading.

"Mr Haskel, you don't need to read the article, we withdraw the question," one of the flanking attorneys said. "We notice that you often use the term 'Brand X' as a term of disparagement. Is that a fair characterization of the phrase?"

My mind raced. Brand X? It seemed too obvious so perhaps it was a trick. But since I had a fool for a lawyer, I pressed on. "I think that is the very definition of the term," I said.

"Very good," the center attorney said, nodding to the attorney on his left. That attorney pushed a second sheath of papers to the attorney nearest the stenographer. "I'd like to enter the following exhibit, the transcript of a speech given by the defendant to the aviation association shown and on the date shown."

Flight Lessons 5: People

"So entered and marked," a third attorney said, pushing the papers to me. It was a speech I had given in California called "The Normalization of Deviance." I wasn't aware that the speech had been recorded. "No need to read the entire speech," the attorney said. "Can you acknowledge you did give a speech to this group on this particular date."

"I remember speaking to this group," I said. "I don't remember the date or the topic, but I can look them up for you, if you want."

"Okay," he said. I pulled out my laptop and allowed it to boot. Each attorney sat silently. I found the speech in question and double-clicked the PowerPoint file. "Yes," I said. "The date and topic were correct." As I spoke, I hit the "Command" and "F" keys and typed "Brand X" in the find box and came up with no results.

"Please turn to page forty-seven and read the highlighted text," the attorney said.

I turned to the page and read the text silently. "Please read aloud." I returned to my laptop and typed in some of the surrounding text. "Mr. Haskel?" the attorney repeated.

"I'm not sure where this transcript comes from," I said. "But these words are not the same as the words in my script."

"Is it possible you went off script?" the attorney asked.

"Yes," I said.

"Then how can you say with certainty that the words in the transcript are not yours?" he asked.

"The phraseology isn't part of my vernacular," I said. "I don't know who took this transcript. A video or audio recording would be very helpful."

The attorneys resumed their whispering until finally the lead attorney cleared his throat. "What did you say, according to your script?"

"The script agrees with my memory," I began. "I said, 'High levels of experience breeds complacency. You will find this in every airline, every corporate aviation management company, even in the smallest flight department. I've seen this in the military. I've seen this in corporate aviation, everything from the best management companies to the worst. Unfortunately, there are more in the worst category than the best.' That's what I said."

"Whom did you mean when you said the worst management companies?" the attorney asked.

"There are several," I said.

"Name them," he said.

"I would rather not," I said.

"Why not?" he asked.

"I went through great pains in that speech not to defame anyone," I said. "I do the same for the website. I am not going to sit here and do what you are accusing me of doing."

"Are you refusing to answer the court?" he said.

"Yes," I said. "Yes, I am."

"We need to do something before he really gets hurt," Kyle said. "He's a good guy, but he's more physical than mental. His first reaction to any problem is to do something physical and sooner or later that knee of his is going to give."

"Yes, all of that is true," I said. "But Sully has a good head on his shoulders, and I think he is smart enough to realize when he can't do a job."

"Maybe so," Kyle said. "He knows A Priori supports us and he's seen how we pilots are about self-critique. In fact, he's good about that too. He keeps telling me about the time he told Sidney about the thrust reverser accumulators. And then he reminds me that we are all here to support each other and that nobody should worry about communicating. He's a CRM poster child."

"As it should be," I said. "Don't you see that in the Air Force too?"

"Not at all," Kyle said. "I think it is pretty rare. Most organizations don't handle bad news well. Sully is a good guy. But I think his time has come."

"You are right," I said. "I think I am too close to the situation and have been putting this off. I'll talk to him. In the meantime, go find me a new mechanic."

I was doing a lot of delegating lately. In fact, I was starting to think of myself as the absentee chief pilot. Or team coach, to use the A Priori job title. Fortunately, I had two pilots who knew how to do my job. Sidney was managing the hangar, our standardization program, and all of our manuals. Kyle was running the safety and training programs. All I had to do was pick up the phone whenever Linda called and fly wherever the other two pilots planned. Most of my time was consumed with the new airplane.

I had made almost all of the cockpit decisions in less than a month. The interior was taking most of my time and days of debating galley design still loomed in my future. Sully was convinced he would be going to GVII school to learn a new airplane. My hints had fallen on deaf ears.

"I saw this many times as a nurse," *The Lovely Mrs. Haskel* said. "A doctor or a nurse knows they aren't as sharp as they used to be but can't let go. Retirement means a big scary change, and not doing anything takes no effort. A doctor who has lost his edge can be very dangerous. We are talking lives at stake. But so are you. Maybe Sully just needs a nudge in the right direction."

"I was trying to get him to make the decision," I said.

"Remember in Hawaii when you were losing engines almost every month?" she asked.

"The mighty 707," I said. "It wasn't so mighty after a while."

"You used to say no to mechanics and other pilots with a joke," she said. "You used to say, 'I can't do that because the lovely Mrs. Haskel won't let me risk lives without her permission. At the time I thought you were talking about your mom. Now I know you were talking about me. Eddie, I will not allow you to risk your life at the hands of a mechanic who isn't at the top of his game."

"Sully would never do that," I said.

"He would never knowingly do that," she said. "But pride does things to a man. One morning he will be in pain but he'll come to work anyway. He can get hurt. You owe it to your passengers. You owe it to me. You owe it to Sully."

"I need the airplane out on the ramp so the sun is right off one of the wings," I said. "It doesn't matter which, but we need direct sunlight into the cabin."

"Okay," Sully said. "You want the APU running?"

"Yes," I said. "I'll be in at two and Elizabeth should be there about three."

Gulfstream had sent a crate of cloth and leather fabric swatches, as well as three boxes of carpet and marble flooring squares. I had flown all over the country with members of the A Priori design team and we had everything narrowed down. Elizabeth was concerned the combinations wouldn't work *in situ.*

I showed up with Sully seated in the tug, still connected to the airplane which he had positioned outside. I could hear the auxiliary power unit running and the sun gleamed off the right wing. "You want the tug disconnected, Eddie?" he asked.

"Yes, please," I said. Sully rose from the tug and walked to the airplane's nose gear to disconnect the strap joining the two. As he bent over his knee buckled. I caught him as he started to fall.

"I'm okay, Eddie" he said. "Really, you can let go. That just happens every now and then." There was no "har, har, har!"

Elizabeth was on time but didn't like any of the samples. I knew my next few months would continue as an interior designer with just a few spare moments left over as a pilot. But one other duty took my immediate attention. After we brought the airplane back into the hangar I sat in the right seat of the tug, with Sully still in the left. From our vantage point, the nose of the airplane was almost close enough to touch. I had a clear view of the left wing; Sully had a view of the right. We sat, quietly.

Flight Lessons 5: People

"Sully, I want you to retire at the end of this year," I said. "I am worried that you could hurt yourself here. You have had a long and distinguished career that you can be very proud of. You owe it to Gwen, your children, and your grandkids to always be there."

"I know, Eddie," he said. "I was just thinking I could help you get the new bird settled first."

"We are going to miss you," I said. "And having you bring in the new airplane would be very beneficial. But it would be selfish of us to risk your health. And it would be selfish of you to do that to your family."

"I'll think about it, Eddie," he said. "Please don't say anything to anyone else."

The next morning, he called. "Gwen and I decided that it is time," he said. "Thanks, Eddie. I guess I just needed a little push."

"Eddie, do you believe in God?" Gary asked. He called out of the blue and the question forced me to stare at the caller ID on my phone. Gary Storm.

"I do, Gary," I said. "Why do you ask?"

"I guess I am not surprised," he said. "Well so do I. I just retired from IFE. Actually, they forced me to retire. Stefano Wayland plays hardball and he made us do some pretty bad stuff. Bad stuff. I am not proud of it, but I did some bad stuff."

"Everybody has a boss," I said. "Sometimes we have to make decisions we aren't proud of."

"Yeah, that about sums it up," he said. "Well one of my bad decisions was to sit with my hands on my lap as our company went after your company. We needed a G450 on account and your company seemed to have an unlimited budget. It seemed like easy pickings. I told them you didn't care about budgets and spent money like a drunken sailor. We could easily take over and cut the budget in half. Mr. Wayland went after your account personally. I guess your CEO called him a few names and he took that personally too.

That's when he sent the lawyers out to get you."

"I was wondering about that," I said. "I never heard back from them."

"They dropped the case," he said. "They never intended to go any further with it. It was just them trying to scare you."

"I appreciate you telling me that," I said. "Mr. Wayland would probably hit the roof if he found out."

"He can go to hell," Gary said. "You have a good life, Eddie. I know we never saw eye to eye and I still think you were a pain in my ass. But I wanted you to know I have moved on and no hard feelings."

"None from me," I said. "Have a nice retirement, I hope to follow you soon."

I sat and reflected. A *Foe* perhaps now a *Friend*? The entire *Friend* versus *Foe* idea had been a bad one. It colored my judgment and typecast people in my mind for future decision making.

The Patriots won the Super Bowl, 13 to 3, over the Rams.

"Didn't they beat the Rams a long time ago to start the dynasty?" I asked.

"Different team," *The Lovely Mrs. Haskel* said. "It was Belichick and Brady and the New England Patriots in the 2001 season. But back then it was the St. Louis Rams and now it is the Los Angeles Rams."

I noticed her enthusiasm for the team started to wane as talk of her beloved Number 12 becoming a free agent started to take hold and was later confirmed. When news that Tom Brady left the New England Patriots for another team came out, she wasn't at all upset. "It is time to move on," she said. "The team goes on, even after the quarterback gets on with his life. They have had a lot of personnel turnover in twenty years. The fundamentals remain because the team's management believes in fundamentals."

I realized she was right. When management has the big picture, believes the big picture, and ensures the entire organization is on the same page, good things happen. I pulled out my MacBook, fired up the HTML page on Crew Resource Management and started to type. When I was finished, I deleted the top warning, "Work in Progress." But it wasn't right. I retyped:

"This will always be a work in progress."

Satisfied, I posted the change for all to see. *The Lovely Mrs. Haskel* turned on the television which had been last tuned to the Football Channel. With the press of a few buttons she moved on to the Tennis Channel. Her team would be there next season.

The team, my team, was doing very well. Kyle lured an Air Force Reserve mechanic to join the team and she turned out to be the finest mechanic I had ever worked with. Sidney and Kyle were both the finest pilots I had ever flown with and both were capable of taking over. Linda, the finest dispatcher in the history of dispatchers, would ensure the team went on no matter who was running the show. Elizabeth was the finest boss I had ever had and was going to be furious. But in a few weeks, I knew, I would become a distant memory. And being put on the no-fly list wouldn't hurt at all. My flying days would soon be over.

Flight Lessons 5: People

Flight Lessons: Management (CRM Beyond the Textbooks)

In the middle eighties, most airlines and military aviation units "got it," that is, they understood it was more cost and mission effective to embrace CRM if it meant keeping airplanes from crashing. The few exceptions included the airlines of Korea, China, the former states of the Soviet Union, and other parts of the world just getting used to flying modern aircraft. The second generation of CRM reinforced the role of cockpit crewmembers and the third generation added cabin crewmembers. Later generations started to incorporate non-flying parts of aviation. These were all good additions.

In fact, many other industries adopted forms of CRM. A hospital operating room, for example, definitely benefits from CRM. But let's focus on aviation here. Third generation CRM has served us well, but the academics cannot leave well enough alone.

The statistical lie about accident rates

You will see in many learned and reputable sources that the annual rate of aviation accidents have fallen precipitously, mainly because of better equipment, training, and operating procedures:

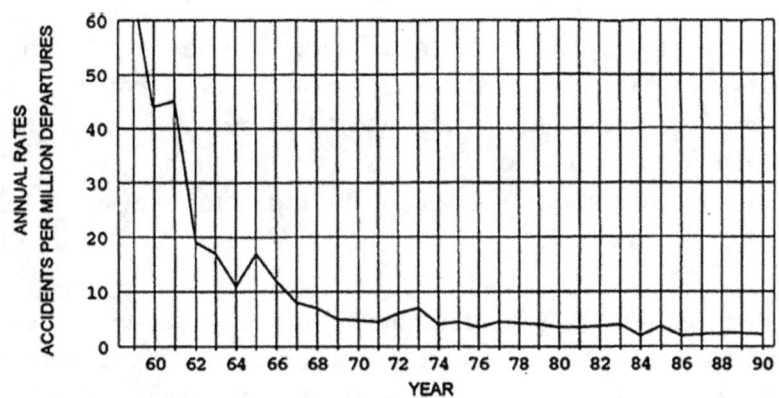

US/Canadian Operators Accident Rates by Year to 1990, from CRM Handbook, figure 1.

Notice the chart is fairly flat from 1986 and on.

But you will read and hear the following lie:

[Crew Resource Management: An Introductory Handbook, pg. 1] As Figure 2 illustrates, as accidents related to equipment weaknesses have decreased, accidents attributed to human weaknesses have increased.

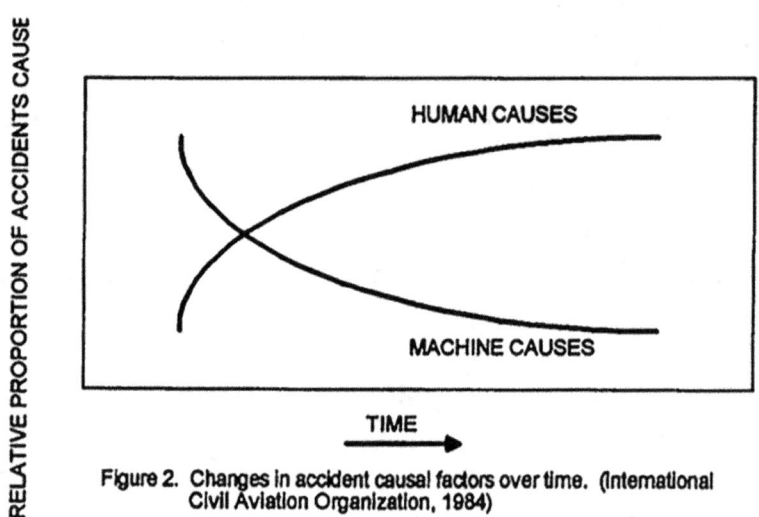

Changes in accident causal factors over time, from CRM Handbook, figure 2.

[Crew Resource Management: An Introductory Handbook, pg. 2] Figure 1 and Figure 2 suggest two points. First, Figure 1 indicates that after a sharp drop in the 1960s, accident rates have leveled off from 1970 through 1990. Second, the trends in causes of accidents illustrated in Figure 2 show that human error has remained a major contributing factor in aviation accidents during these latter years.

Figure 1 seems to show the accident rate has leveled off and we aren't getting any better. This is a distortion caused by the linear scale of the vertcal axis. It is hard to see a trend when the changes are small relative to the scale.

Flight Lessons 5: People

The second chart is a lie of improperly used statistics. The chart clearly says "Relative proportion of accidents cause." In plain English:

1. The number of accidents has gone down, way down.
2. The number of accidents caused by machines has gone down, way down.
3. The number of accidents caused by humans has gone down, but not as far down as those cause by machines.

So why is overplaying the problem a problem when it comes to training? Because the problem has changed. The problem in aviation used to be a culture that gave the captain complete authority and discouraged any kind of resistance to that authority. We are over that. While it may be true that not every pilot fully embraces CRM, the vast majority of them say they do. That word, "say," is important. Because the new problem is that we now have a culture that expects all flight crews to embrace CRM and that we have some pilots that may not know how to do that, or are doing that in thoughts only. We have a new problem:

- Some captains think they follow CRM principles but have never really been tested to see if they "walk the talk."
- Some captains do not embrace CRM principles, but play act the role in training and never get tested on their true convictions.
- Some captains do not know how to foster a good CRM environment among unfamiliar crews.
- Some captains do not know how to deal with unfamiliar crews that may fall short of the standards set by the crews they are familiar with.
- Some crewmembers do not know how to deal with these captains in a "live" situation, that is, a situation outside the contrive situations in the classroom or with captains other than those they are very familiar with.

James Albright

Bringing management into the fold of CRM

The fundamentals learned in the second generation of CRM (given at the end of Part Three) remain sound when the captain and the crew fully understand and embrace those fundamentals. In the days before CRM the captain was the problem. We addressed that in the first generation of CRM and followed up with the rest of the crew in generations two and three. Our new focus returns to captains who (a) do not believe in CRM, (b) are play acting CRM when in training or during evaluations, or (c) can only adhere to CRM tenets under ideal conditions. While uniquely talented non-captains or fellow captains could fix the situation, this is rarely the case. The problem is made worse in organizations where several CRM-poor captains can thrive in an organization that doesn't know better. What is the cure?

1) Management must become CRM-literate and understand the importance of having captains who can listen to and properly manage a crew.

2) Management must learn how to detect captains who do not "walk the CRM talk."

a. Find independent Safety Management System auditors with a track record of issuing frank, honest reports. You can help in this process by making clear you will not be using the same auditor twice because you don't want the auditor to think "sugar coating" the results will invite future visits (and income).

b. Invite peer reviews from other flight departments.

c. Spend time in the cockpit during engine start, taxi, takeoff, en route, approach, landing, and taxi to parking. Pay special attention to the free flow of information between crewmembers.

3) Management should encourage personnel transitions from job to job within the flight department as well as outside. The person running the flight department should not be allowed to remain in position for more than ten years, or perhaps much less. Transitioning such pilots to a per diem basis may allow some flexibility and provide for "new blood" to prevent complacency to become institutionalized.

Postscript

My introduction to Crew Resource Management was by an Air Force captain who cut a line through the cockpit with his hand and said, "Everything on this side of the cockpit belongs to me. Everything on that side of the cockpit belongs to us."

But the Air Force figured it out about the same time most major U.S. airlines did. It makes no sense to crash airplanes because the crew isn't working together as a team; you can't meet a military mission and you can't make a profit in a civilian company. Twenty years in the Air Force taught me the benefits of good Crew Resource Management by demonstrating first how things are without it, and then evolving to how things are with it. By the time I put away my uniform for good, I thought I had a handle on CRM.

Twenty years as a civilian pilot reinforced what I already knew, but also helped me understand why CRM often fails. Almost every pilot believes they are model citizens of the crew resource management world. Beauty is in the eye of the beholder, and so is good CRM. Most criticism against dysfunctional pilots are behind their backs, insuring they remain oblivious.

And there lies the secret of why CRM so often fails: we pilots can be quick to identify another pilot's CRM shortcomings but can be blind to our own. Industry's answer has been predictable, but you cannot evaluate CRM with a 25-question quiz or a 4-hour simulator session. It can only be evaluated "out there," in the real world.

The secret to really good CRM is empathy for others and the willingness to accept and act on criticism with an open mind. The secret to ensuring good CRM is having higher levels of management involved in the process, looking for signs of open communications and evolving procedures. Standard operating procedures that haven't changed in years are not signs of SOPs that were perfect to begin with, they are signs of an aviation culture that is unwilling to be self-critical or listen to anyone other than those in charge.

I hope these stories from my twenty years as a civilian pilot demonstrate that pilots who treat each other with respect are more likely to listen when they need to. Pilots with enough humility to acknowledge their own faults tend to be open to outside criticism. Saying you have thick skin isn't enough.

CRM Case Studies

The following case studies can be found at
https://www.code7700.com/case_studies.htm

1) Air Blue ABQ-202 (2010) — Despite several warnings from his first officer and the terrain warning system, the captain flew the aircraft into a mountain killing everyone onboard. The captain had over 15 times the flying time of the first officer, and browbeat and berated him to the point where was little more than a passenger, unwilling to speak up or take command to prevent disaster.

2) Air Florida 90 (1982) — An amiable captain with inadequate experience dealing with icing conditions was paired with a first officer who had the right answer but unwilling to speak forcefully. Most everyone on board was killed.

3) Air Illinois 710 (1983) — A captain with an internal drive to keep the schedule and a reputation of getting angry with first officers decided to press on to his destination after an electrical failure. His destination was IFR, over 30 minutes away. He could have turned back to his departure airport, which was VFR. All aboard were killed.

4) Allegheny Airlines 453 (1978) — A complete lack of discipline in the cockpit is evidenced by sloppy procedures, the absence of required call outs, and stabilized approach monitoring. The lack of crew resource management destroyed the airplane.

5) Eastern Airlines 401 (1972) — The pilots failed to continuously monitor the airplane while troubleshooting a gear position light and allowed the airplane to descend into the Everglades, killing all on board.

6) Galaxy Airlines 203 (1985) — A breakdown in crew coordination following an unexpected vibration shortly after takeoff led to a loss of control of the airplane and loss of all but one person on board.

7) Japan Air Lines 8054 (1977) — The crew was unwilling to confront an intoxicated captain who over-rotated into a stall, lost control of the aircraft and killed all on board.

8) Pan Am 115 (1959) — An inept copilot made several mistakes that plunged the aircraft into a spiraling dive. While the captain was able

to recover, the question that should have been asked but wasn't is this: what about the Pan Am culture allowed such a pilot into the captain's seat of their flagship aircraft?

9) Pan Am 212 (1964) — The captain deviated from the ILS glide slope and ended up landing too long to stop on the remaining runway. While nobody was killed, the aircraft was damaged beyond repair.

10) Pan Am 292 (1965) — After the captain deviated from weather visually, the crew lost position awareness and descended too early into the terrain.

11) Pan Am 001 (1968) — The crew misset their altimeters on approach (millibars versus inches) and flew too low on approach and crashed.

12) Pan Am 217 (1968) — The crew flew into the ocean, perhaps because of the visual illusion of the dark ocean against a dark sky.

13) Pan Am 799 (1968) — The crew attempted to takeoff without the flaps set.

14) Pan Am 6005 (1971) — The captain misflew the approach and impacted a mountain short of the runway.

15) Pan Am 816 (1973) — An instrument failure might have distracted the crew after takeoff; they flew a descending turn into the ocean.

16) Pan Am 160 (1973) — Uncontrollable smoke in the cockpit contributed to a number of CRM errors that left the aircraft unflyable.

17) Pan Am 806 1974) — The crew failed to recognize an excessive descent rate caused by a recoverable windshear encounter.

18) Pan Am 812 (1974) — The crew turned and descended 30 nautical miles early, opting to bet their lives on one ADF needle that had swung (indicating station passage) while the other remained steady, pointing ahead.

19) United Airlines 173 (1978) — A captain not listening to the crew and a crew not being assertive enough caused the loss of an airplane and many lives.

20) United Airlines 232 (1989) — The mishap was caused by shortsighted certification rules that led to an engine failure that took out the primary flight control systems. Excellent CRM saved many lives that day.

References

Advisory Circular 120-51E, Crew Resource Management Training, 1/22/04, U.S. Department of Transportation

Boeing Commercial Airplanes, Statistical Summary of Commercial Jet Airplane Accidents, Worldwide Operations 1959 - 2012, 2013

Cortés, Antonio; Cusick, Stephen; Rodrigues, Clarence, Commercial Aviation Safety, McGraw Hill Education, New York, NY, 2017.

Cortés, Antonio, CRM Leadership & Followership 2.0, ERAU Department of Aeronautical Science, 2008

Crew Resource Management: An Introductory Handbook, DOT/FAA/RD-92/26, DOT-VNTSC-FAA-92-8, Research and Development Service, Washington, DC, August 1992

Dekker, Sidney and Lundström, Johan, From Threat and Error Management (TEM) to Resilience, Journal of Human Factors and Aerospace Safety, May 2007

Flight Safety Foundation, Aviation Safety World, "Pressing the Approach," December 2006

Gann, Ernest K., Fate is the Hunter: A Pilot's Memoir, 1961, Simon & Schuster, New York

Gandt, Robert, Skygods: The Fall of Pan Am, 2012, Wm. Morrow Company, Inc., New York

Gawande, Atul., The Checklist Manifesto: How to Get Things Right, 2009, Metropolitan Boos, Henry Holt and Company, LLC, New York.

Helmreich, Robert L., Klinect, James R., Wilhem, John A., Models of Threat, Error, and CRM in Flight Operations, University of Texas

Kanki, Barbara; Helmreich, Robert; and Anca, José, Crew Resource Management, Academic Press, Amsterdam, 2010.

Lutat, Christopher J. and Swah, S. Ryan, Automation Airmanship, McGraw Hill Education, London, 2013.

James Albright is an average pilot with average stick and rudder skills, but has an above average desire to learn and instruct. He spent twenty years in the United States Air Force as an aircraft commander, instructor pilot, evaluator pilot, and squadron commander. After retiring as a lieutenant colonel, he went on to fly for several private and commercial operators as an international captain, check airman, and chief pilot. His logbook includes the T-37B, T-38A, KC-135A, Boeing 707, Boeing 747, Challenger 604, and the Gulfstream III, IV, V, G450, and GVII.

His website, www.code7700.com attracts around five million hits each month and his articles have appeared in several magazines, most notably Business & Commercial Aviation.

While he claims to be devoid of ego, that can hardly be true of someone willing to write a five-volume set of flight lessons based on his own experiences.

www.ingramcontent.com/pod-product-compliance
Lightning Source LLC
Chambersburg PA
CBHW050620300426
44112CB00012B/1593